K

Managing in the Public Sector

University of Northumbria at Newcastle

Titles in the Institute of Management Series

NVQ Level 3

The Competent First-Line Manager
Shields

Certificate (NVQ Level 4)

The Management Task (Second edition)
Dixon

Managing Financial Resources (Second edition)
Broadbent and Cullen

Managing Information
Wilson

Managing People (Second edition)
Thomson

Meeting Customer Needs (Second edition)
Smith

Personal Effectiveness (Second edition)
Murdock and Scutt

Diploma (NVQ Level 5)

Developing Human Resources
Thomson and Mabey

Managerial Finance
Parkinson

Managing an Effective Operation
Fowler and Graves

Managing Knowledge
Wilson

Managing in the Public Sector
Blundell and Murdock

Managing Quality
Wilson, McBride and Bell

Managing Schools
Whitaker

Managing in the Single European Market
Brown

Marketing
Lancaster and Reynolds

Tutor support

NVQ Handbook: practical guidelines for providers and assessors
Walton

Managing in the Public Sector

Brian Blundell and Alex Murdock

Published in association with
The Institute of Management

This book is dedicated to Eric and Gene Murdock

Butterworth-Heinemann
Linacre House, Jordan Hill, Oxford OX2 8DP
A division of Reed Educational and Professional Publishing Ltd

℞ A member of the Reed Elsevier plc group

OXFORD   BOSTON   JOHANNESBURG
MELBOURNE   NEW DELHI   SINGAPORE

First published 1997

British Library Cataloguing in Publication Data
A catalogue record for this book is available from the British Library

ISBN 0 7506 2195 8

Printed and bound in Great Britain by
Biddles Ltd, Guildford and King's Lynn

Contents

Series adviser's preface

This book is one of a series designed for people wanting to develop their capabilities as managers. You might think that there isn't anything very new in that. In one way you would be right. The fact that very many people want to learn to become better managers is not new, and for many years a wide range of approaches to such learning and development has been available. These have included courses, leading to formal qualifications, organizationally-based management development programmes and a whole variety of self-study materials. A copious literature, extending from academic text-books to sometimes idiosyncratic prescriptions from successful managers and consultants, has existed to aid – or perhaps confuse – the potential seeker after managerial truth and enlightenment.

So what is new about this series? In fact, a great deal – marking in some ways a revolution in our thinking both about the art of managing and also the process of developing managers.

Where did it all begin! Like most revolutions, although there may be a single, identifiable act that precipitated the uprising, the roots of discontent are many and long-established. The debate about the performance of British managers, the way managers are educated and trained, and the extent to which shortcomings in both these areas have contributed to our economic decline, has been running for several decades.

Until recently, this debate had been marked by periods of frenetic activity – stimulated by some report or enquiry and perhaps ending in some new initiatives or policy changes – followed by relatively long periods of comparative calm. But the underlying causes for concern persisted. Basically, the majority of managers in the UK appeared to have little or no training for their role, certainly far less than their counterparts in our major competitor nations. And there was concern about the nature, style and appropriateness of the management education and training that was available.

The catalyst for this latest revolution came in late 1986 and early 1987, when three major reports reopened the whole issue. The 1987 reports were *The Making of British Managers* by John Constable and Roger McCormick, carried out for the British Institute of Management and the CBI, and *The Making of Managers* by Charles Handy, carried out for the (then) Manpower Services Commission, National Economic Development Office and British Institute of Management. The 1986 report, which often receives less recognition than it deserves as a key contribution to the recent changes was *Management Training: context and process* by Iain Mangham and Mick Silver, carried out for the Economic and Social Research Council and the Department of Trade and Industry.

It is not the place to review in detail what the reports said. Indeed, they and their consequences are discussed in several places in this series of books. But essentially they confirmed that:

- British managers were undertrained by comparison with their counterparts internationally.
- The majority of employers invested far too little in training and developing their managers.
- Many employers found it difficult to specify with any degree of detail just what it was that they required successful managers to be able to do.

The Constable/McCormick and Handy reports advanced various recommendations for addressing these problems, involving an expansion of management education and development, a reformed structure of qualifications and a commitment from employers to a code of practice for management development. While this analysis was not new, and had echoes of much that had been said in earlier debates, this time a few leading individuals determined that the response should be both radical and permanent. The response was coordinated by the newly-established Council for Management Education and Development (now the National Forum for Management Education and Development (NFMED)) under the energetic and visionary leadership of Bob (now Sir Bob) Reid, formerly of Shell UK and the British Railways Board.

Under the umbrella of NFMED a series of employer-led working parties tackled the problem of defining what it was that managers should be able to do, and how this differed for people at different levels in their organizations; how this satisfactory ability to perform might be verified; and how an appropriate structure of management qualifications could be put in place. This work drew upon the methods used to specify vocational standards in industry and commerce, and led to the development and introduction of competence-based management standards and qualifications. In this context, competence is defined as the ability to perform the activities within an occupation or function to the standards expected in employment.

It is this competence-based approach that is new in our thinking about the manager's capabilities. It is also what is new about this series of books, in that they are designed to support both this new structure of management standards, and of development activities based on it. The series was originally commissioned to support the Institute of Management's Certificate and Diploma qualifications, which were one of the first to be based on the new standards. However, these books are equally appropriate to any university, college or indeed company course leading to a certificate in management or diploma in management studies.

The standards were specified through an extensive process of consultation with a large number of managers in organizations of many different types and sizes. They are therefore employment based and employer-supported. And they fill the gap that Mangham and Silver identified – now we do have a language to describe what it is employers want their managers to be able to do – at least in part.

If you are engaged in any form of management development leading to a certificate or diploma qualification conforming to the national management standards, then you are probably already familiar with most of the key ideas on which the standards are based. To achieve their key purpose, which is defined as achieving the organization's objectives and continuously improving its performance, managers need to perform four key roles: managing operations, managing finance, managing people and managing information. Each of these key roles has a sub-structure of units and elements, each with associated performance and assessment criteria.

The reason for the qualification 'in part' is that organizations are different, and jobs within them are different. Thus the generic management standards probably do not cover all the management competences that you may need to possess in your job. There are almost certainly additional things, specific to your own situation in your own organization, that you need to be able to do. The standards are necessary, but almost certainly not sufficient. Only you, in discussion with your boss, will be able to decide what other capabilities you need to possess. But the standards are a place to start, a basis on which to build. Once you have demonstrated your proficiency against the standards, it will stand you in good stead as you progress through your organization, or change jobs.

So how do the new standards change the process by which you develop yourself as a manager? They change the process of development, or of gaining a management qualification, quite a lot. It is no longer a question of acquiring information and facts, perhaps by being 'taught' in some classroom environment, and then being tested to see what you can recall. It involves demonstrating, in a quite specific way, that you can do certain things to a particular standard of performance. And because of this, it puts a much greater onus on you to manage your own development, to decide how you can demonstrate any particular competence, what evidence you need to present, and how you can collect it. Of course, there will always be people to advise and guide you in this, if you need help.

But there is another dimension, and it is to this that this series of books is addressed. While the standards stress ability to perform, they do not ignore the traditional knowledge base that has been associated with 'management studies'. Rather, they set this in a different context. The standards are supported by 'underpinning knowledge and understanding' which has three components:

- Purpose and context, which is knowledge and understanding of the manager's objectives, and of the relevant organizational and environmental influences, opportunities and values.
- Principles and methods, which is knowledge and understanding of the theories, models, principles, methods and techniques that provide the basis of competent managerial performance.
- Data, which is knowledge and understanding of specific facts likely to be important to meeting the standards.

Possession of the relevant knowledge and understanding underpinning the standards is needed to support competent managerial performance as specified in the standards. It also has an important role in supporting the transferability of management capabilities. It helps to ensure that you have done more than learned 'the way we do things around here' in your own organization. It indicates a recognition of the wider things which underpin competence, and that you will be able to change jobs or organizations and still be able to perform effectively.

These books cover the knowledge and understanding underpinning the management standards, most specifically in the category of principles and methods. But their coverage is not limited to the minimum required by the standards, and extends in both depth and breadth in many areas. The authors have tried to approach these underlying principles and methods in a practical way. They use many short cases and examples which we hope will demonstrate how, in practice, the principles and methods, and knowledge of purpose and context plus data, support the ability to perform as required by the management standards. In particular we hope that this type of presentation will enable you to identify and learn from similar examples in your own managerial work.

You will already have noticed that one consequence of this new focus on the standards is that the traditional 'functional' packages of knowledge and theory do not appear. The standard textbook titles such as 'quantitative methods', 'production management', 'organizational behaviour' etc. disappear. Instead, principles and methods have been collected together in clusters that more closely match the key roles within the standards. You will also find a small degree of overlap in some of the volumes, because some principles and methods support several of the individual units within the standards. We hope you will find this useful reinforcement.

Having described the positive aspects of standards-based management development, it would be wrong to finish without a few cautionary remarks. The developments described above may seem simple, logical and uncontroversial. It did not always seem that way in the years of work which led up to the introduction of the standards. To revert to the revolution analogy, the process has been marked by ideological conflict and battles over sovereignty and territory. It has sometimes been unclear which side various parties are on

– and indeed how many sides there are! The revolution, if well advanced, is not at an end. Guerilla warfare continues in parts of the territory.

Perhaps the best way of describing this is to say that, while competence-based standards are widely recognized as at least a major part of the answer to improving managerial performance, they are not the whole answer. There is still some debate about the way competences are defined, and whether those in the standards are the most appropriate on which to base assessment of managerial performance. There are other models of management competences than those in the standards.

There is also a danger in separating management performance into a set of discrete components. The whole is, and needs to be, more than the sum of the parts. Just like bowling an off-break in cricket, practising a golf swing or forehand drive in tennis, you have to combine all the separate movements into a smooth, flowing action. How you combine the competences, and build on them, will mark your own individual style as a manager.

We should also be careful not to see the standards as set in stone. They determine what today's managers need to be able to do. As the arena in which managers operate changes, then so will the standards. The lesson for all of us as managers is that we need to go on learning and developing, acquiring new skills or refining existing ones. Obtaining your certificate or diploma is like passing a mile post, not crossing the finishing line.

All the changes and developments of recent years have brought management qualifications, and the processes by which they are gained, much closer to your job as a manager. We hope these books support this process by providing bridges between your own experience and the underlying principles and methods which will help you to demonstrate your competence. Already, there is a lot of evidence that managers enjoy the challenge of demonstrating competence, and find immediate benefits in their jobs from the programmes based on these new-style qualifications. We hope you do too. Good luck in your career development.

Paul Jervis

Acknowledgements

The authors gratefully acknowledge the support and forbearance of their partners Sarah and Margit.

Part One   Introduction

1 Using the book effectively

Aims and learning objectives

Welcome to *Managing in the Public Sector*. This book is a product in the same way that an ice cream or a vacuum cleaner is, in that we have produced it with the overall aim of meeting a particular need. The need we set out to meet is that of the middle level manager in the public (or not for profit) sector who is considering further training and/or qualification. If you are such a person and you are considering a management qualification based upon the Management Charter Initiative standards then you will find that this book caters for you. It is written by two authors who have considerable public sector work experience as both professionals and as managers.

The particular aims of this chapter are to:

- introduce the book to you and explain the way it is set out
- offer some guidance on how you might use the book
- discuss the concept of managerial competence and competency
- outline the background of the Management Charter Initiative (MCI) and the development of management education in the UK
- give guidance on the demonstration of underpinning knowledge and gathering evidence for a portfolio to satisfy the requirements of the Middle Management Standards (National Vocational Qualification level 5)
- introduce other sources of information of value to the public sector manager.

At the end of this chapter you will be able to:

- explain what managerial competence and competency are
- understand the place of Management Charter Initiative (MCI) standards in the overall context of managerial education and training in the UK. In particular you will be aware of how the public sector have used these standards
- start acquiring or reinforcing your underpinning knowledge about management in the public sector in the UK
- understand the nature of portfolio evidence used to demonstrate competence for the purpose of seeking a National Vocational Qualification (NVQ) Award.

Layout of the book

The book is set out in a particular way to make it easier for you to access the contents. Rather than simply using chapters we have also divided the book into 'parts'. The first part seeks to introduce the book, the role of 'competence' in management development and National Vocational Qualifications (NVQs). It also introduces some of the key elements of the MCI standards at middle manager level.

The second part (Understanding the Public Sector) which includes Chapters 2, 3 and 4 largely focuses upon the general background that distinguishes the environment of the public sector manager. In effect it covers the overall underpinning knowledge that you require as a manager in the public sector. To some extent this should be familiar territory to you. However the chapters will provide the link between your experience and the theoretical work of a number of writers in both the area of management in general and the public sector in particular. You should also find that these chapters enable you to appreciate the key themes which are important across the whole public sector environment and make links between your organization and other areas (i.e. charities and voluntary organizations, the National Health Service, central government and local government).

The third part (The Competent Manager in the Public Sector) is where we focus upon the key roles which define the MCI standards. These are covered in Chapters 5, 6, 7 and 8, with the main focus of each chapter being indicated by the title. Many managers have a particular role specialism whether it be finance, human resource management, operations or whatever. However, in each chapter we seek to cover the key roles from a public sector perspective using appropriate examples to illustrate good practice.

The fourth part (Broader Issues and the Public Sector) introduces issues which you as a middle level manager need to be aware of in your current and future role. Strategic planning and strategic management is covered because you need to be able to understand and practise this. Chapter 10 addresses the growing importance of performance criteria and in particular the impact of citizen (customer) charters. The public sector perspective is, we believe, significantly different from that of the private for-profit sector. These chapters seek to bring out the flavour of the public and not-for-profit sector.

The final part (Bringing it All Together) aims to bring issues together and take a look at the future, summarizes the key points emerging from the preceding parts of the book and suggests ways in which you can continue to develop your managerial competencies.

How to use the book

You will notice that we set out each chapter in a particular way. At the beginning of each chapter we indicate what the aims and learning objectives of the chapter are. At the end of each chapter we offer a summary and also action and discussion points and a guide to further reading. We believe that you, the reader, will benefit from this accessible and clear format. Your time is a scarce commodity and in your work you rightly expect things to be set out in as straightforward a fashion as possible.

The majority of managers who read this book will be considering or undertaking management training or qualifications. Therefore you may wish to look for information to help you gain the understanding for a particular aspect of a qualification. If this is NVQ-based using the MCI standards then you should find the particular chapters dealing with it easy to identify. We have also provided, in Appendix A, a matrix which maps the content of the chapters to the main requirements of the Middle Management Standards (NVQ level 5). At the end of each chapter you will find a number of suggestions for action you can take to develop and demonstrate your managerial competence. Each of these action points will be referenced to a particular Unit of Competence in the matrix. If you successfully complete every activity you will have approached each Unit of Competence from at least four, and as many as nine, different angles.

In one of the James Bond novels 'M', his boss, observes that 'shooting the hell out of a piece of cardboard proves nothing'. Similarly you cannot expect to somehow acquire managerial competence merely by reading (and rereading) this or any other book. Rather you have to link the contents of the book with your day-to-day activities in the workplace. The action points at the end of each chapter are intended for this purpose. Because they are also based upon the MCI Middle Management Standards these action points should help you to apply the concepts in this book to your work as a manager.

The suggested further reading is given for you to explore aspects of each chapter further. We provide our own comments about the further reading to save you time. The books recommended as further reading may not necessarily be the ones most esteemed in academic terms. Academics often write for very specialized readers who are comfortable with technical terms and who do not value ease of presentation as much as the more general reader. The description of a PhD dissertation as something written by one for an audience of four springs to mind. Therefore we indicate for each suggested reading our opinion of its ease of readability for the average middle level manager. Quite possibly you may have more academic leaning than the average manager. In which case we would encourage you to follow up the more specialist recommended reading.

Nature of managerial competency

In the debate leading to the introduction of management standards in the UK there was a considerable amount of discussion about competence. Part of the discussion was about the difference between competence and competency. Purists in the field will maintain the need to distinguish between these. A practical academic writing on the subject offers the following distinction (Weightman, 1995).

- Competence/competences underline the behaviours thought necessary to achieve a desired outcome.
- Competency/competencies are things you can demonstrate . . . where it is clear when the behaviour is successful.

The MCI standards are based around the second definition – that of competency. In short they seek to set out things which you demonstrate in order to show that you meet the standards. However as Jane Weightman points out management skills are more subtle and their demonstration requires knowledge and understanding.

She also notes that the need for transferable qualifications in the European Community has fostered a greater interest in competencies. We would add that the need to address issues of equality of opportunity within the workplace also has a lot to do with the competency movement. Demonstration of competency is a fairer way to decide on promotion and ability than simple possession of academic degrees, status of school attended, personal attractiveness or social class (all of which have been widely used in both the private and public sector).

Because competency is about demonstrating performance and managers usually work through other people this creates an interesting challenge for managerial competency. When you take a driving test, which involves demonstrating competency, you expect the car to behave predictably. When you press the accelerator or the brake you expect the car to speed up or slow down. However when you as a manager seek to demonstrate competency then you find that you need to rely upon the co-operation of other people to do it.

There is a story told about Harry Truman, an American President who was succeeded by 'Ike' Eisenhower. Eisenhower had previously been an army General. Truman made a comment to the effect of: 'Poor Ike, he'll come into the White House and say do this and do that but nothing will happen because this isn't like the Army'. Truman's comments were in fact unfair on Eisenhower. He had much experience of working with politicians and competing generals during the Second World War and knew how to persuade, influence and plead to get his way. However they do capture a key aspect of managerial competency. A manager who simply issues orders and directives is not necessarily competent *even if* those orders and directives are exactly right to resolve the problem. People, and organizations, are not machines simply to be driven. People need to understand why an action is required – better still they should be involved in decisions and feel motivated to carry them through. Managerial competency is demonstrated by recognizing this and accomplishing objectives through others rather than by riding rough-shod over people.

Managing yourself and managing others

This gets to the heart of our 'product'. We want you to find that in using, rather than just reading, this book you have a real developmental experience, and that this spills over into your management of others. Whenever we are helping managers to learn we always start from the premise that if you cannot manage and develop yourself you will have little chance of managing and developing others. Good management is built upon sound planning which, in turn, requires the skills of effective analysis. As a manager you need to be able to analyse your own behaviour and that of others, both as individuals and in teams. You need to be able to understand what is happening in your organization and how this relates to your organization's relationship with its external environment (that is all the people, agencies, opportunities and threats which have an important influence on your organization, but are not part of it). We will be encouraging you to develop your understanding and analytical skills by broadly following the process known as 'experiential learning'.

In essence experiential learning occurs when somebody has an experience (i.e. in the context of managerial learning takes some managerial action), reflects on that experience, draws some general lessons from that experience (i.e. develops a 'theory' about what happened and why) and then uses that theory to plan for, or experiment with, the next experience. Then the whole cycle starts again. It is relatively easily to get stuck at various parts of the cycle (for example to spend so much time reflecting on what went wrong that you are unable to move on) or to miss one of the stages out (for example to go from reflection to planning next actions without really using your reflection to develop a coherent theory to guide your actions).

Used effectively, experiential learning can be a powerful process for developing yourself, others, teams and whole organizations. Just reflect for a moment on your approach to developing your own knowledge and skills, helping others to enhance their own performance, and your contribution to team development. How much time do you take to review your progress at work and your development as a manager? When a member of your staff has just dealt with a particularly difficult situation or project do you help them reflect on the experience and use it to plan ways of dealing with the next similar issue even more effectively? At the end of a long team meeting, does the team take a few minutes to review the effectiveness of the meeting, decide what contributed to the relative level of effectiveness (and ineffectiveness) and plan to be even more effective at the next meeting. In our experience it is not uncommon for teams to meet for three hours, only adequately cover the first three agenda items, rush the rest through in the last ten minutes, and *still* not allow five minutes for a team review. This is really wasteful of precious organizational resources, particularly time and the talents of people.

It was, perhaps, because of a lack of such conscious and planned management and team development activities that, towards the end of the 1970s, serious concern began to be expressed about the quality of management in the UK, compared with many of our international competitors, leading to a review of management education and development, which we will discuss next.

Background of management qualifications/training

In the 1980s two influential reports appeared which examined the situation of management education in the UK (Constable and McCormack, 1987; Handy, 1987). They drew attention to a need for more management education and commented on the lack of formal training for managers.

Since then there has been a great growth in educational provision particularly in terms of MBA courses. Indeed the current MBA provision exceeds the targets suggested by the reports. However this growth in MBA provision has been marked by a considerable variety in quality in terms of the course content, teaching and course participants. Currently there are two potential accrediting bodies (the Association of MBAs and the Association of Business Schools). The majority of UK MBA courses are, at the time of writing, accredited by neither body. Currently there are senior management standards being piloted by the Management Charter Initiative which are aimed at MBA level. However we believe that it may be some time before these become widely accepted in what is a confused and congested MBA market.

At the level of Diploma in Management Studies there has been a long tradition of academic provision. The introduction, by the MCI, of Junior Management Standards (M1) led to a number of academic and accrediting bodies breaking the Diploma in Management Studies into two parts. The first part was mapped onto the Junior Management Standards and often was associated with the award of a Certificate in Management. There has been a considerable degree of success in the adoption of the Junior Management Standards. In particular they have significantly influenced the delivery and approach of management education even when the providers or participants have not actually registered for Management NVQ level 4.

The second part is likely to become increasingly linked to the Middle Management Standards (M2). In our experience there has been a degree of reluctance on the part of higher education institutions to adopt wholeheartedly the standards at Diploma level. This is largely associated with concerns over the need to protect and foster

Carlisle Library
CheckOut Receipt

09/12/2003
02:45 pm

Item:Management for the public domain :
enabling the learning society
Due Date: 14/01/2004 23:59

Item:Managing in the public sector
Due Date: 14/01/2004 23:59

Thank You for using
the 3M SelfCheck System!

01228 404660

academic learning. Nevertheless the concept of competence, having become established at the Certificate level, is likely to make progress here.

MCI and Management Standards

The Management Charter Initiative is an official organization which takes a leading role in developing management standards. Interestingly it is not in itself an awarding body but rather it accredits the programmes of other organizations.

The management standards are not set in stone and are likely to undergo change and adjustment. This is true of all occupational standards and management ones are no different. Just as you might be concerned if your plumber or dentist was assessed by standards which had not been updated for fifteen years so it will be the case that the kinds of competence required by managers will alter in the light of changes in knowledge.

For example the earlier editions of the management standards stressed recruitment and selection skills. The skills associated with reducing the workforce through lay-off and redundancy are not specifically mentioned. However, particularly in certain sectors of the economy, this has been a key activity for managers in the past few years and we expect the new standards to reflect this by including an element concerned with dismissing people who are redundant.

Therefore we would advise the reader to be alert to the fact that the competencies set out by the MCI (or indeed by any validating body) are almost certainly not the whole story as to what is required of a manager in the current time frame and immediate future. An important component of the competencies of middle level managers is to be able to scan the environment in which they work and be able to predict what skills will be required in the future.

Nature of underpinning knowledge

A key aspect of demonstrating managerial competency lies in what is called the underpinning knowledge. The underpinning knowledge is the understanding which enables you not simply to engage in an demonstration of competence but also to appreciate the factors which made it successful.

An example might be drawn from a different field to illustrate. Let us suppose that your washing machine packs up and you call an engineer. The engineer listens to your account of what has happened and then leans over the machine and makes a brief adjustment. The machine works. It has all taken about five minutes. The engineer then presents a bill for £30 and you object to this amount for five minutes' work – after all it represents some £360 per hour. The engineer thinks for a moment and the rewrites the bill – '£1 for labour and £29 for knowledge'.

We intend that this book should give you much of the underpinning knowledge associated with being a competent middle level manager in the public sector. It will not furnish you with *all* the knowledge since some of that will be specific to your own organization. However we hope that it will give you a broader picture of the public sector than you probably have acquired from your own organizational and occupational perspective. It should enable you to consider a wider range of managerial possibilities within the public not-for-profit sector.

Use of portfolios in management education

If you have already started on an NVQ route in management education then you will almost certainly know what a portfolio is. In this context a portfolio represents a collection of material gathered for the purpose of showing your managerial competency.

The portfolio should contain a variety of material which is linked to the various MCI standards. Some of this will be direct evidence such as reports which you might have prepared for your work. It may also include witness statements from colleagues, your boss and other people which attest to your competency in a particular element of the standards. It should also contain evidence that you possess the underpinning knowledge.

It is important to stress that a good portfolio will contain a range of supportive evidence. Some of this may not come from your workplace at all. Almost everyone has a richness of experience outside of the workplace. Perhaps you have been a school governor or keep the accounts for a local organization. Such experience can be very useful in demonstrating competency especially where evidence from the workplace is limited or not recent.

We have designed this book with the construction of a portfolio in mind. Obviously there are many other sources of information that you can use as well as this book to keep your portfolio up to date and ensure that you are aware of the latest issues and examples of good practice in public sector management. The next section reviews some of these other sources and resources.

Other sources of information

Journals

Public sector management is blessed with a wide range of journals addressing its needs. Some of these have a more academic focus, while others concentrate on providing news of developments without necessarily going into the depth of analysis that you might expect from an academic publication. Both types are of value to you as a manager and we will briefly review some journals which we think may be of particular use to you.

Health Service Journal
A weekly journal offering up-to-the-minute news together with articles featuring all aspects of health service management. Offers some excellent case examples and models of good practice.

International Journal of Public Sector Management
Internationally focused, but with good coverage of the UK. Tends to be well written and both academically credible and practically oriented. Worth putting on your list of journals to consult regularly.

Local Government Chronicle
Good for both news items and longer articles in the area of local government and its relationship with the broader environment.

Local Government Policy Making
An academic journal worth exploring when you want to really ground your underpinning knowledge and understanding on in-depth analysis.

Management Decision
One of the more academically focused journals and worth scanning for in-depth analysis of the processes of decision making in organizations, including public sector examples.

Management Learning
A journal concentrating on the processes of management education and development with a high incidence of case examples drawn from all areas of the public sector.

Municipal Journal
Offers a wide coverage of local government issues, with some concentration on the management of technical services.

Non-profit and Voluntary Sector Quarterly
Useful, practical, journal offering an analysis of current issues together with debate and material for practical application.

People Management
The journal of the Institute of Personnel and Development. Considers 'people' issues across all sectors of the economy, with frequent articles reporting on the pubic sector and regular news updates.

Personnel Today
Distributed (free) to people on its controlled circulation list. Tends to have shorter articles than *People Management* and offers a succinct analysis of current issues and developments in human resource management and development.

Public Administration
Good coverage of the sector, academically sound and practically useful.

Public Money and Management
Striking a good balance between academic depth and practical application. Covers both the 'money' and the 'management' aspects very well. Another one for your 'consult regularly' list.

Voluntas
A more academically oriented journal with an international coverage, very good for developing the breadth and depth of your underpinning knowledge and understanding.

We live in the information age and that is as true for managers in the public sector as for anyone else. Whilst books and journals represent an important source of information there are other forms of media that offer certain advantages.

The press

The national and local press are a vital source of topical information. Indeed John Naisbit, an American futurologist, draws much of his data on emerging global trends from local newspapers.

Most UK public managers are well acquainted with the *Guardian* newspaper if only to search for jobs. The Wednesday edition is the minimum essential reading in order to keep abreast of public sector issues. The *Independent* has also established a good reputation for coverage in this area. The clarity of writing and broader sweep of the *Financial Times* has much to commend it – even though it may not earn you much 'street credibility' in certain areas of the public sector! A thoughtful public sector manager would not neglect the wider press spectrum. Some of the writing in the *Daily Telegraph* provides a good barometer of informed opinion on the right of the political spectrum.

If you have any accountability to local politicians then you neglect your local press at your peril. If there is any kind of local concern raised via the press that can impact upon you then you can bet good money that there will be strong political interest in your response.

Radio

The comments about local press are also true, though to a varying extent, of local radio. However what we would like to focus upon here is the potential offered by national radio to inform and improve your knowledge and effectiveness.

Radio programmes, particularly some of those on Radio 4, are often of a very high quality and can pick up on complex issues before they get reported as TV documentaries. We would highlight in particular the following Radio 4 programmes which often cover matters of major relevance to public sector managers. The usual times of broadcast are given although these can change:

Analysis (Thursday evenings – repeated Sunday afternoon)
This is a wide-ranging programme which often covers highly relevant issues. It tends to have a political or philosophical orientation. It is well informed and balanced. The presenters are usually nationally respected experts who in turn draw upon the best sources. Listening to this 45-minute programme can sometimes be more effective than reading several books on the subject.

File on 4 (Tuesday evenings – repeated Saturday afternoon)
This programme usually focuses upon UK topical issues with a very strong public sector focus. In our opinion it is more journalistic than *Analysis* but usually manages to strike a balance. The issues the programme covers are sometimes subsequently picked up in later TV documentaries. There is little doubt in our view that a public sector

manager who listens to this programme will both be better informed and also be alerted to 'public sector banana skins'.

In Business (Sunday evenings)
Whilst this programme, by its very title, is not specifically addressed to the public sector manager, there is often a highly relevant managerial content. Programmes have looked at such areas as stakeholding, CCT, outsourcing and the changing nature of work.

Other regular Radio 4 programmes that are worth mentioning include:

Costing the Earth because of the likely need for all managers to become more environmentally aware.

The Net for those managers who wish to keep abreast of IT developments (and this really should include *all* managers).

A significant advantage of using radio programmes as a source of information is that you can easily tape them and play the tapes whilst commuting or travelling.

Television

Whilst the UK is not blessed (or cursed?!) yet with the range of TV channels that exist in the USA there is still plenty to choose from. Britain has a well-earned reputation for producing high quality documentary programmes.

In our experience some of these programmes have been particularly useful for public sector managers. Indeed for some time management lecturers have made use of such programmes to assist in teaching.

Public Eye and *Panorama* are both programmes which often pick up on major issues in the public domain. They are usually carefully researched and seek to provide a balanced picture.

Just as the local and regional press can be an important source of comment on local issues, so can the regional TV news programmes.

There has been a rapid growth in the use of TV as an information medium especially with the use of video recorders to tape programmes broadcast in the early hours. The penetration of the public sector here has been quite remarkable. Currently 'The Learning Channel' offers Voluntary Sector TV, Royal College of Nursing and the Benefit Agency.

Computer-based media

As we write this our university is building a large extension building for its library. This extension will not be noted for its large holdings of books and long isles of shelved journals. Rather users will access information via electronic databases.

It is hard to exaggerate the impact of IT. The leisurely search along dusty shelves will be replaced by the computer screen and 'search algorithms'. As a manager, when you are required to produce a report on a subject, you can access much, if not all, the relevant information without opening a book – indeed perhaps without leaving your desk.

Almost all the major broadsheet journals and newspapers are now accessible via computer searches. We do not seek to provide you with detailed instruction on how to do this here because it is a skill only acquired through practice. But make no mistake it is a skill which you must acquire if you wish to function efficiently to and beyond the millennium and we think that it is important to alert you to some of the main sources of electronically mediated information and discussion. You are increasingly likely to be able to access some, if not all, of these resources from work. If not you will be able to do so from a university or college library, or possibly from your local public library (we have drawn on information from South Bank University Library and Learning Resources Department in preparing this section, and gratefully acknowledge their help).

CD-ROM (Compact Disc Read Only Memory)

These are computer-read discs which contain indexes or abstracts of articles covering a number of journals in a particular subject area. Examples of CD-ROMs of particular interest to public sector managers include:

ABI/INFORM, indexing over 1000 business journals covering business, finance and management. ABI/INFORM tends to concentrate on American journals but does include others from across the world.
Child Data, indexing books, journals and reports in the National Children's Bureau Library. Covers health, education and welfare of children and young people.
CINAHL (Cumulative Index to Nursing and Allied Health Literature) with references from virtually all English language nursing and allied journals.
ERIC (Education Resources Information Centre). The national US database for education, although it does index some British journals.
PAIS (Public Affairs Information Service). Again an American database covering public policy, business, economics, government and other social sciences, with some British and much European material.
VOLNET. Contains references to articles, press items, reports and other publications in areas such as community development, social policy and child policy together with information from agencies such as the Community Development Foundation and Barnardos.
Newspapers and journals. CD-ROMS are available giving the full text of journals such as the *Economist* and newspapers including the *Financial Times*, the *Guardian* and the *Observer*.

The Internet and the World Wide Web

The Internet is the name for the system which links millions of computers throughout the world, allowing them to communicate with each other. The World Wide Web (WWW) is a service on the Internet which uses special computer software to give users access to the information on the Internet. WWW is becoming the standard way of navigating around the Internet.

Once you have access to the Internet you will find it, in turns, invaluable and valueless; fascinating and frustrating; a time-saver and a time-waster! The Internet can be used for sending and receiving electronic-mail (e-mail); searching library catalogues around the world; accessing information such as reference material; databases; and discussing issues of common interest with a wide range of people (sometimes known as mailing lists or newsgroups). Each site on the Internet has its own address on the WWW known as its Uniform Resource Locator (URL). There are obviously thousands of addresses on the Internet but to give you some indication of the resources available on the Internet we have drawn up the following short list of sites which may be of particular interest to managers in the public sector:

HM Treasury Information. URL http://www.hm-treasury.gov.uk/
Contains items such as the full text of H.M. Treasury publications, including press releases, ministers' speeches, minutes of the Chancellor's monthly meetings, and full details of the Budget.
HMSO. URL http://www.hmso.gov.uk/
Contains the HMSO catalogue (including abstracts) and details of HMSO bookshops and stockists.
Central Statistical Office (CSO). URL http://www.emap.com/cso/welcome.htm
Contains information about the CSO and its publications and 'Statistic of the Day'!
CCTA Government Information Service. URL http://www.open.gov.uk/
CCTA is the UK Government's Centre for Information Systems. This pilot Web site includes information on the Citizen's Charter Unit, and will include information on local government services.
GreenNet. URL http://www.gn.apc.org/
GreenNet is designed for use by environment, peace, human rights and development groups. Together with many other sites it also contains links to other related resources.
Gingerbread Group. URL http://www.demon.co.uk/charities/ginger/
The Gingerbread group is a support organization for single parent families in England and Wales. Their Web site contains information about Gingerbread, local and regional groups, related organizations, information on their advice line and details of their publications.
RNIB. URL http://www.rnib.org.uk/
Provided by the Royal National Institute for the Blind and containing information about the Institute, details of the services it provides, press releases, fact sheets, product information and related sites of interest.
Voluntary Organizations Internet Server (VOIS). URL http://www.vois.org.uk/
This site currently contains information for the National Council for Voluntary Organizations (NCVO), Partners in the Countryside, Shelter, National Council for Social Concern, Volunteer Centre UK, and VOIS itself.
UKSOCWORK. URL http://www.nisw.org.uk/net/listserv/uk.html/
Established by the National Institute for Social Work and providing a broad forum for discussion of topics of common interest to those in social work, and related services.
ESRC Data Archive. URL http://dawww.essex.ac.uk/
Houses the largest collection of accessible computer-readable data in the social sciences and humanities in the UK. Founded in 1967, it now contains approximately 4500 datasets.

Similarly access is also available to governmental, not-for-profit and other public sector and related organizations across the world. The American governmental services appear to be particularly open. But beware, as we said earlier once you start to 'trawl the net' you can find yourself spending hours pursuing seemingly interesting leads to no avail. There is, however, some really useful material out there, once you know where to find it.

Summary

In this part of the book we have set its purpose in the context of helping you continue to develop your managerial competence, and gaining formal recognition through NVQs and other qualifications if you wish. We have explained that the book sets out to ensure that you have the necessary knowledge and understanding to underpin your managerial competence: in particular we have suggested that knowledge, understanding and competence may best be tested and developed through using an experiential learning approach. As a manager you may find this approach to be as valuable in managing the development of your staff, your team and the whole organization as it is for yourself. Management in the public sector is a fast-moving subject and to maintain your competence you need to be continually updating your knowledge and skills, through using this book, and accessing some of the other resources we have mentioned above we hope that you will be able to achieve this.

Action points and discussion points

(Items in italics are intended to encourage the reader to develop greater intellectual awareness, items in plain type are focused upon work-related activity.)

Review internal and external operating environments

Prepare a review of your current sources of information which you use in developing your managerial competence. Which categories do they fall into? What other sources could/should you be using?

Set yourself a small research project and use some of the computer-based media to gather data on your research. If you are already familiar with some of the resources, experiment with other ones. Join a newsgroup or other forum on the Internet and discuss the results of your research with other people.

Manage self to optimize performance

If you are not already doing so, begin to construct a portfolio of material which you can use as 'evidence' of your managerial competence (even if you are not contemplating presenting your portfolio for a qualification it can still be invaluable when preparing job applications and for interviews).

Tune into one of the television or radio programmes featured in this chapter and make notes of the programme as if you were attending a formal lecture. Review your notes and critique the programme. What were the main points it was making? How valid are they in your opinion? Where do they match, and differ from, your own managerial experience? What have you learnt from the programme? What other questions has it raised for you?

Maintain effective working relationships

Take a piece of paper and draw a circle in the middle of it to represent yourself at work. Now add circles for all the other people you have significant working relationships with (you could put the more important relationships nearer to your circle, and the less important ones further away). Taking each relationship in turn ask yourself what you expect of the other person, and what they expect of you (in doing this you will be conducting a 'role analysis'). The next step is to identify where you are not getting what you expect, or not fully providing what others expect of you. Why is this? What are the implications of these gaps for your work? How can the gaps be tackled and reduced?

List the criteria, in your opinion, of an effective working relationship (and think about how you are defining 'effective' in this context). Use appropriate opportunities to test out your list with other people at work (you might want to do this formally as part of feedback on your performance as a manager during supervision or appraisal sessions with your staff or less formally through individual or team discussions). How has your list changed as a result of these consultations? How well do you perform against these criteria? What are the five main steps that you can take to develop your working relationships?

Develop teams and individuals to enhance performance

Reflect on the way you help others learn at work. What techniques do you use? How effective are they? How do you help people who are having difficulty meeting the performance standards expected of them? Could more attention to the experiential learning cycle improve you own performance in managing yourself and other people?

Develop teams and individuals to enhance performance/Develop management teams

How effective are the teams of which you are a manager, leader or member? What differentiates, in your experience, really effective teams from less effective ones? How can you use this information to develop your own competence as a manager?

Do some research away from your workplace with people you know. Get them talking about their experience of teams, both as participants and observers. As soon as you have the opportunity jot down the main points arising from these discussions (you may get some odd looks if you are scribbling frantically while they are talking). Once you have collected a dozen or so sets of comments analyse your 'data'. Think about ways which you can use to categorize what you have heard (e.g. 'Work Teams', 'Sports Teams', 'Formal Teams', 'Informal Teams', 'Good Teams', 'Bad Teams', etc.) and then note the comments made against each category. What does this tell you about the way people see teams? What are the implications for your own work in teams, both as a manager and as a participant?

Part Two   Understanding the Public Sector

2 The public sector environment

Aims and learning objectives

The aims of this chapter are to introduce you to the public sector in the United Kingdom with a particular focus upon the key theoretical concepts that assist in understanding it. By the end of this chapter you should possess a general idea of the scope of the public sector and be able to contrast the public and private sector on a conceptual level.

At the end of this chapter and associated activities and reading you will be able to:

- appreciate the way in which the public administration/bureaucratic approaches have come to be replaced by what has been described as new public management
- understand the effect of 'New Right' thinking which has influenced much of the reform activity of the last four Conservative Governments
- use theory to understand the behaviour, culture and structure of public sector organizations.

In competence terms this chapter provides an overall understanding of the public sector. The reader wishing to develop a closer understanding of particular theoretical approaches should follow the guidelines for further reading at the end of the chapter and the references within the text (see the Bibliography at the end of the book).

Theoretical underpinnings

The scope of the public sector

The public sector impacts upon all people who live in the UK and indeed many who do not. If you are reading this book from the perspective of a manager in the public sector you will need little convincing of this. But suppose a visitor from abroad picks up the book. How might the public sector in this country have affected him or her? They do not live in this country; they do not work here; they (probably) do not pay direct taxes in this country.

The comments we will make about these overseas visitors are generally applicable to the public sector in most countries and are illustrative of the scope and importance of the public sector in general.

Let us consider the way the public sector might have an impact.

- The first effect is before our guests even arrive. If they originate from outside the European Community they might have had to obtain a visa before setting off. Whether they require such a visa will depend upon the law on the one hand, and on the other hand the discretion of public officials charged with regulating entry of overseas visitors.
- When our visitors arrive they will quickly encounter a whole welter of official requirements. The official requirements range from strict legal constraints (such as driving on the left) to more discretionary ones (such as parking or access to areas of public parks).
- They will often enjoy public provisions for things they have not had to pay for. There is no charge for walking in most parks or tolls for driving on our roads. Our guests will be able to do this without having directly paid towards it in the way that taxpayers of the country have.
- The visitors will also have access to public services such as the police without incurring a charge. In some circumstances they would also have access to fire or health services though increasingly these services are becoming less freely available.

Here we see the relevance of the public services to those who have not contributed to them through direct taxation and have no say through the political process. How much greater is the scope of the public sector to those who have an attachment through domicile, citizenship, employment, the ballot box etc.

The size of the public sector in the United Kingdom can be seen in terms of employment in the following table (Table 2.1). The trends over time are also shown. Over the period 1971–81 employment in the public sector has grown overall and within sectors. However since 1981 we have seen a reduction in public sector employment. This has been particularly pronounced in central government and public corporations through the 'Next Steps' agency programme and various privatizations. In the National Health Service (NHS) the trend has been associated with a transfer of staff to the NHS Trusts.

Philosophical aspects

As the previous section has shown the make-up of the public sector has changed considerably over the past twenty years. Though the public sector continues to be a major employer the numbers employed have fallen. This is not a matter of circumstance but rather as a consequence of policy. This policy in turn is based upon a new philosophical approach to the public sector. The general characteristics of this approach have been called 'the New Right'. It is essen-

Table 2.1 UK public sector manpower, 1971–1994 (*mid-year counts*)

	Total employed ('000)			% change	% change
	1971	*1981*	*1994*	*1971–81*	*1981–94*
Total workforce	24 533	24 489	25 304	–0.2%	3.3%
Private sector	17 906	17 304	19 701	–3.4%	13.9%
Public sector	6 627	7 185	5 290	8.4%	–26.4%
Breakdown of public sector					
Central government	1 966	2 419	1 215	23.0%	–49.8%
Local authorities	2 652	2 899	2 642	9.3%	–8.9%
Public corporations	2 009	1 867	1 433	–7.1%	–23.2%
NHS Trusts	0	0	966	n/a	n/a
NHS (non Trusts)	785	1 207	205	53.8%	–83.0%
Total NHS	785	1 207	1 171	53.8%	–3.0%

Source: HMSO (1995).

tial to understand the characteristics of 'New Right' philosophies in order to understand how the changes in the public sector have come about. We would direct the reader to the recommended reading at the end of this chapter if they wish to explore these further.

Customer approach

Traditionally the public sector often viewed those people seeking services as clients. The public official applies rules and judgement and allocates resources on this basis. The only choice accorded to the client was the choice to refuse or accept. In certain circumstances not even this choice was allowed.

The New Right portrays the recipient of public services as a customer. The customer concept draws upon private sector models and implies an ability to not only choose between providers but also to influence (or even determine) the nature of what they are offered.

The concept of the market

The New Right believes in the power of the marketplace to determine both price and product issues in the public sector. In order for the marketplace to operate there needs to be competition between providers for the customer. If the only choice offered to the customer is to buy from one supplier then competition cannot be seen to exist.

Therefore if you want to introduce the market into the public sector then you must foster competition between different suppliers.

Individualism and self-reliance

Milton and Rose Friedman wrote a book called *Free to Choose* (1980) in which they praised the concepts of political and economic freedom. Their words are worth quoting (p. 65):

> An essential part of economic freedom is freedom to choose how to use our income: how much to spend on ourselves and on what items; how much to save and in what form; how much to give away and to whom.

The Friedmans' comment that this freedom is different from the freedom to vote for a government. The reason is that when you vote you usually have to compromise in terms of the choice between alternatives. Hence they say (p. 66, original emphasis):

> The ballot box produces conformity without unanimity; the marketplace unanimity without conformity. *That is why it is desirable to use the ballot box, so far as possible, only for those decisions where conformity is essential.*

Therefore the New Right moves beyond simply 'liberalizing the market' but rather stresses the primacy of the individual and favours an active distrust of the state. Writing from a 'non' New Right perspective Samuel Brittan (1988, p. 212) comments that the New Economic Right:

> goes much further than market liberalism towards laissez-faire in its economic teaching, has little place for redistribution, and accepts the pattern of ownership which emerges from effort, luck and inheritance. It is profoundly suspicious of public action to cope with 'externalities' and places great emphasis on denationalization and low government spending.

For those unfamiliar with economic concepts 'externalities' are the impacts of economic activities which do not cost or benefit those people engaged in the activity. An obvious example is that bright lights of a shopping centre may have an impact upon those living nearby.

Purchaser/provider split

The separation of the role of purchasing from that of provision is regarded as essential in the transformation of public services. It has been described by Rodney Brook as the concept which underpins government thinking on the public sector (Pollitt and Harrison, 1992, p. 36). The development of 'arms length' arrangements is now familiar in both local government and in the health sector. Interestingly there are areas of the public sector where this split has operated for many years. For those readers familiar with social services the 'purchasing' of out-of-county (or out-of-borough) placements for adults or children in need of residential provision represented a form of purchaser–provider split. The social worker 'purchases' residential care for a client from a provider who is not the social worker's employer.

Contract culture

Inherent in the separation of purchaser and provider has been the growth of a 'contract culture'. This represents a significant move away from the previous reliance upon either management authority or professional pressures to obtain results. Instead of services being managed through a hierarchy or by professional standards reliance is now placed upon monitoring performance against contractual requirements.

Compulsory Competitive Tendering (CCT) is the obvious proof of the spread of this contract culture. The process of setting up CCT led to often highly specified and lengthy contract documents. With the move of CCT into the 'white collar' and professional areas of the public sector the new jargon of 'Service Level Agreement' has emerged.

Performance orientation

Staff working in a contractual situation are far more subject to performance measures. The concept that 'what can be measured should be measured' and that 'what is measured is done' stems from management theorists such as W. Edwards Deming (1982). The public sector has traditionally been orientated towards process rather than outcomes. It was not so important to do the right thing as to do it in the right way.

Pay and conditions flexibility

Variation in pay and conditions is associated with the adoption of the contract culture and performance measurement. Once you look at achievement against targets and the use of reward systems to promote this you move away from traditional public sector structures. The past tradition of seniority leading to promotion and payment for adhering to a process does not sit well in an outcome and results driven environment. Similarly the rate and conditions of service become less associated with the job and increasingly are related to the individual job performer.

The private/public sector continuum

This section will be based around Tomkins' typology (Tomkins, 1987). He suggests that there is no clear division which marks out the private from the public sector in respect of organizational forms. Rather he views it as a continuum ranging from fully private to fully public.

The previous section outlining the New Right perception may imply that there is no gradation between public and private – in effect almost all should be in the private. However in reality there is a continuum between the two. Cyril Tomkins provides one way of looking at this which offers a number of interim stages. This is shown in Figure 2.1.

Tomkins challenges some of the assumptions of the private sector being always more competitive than public sector. He also notes that considerations other than cost might weigh in the balance. So in discussing his continuum it is important not to assume that the continuum of competitiveness would automatically correspond.

The continuum has *fully private* organizations at one end. The nature of private ownership means that the company or organization is free to pursue its activities as long as it remains within the law of the land. Thus Richard Branson decided to sell his record business and move into airlines. He then moved into soft drinks and is now offering financial services. Within the category of private ownership are companies which have shareholders. Most household name companies such as Marks & Spencer would be found here. So also we would find formerly nationalized industries that are now fully privatized (such as the National Freight Corporation). The ownership of such enterprises is vested in the shareholders. In the example of the National Freight Corporation much of the shareholding is held by the staff themselves.

The next category is private with *part State ownership*. Many parts of the public sector pass through this stage as they are privatized. They are, in effect, privatized in stages. Here the organization is not

- Fully private
- Private with part State ownership
- Joint ventures
- Private regulated
- Public infrastructure: private operations
- Contracted out
- Public with 'managed' competition
- Public without competition

Figure 2.1 *The private–public continuum*

Source: Tomkins, C. R. (1987). *Achieving Economy, Efficiency and Effectiveness in the Public Sector*. Kegan Paul (p. 21).

necessarily free to act. The Government shareholding may act as a potential (or actual) restraint.

The prominence which has attached to pay rises (and overall remuneration) of the chief executives of these enterprises is a case in point. Compare the attention paid in Parliament to the salary level of Cedric Brown of British Gas with the reaction to the (similarly substantial) salary which Lord King, Chairman of British Airways received. A key difference was the presence of public ownership. Yet both organizations were originally clearly in the public sector.

Tomkins comments that the presence of a social issue might cause the State to maintain a measure of ownership in what could otherwise be a fully privatized operation. In the case of British Gas and British Airways a clear distinction was that most UK residents are customers of British Gas and do not perceive any evident competition in the market to supply them with gas. When you decide to fly there is almost always a choice of airline.

Joint ventures are to be found where there is a need to undertake some kind or project but it is seen as inappropriate for the public sector to assume the risk. The various inner city development corporations can be seen as an example. The government wishes to exercise a significant degree of control yet views the operation as requiring private sector capital (and probably expertise) for it to be effective. Examples of this include development corporations or inner city partnerships.

In the *Private regulated* sector we find natural monopolies or nationalized industries which have been sold into private ownership. The state continues to regulate usually by means of a pricing formula. The water industry is an example of such a natural monopoly.

In *Public infrastructure: Private operations* the State maintains ownership of the infrastructure but brings in private operators to run it. This is shown by various bridge-building projects where the bridge itself is in the public sector but it is operated by a private company. Interestingly for Eurotunnel shareholders the tunnel itself is leased to Eurotunnel and the ownership will revert to the State when the lease expires.

The UK public sector is full of examples of *Contracting out*. Local authority cleaning and refuse collection services were early examples. The contracting out may be (and often is) to the local authority itself under a purchaser/provider split.

Public with 'managed' competition – the internal market in the National Health Service would be an example of this. It has been described as a 'quasi-market'.

Public without competition – here the state regards competition as inappropriate and therefore maintains public ownership and operations. Obvious examples would be the armed forces and security services such as MI5.

From public administration to new public management

The history of the past fifteen years or so in the public sector has been one of a move from a 'public administration' approach to something which has been called New Public Management (Gunn, 1988; Willcocks and Harrow 1992). The traditional public administration approach was characterized by the following differences which Sue Dopson and Rosemary Stewart stressed in a key article (1990). They report on the results of major research study looking at the attitudes to change of middle managers. They compared several public sector organizations including Inland Revenue, NHS and Her Majesty's Stationery Office. They also looked at private sector organizations including a manufacturing company and a car parts distributor.

Figure 2.2 summarizes the key elements of the public administration tradition as described by Dopson and Stewart. If you have been in the public sector for over ten years you may well identify with many if not all of these elements. Indeed in some organizations they still exercise a considerable effect. But in a large part of the public sector they have been eroded by the emergence of a new public management perspective.

- Critical factors in the environment
  The public sector is less efficient or cost orientated than the private sector.
  Stakeholder interests are wider than in the private sector.
  The private sector has a clearer idea of who their customers are.
  It is harder for public sector managers to analyse their environment.

- Organizational constraints for public sector managers
  Policy directives are less clear for public sector managers.
  Decision making is more open and hence problematic.
  There is greater lobbying from pressure groups.
  The time constraints tend to be 'artificial'.
  Coalitions behind policy are more unstable and liable to disintegrate.
  Professional structures are very influential.
  Payment systems are less reward oriented.
  Strategic management is rare.

- Managers' responsibility and influence
  Accountability is more complex.
  Problems in influencing inputs.
  Difficulties in measuring outcomes.

Figure 2.2 *The public administration tradition summarized*

Source: Dopson and Stewart (1990).

The new public management is significantly influenced by the introduction of private sector practices and techniques. In 1988 Gunn published an influential and much quoted article, in which he noted:

Many of us have been raised in the tradition that management in the public sector is different from business management and that little, if anything, can be learned across the sectoral divide . . . this [is] the 'public administration' or 'classical' perspective. A more recent and equally simplistic view holds that the government has everything to learn from more efficient practices in the private sector . . . this [is] the 'business management' perspective (Gunn, 1988, p. 21).

He then continues to suggest that there might be a third perspective which he calls 'public management'. He draws upon American influences in defining public management, citing an American authority who describes it as 'a merger of the normative orientation of traditional public administration and the instrumental orientation of general management' (Gunn, 1988, p. 24). This has the strong implication that there are merits in both influences.

Gunn suggests various areas of the public sector where business practices and techniques could offer a great deal. Strategic management, purchasing and procurement and performance indicators are three areas he mentions. Significantly all of these areas have shown considerable responsiveness to business methods in the years following the publication of Gunn's article.

Subsequently two American authors, Osborne and Gaebler (1992), published a very influential account of the development and practice of public management in the USA. Perhaps significantly neither were academics and one (Gaebler) was a former city manager. The book became required reading for a number of top British civil servants and the authors have become minor celebrities on the speakers' circuit. Their ten maxims are as follows:

- Steering rather than rowing.
- Empowering rather than serving.
- Injecting competition into service delivery.
- Transforming rule driven organizations.
- Funding outcomes rather than inputs.
- Meeting customer not bureaucracy needs.
- Earning rather than spending.
- Prevention rather than cure.
- Participation rather than hierarchy.
- Getting change via the market.

In Table 2.2 we describe these ten maxims briefly and draw out their implications for the UK.

Domain theory

In work with public managers we have often encountered considerable resistance to the application of models of management beha-

Table 2.2 (continued)

Maxim	UK implications
6 Meeting customer not bureaucracy needs • Peters and Waterman concept of 'Close to Customer' • Growth in use of surveys to identify service needs • Development of TQM in local services • Giving people choices (example of giving education choices to military veterans)	• Growing use of charters • BS 5750 • Student grants as example – impact on higher/further education
7 Earning rather than spending • Traditional government focus upon expenditure • Now move towards income generation • Growth of barter (land for facilities) and joint ventures • Increase in fee charging • Investing for profit (entrepreneurialism) • Costing services	• Numerous examples in local government – Westminster, Hammersmith and Fulham • Still seen as at variance with values • Not often rewarded (either locally or centrally)
8 Prevention rather than cure • Tradition is to wait for something to break then fix it • Prevention involves future proofing – preventive maintenance • Incentives often are towards cure rather than prevention • Prevention becoming significant with environmental issues • Need to change incentives – strategic planning issues	• Often tied to rules and procedures and legal requirements • Recycling as example where it's beginning to happen

9 Participation rather than hierarchy
• Centralization is often the usual reaction to problems
• However decentralized responses are more:
  – flexible
  – effective
  – innovative
  – committed
  – productive
Knowledge often held locally
They suggest that decentralized and participative management is better than hierarchy and draw attention to a range of team-based approaches
	• Work force insecurity makes it difficult
	• White collar/blue collar, Professional/managerial, department divisions all still exist to some extent and impede participative management
	• However it is a growing trend in number of authorities

10 Getting change via the market
• They suggest that government can achieve change via structuring the market
• Examples such as requiring large deposits on bottles to reduce littering
• Concept is of moving away from 'programmes' to market regulation
• Change via 'programmes' or civil servants is slow – via the market it can occur quickly
• Ways of restructuring the market include:
  – rule setting
  – furnishing consumer information
  – creating demand
  – investment policy
  – use of taxation
  – charging fees
	• Often used implicitly (viz. through fees/eligibility)
	• Examples – private residential care, parking regulations, environmental health

Table 2.2 Summary of Osborne and Gaebler's ten maxims and their application to public management in the UK

Maxim	UK implications
1 Steering rather than rowing • Government is moving to a situation where policy decisions (steering) is separated from service delivery (rowing) • Government becomes a purchaser rather than a provider • Local government thus can utilize specialist providers • Government co-ordinates efforts and avoids becoming constrained by programme/service ownership	• Increasing use of voluntary organizations/private sector to provide service aspects • Increased sophistication of inspection/evaluation • Strategic focus using purchasing decisions to effect policy change • Suggestion of where the 'boundary' of privatization might lie • Tendency for political interference in operational issues (viz. the current local government reorganization)
2 Empowering rather than serving • Long tradition of self help – the rich diversity of associations and voluntarism • Problems associated with 'clienthood' • US experience particularly with schools, AIDS and housing – contrast between failure of professionals/bureaucrats and effect of local management • Associated with 'communitization' movement	• Current obsession with concept of community • Encouragement of voluntarism/empowerment (tenants/schools) • Issues of quangoization (lack of local autonomy) • Funding capture of voluntary organizations
3 Injecting competition into service delivery • They suggest competition leads to: – efficiency/cost savings – more customer response – innovation – higher staff morale • They offer examples of improvements in school education resulting from more competition	• CCT has led to some cost savings • TUPE has created a major obstacle • Is it 'real' competition or a managed market?
4 Transforming rule driven organizations • Traditional bureaucracies operate through rules • When things go wrong new rules are the response • Mission driven organizations: – look at the result rather than the process – are more flexible/efficient/innovative • Concept of reduction of red tape and rule reduction: – sunset laws (rules with an expiry date) – review bodies – zero based budgets – carry over budgets	• Move towards mission based budgets (Tower Hamlets) • Growth of voluntary and private sector role in service delivery • Lack of sophisticated monitoring – creates opportunities • Lack of written constitution – the rules are the only restraint • Lack of reward for risk taking – penalty for failure? • Concerns about accountability/corruption
5 Funding outcomes rather than inputs • Tradition of measuring activity rather than outcome • Many states in US are moving to outcome measures and performance (as opposed to activity/expenditure) indicators • Hence move away from issues such as staffing numbers or budget codes • Increased focus on 'customer satisfaction'/measurement of critical outcome variables (viz. air quality)	• Happening where outcomes can be measured (viz. leisure services) • Problems where outcomes harder to measure or no obvious customer • Likely to increase with decentralization

viour which the managers regard as rooted in the bureaucratic environment. In the search for a theoretical model which has validity for public sector managers writers such as Willcocks and Harrow (1992) have made use of 'domain theory'. This theory can be tracked back to work by Kouzes and Mico (1979).

The approach by Kouzes and Mico has been picked up by various authors in the UK and hence is well worth considering in some detail (Willcocks and Harrow, 1992). Essentially they suggest that there are limitations in the application of bureaucratic theory to what they describe as 'human service organizations'. The management domain focuses upon linear command structures which are illustrated by the organization chart.

Kouzes and Mico believe that human service organizations are different. Such organizations operate in health, education and social services and are significantly different from business (for profit) organizations. Their research led them to believe that within human service organizations there are different viewpoints depending upon whether the perspective was one of policy, management or service. These represented the 'domains' of the human service organization.

It is quite conceivable and indeed very likely that people will look at a particular issue through the perspective of their 'domain'. This effect is quite well known in psychology and Kouzes and Mico applied it here to public sector organizations.

They outline three domains which exist in human service organizations.

The policy (or political) domain

Here the focus is upon parliamentary democracy and the consent of the governed. A certain amount of disagreement is acceptable. Decision making has an equitable (or fair) aspect. Respect for law is stressed.

The managerial domain

The stress is here upon rational decision making and communication through organizational hierarchies. Cost effectiveness is important and bureaucratic practices are seen as positive. Information is a key ingredient.

The professional domain

This is the realm of the expert who is client focused. Professional behaviour and standards of conduct are very important. Problem solving is seen as happening on a non-hierarchical basis with a high degree of respect for the individual.

This can be illustrated by an example in the UK context. In October 1995 the Head of the Prison Service, Derek Lewis, was sacked by the Home Secretary, Michael Howard. Mr Lewis stated publicly that he felt that the Home Secretary had intervened in the operational aspects of the Prison Service. Mr Howard maintained that he had only responsibility for policy and that the operational shortcomings highlighted by a report into escapes were the responsibility of Mr Lewis. It is quite conceivable that both Mr Lewis and Mr Howard sincerely and strongly believe in their respective statements. Domain theory can explain this apparent paradox.

Mr Lewis would naturally regard himself as the 'manager' of the Prison Service. Operational matters come within his responsibility and this is his domain. Mr Howard, as a politician responsible to Parliament for the Prison Service, sees himself as making policy. His is the political or policy domain. The perception of the issues are strongly affected by their respective domains. In the event the matter went to court and Mr Lewis received a very substantial sum of money.

Organization and structure

Concepts of bureaucracy

This section will describe and assess the impact of the bureaucratic model in the public sector using both Weber's typology and later work by Downs and Crozier.

The term 'bureaucracy' is widely used in the organization context. Originally the term was developed by a sociologist called Max Weber. He described bureaucracy as an 'ideal type' . He looked at organizations from the perspective of what constituted authority in society. Hence bureaucracy was applicable to all organizations, not simply to those in the public sector.

He looked at the varieties of legitimate authority and suggested that there were three types based upon their claims to be legitimate:

- Rational claims which derive from rules and laws. Thus the person claims authority because they 'legally' possess it. The basis of obedience is impersonal and rooted in the office rather than the individual who occupies it.
- Traditional claims which owe their strength to past practice. The basis of obedience is to the person (such as the king or queen) but is governed by custom and practice.
- Charismatic claims whereby the individual lays claim to authority by virtue of some strength of character or personality. Some leaders of religious cults would be an example of this.

Bureaucracy bases its claim to legitimacy upon the first of these varieties and the following factors are drawn from Weber to identify the bureaucratic model:

- The existence of rules which govern the exercise of authority.
- There are boundaries or areas of competence within which authority is exercised.
- A hierarchy which means lower staff are responsible to higher staff with rights of appeal upwards.
- Training of staff in the conduct of their work.
- The organization is not 'owned' by those who administer it.
- Written records of decisions and actions are kept.
- The person holding the office cannot personally benefit from it through, for example, selling the right to hold the office or accepting bribes. In short the office holder is expected to act objectively and independently by reference to the rules.

Weber sees the way in which administrative staff are appointed and function as central to the notion of bureaucracy in its purest form. He adds factors such as:

- free selection on the basis of technical qualifications
- payment by fixed salaries with pension entitlements
- the office being seen as at least the primary source of income
- a promotion system such that the person has a career.

The thoughtful reader will identify this as a model which is not easily applicable in much of the public sector nowadays. None the less it is important to understand the power which the concept has exercised over organizational theory. Weber observed (Pugh, 1990, p. 9):

> This type of organization [monocratic bureaucratic structure] is in principle applicable with equal facility to a wide range of different fields. It may be applied in profit-making business or in charitable organizations, or in any number of other types of private enterprise serving ideal or material ends. It is equally applicable to political and religious organizations.

Weber saw bureaucracy as representing a superior type in respect of the following:

- precision
- stability
- discipline
- reliability.

Organization culture

In this section we will look at a theoretical approach to organizations which is introduced to managers taking academic programmes and which we have found public sector managers find particularly useful,

(Handy, 1993). The approach was developed by Charles Handy (who acknowledges his debt to Roger Harrison). The approach involves thinking about organizations in terms of different cultures. We would stress that the cultures described are 'ideal or perfect' types. In reality most organizations have features of more than one culture.

The power culture

This is typically found in entrepreneurial organizations where there is a strong central figure. Handy likens it to a club culture in that the members' power base is based upon being 'in tune' with those in charge. Handy symbolizes it with a spider's web and stresses that the encircling lines are as important as those which radiate out.

People are often recruited informally to such organizations. Once recruited they are trusted – often with large responsibilities. Such a culture sets little store by rule books or written procedures. Job descriptions are also not used. Rather the member is expected to 'do what is right'. If he/she gets it right then rewards follow. If not then the person is often out, and fast. It is the ends rather than the means which tend to be important.

Such cultures are capable of fast decision making and the leaders are often famous (Ralph Halpern of Burtons) or infamous (Robert Maxwell). There can be obvious succession problems if the 'spider' dies/leaves. Also there is a problem of growth because of the increased complexity which it brings.

A person in such a culture when asked what they do might say 'I work for (Robert Maxwell)'. She/he would tend to think intuitively, like soft data, take in the 'big picture and see the solution to a problem as lying with a person (replace X). She/he would value power over people and events.

The role culture

This is the 'conventional' view of an organization. The culture is based around the task. The word 'bureaucracy' is often used – though not in its negative meaning. It has been true of many large organizations such as life insurance companies and much of the public sector.

Handy likens it to a resembling a temple with a rational and sup- ported hierarchical structure. Rules and procedures abound and are strongly supported. Logic governs both the structure and decision making in this organization. There is functional division of work with co-ordination from the top.

Power arises from the position held and people are expected to fulfil their laid-down roles. Continuity and stability is sought and the organization operates well in such a setting. However it copes less well if the environment is unstable and sudden changes of direction are needed.

A person in such a culture when asked what they do might say 'I work for (the Department of Trade and I am a Principal Officer)'. She/he would be logical and sequential in their approach. Learning would arise from acquiring more skill and knowledge. Activities are broken down into separate events. Authority to act is a key concept and organization charts an essential guide. A problem is seen in terms of responsibilities or rules rather than the individual person.

The task culture

The focus here is the solution of problems and in particular how to bring resources together to do this. Its symbol is a net where the strength lies in the weaving of the strands.

It is typical of project style organizations such as construction or research companies and recognizes expertise as a source of power. Hence people who know their job or skill fit well. Age, seniority or position are less significant. It is adaptable and is often in a constant state of flux.

However it is not so capable where repeated and predictable operations are required. Neither is it well suited to delivering economies of scale and cost focused strategies. Rather it is aimed at the provision of solutions to problems.

A person in such a culture when asked what they do might say 'I am (a marketing executive with Southwark Enterprise)'. She/he regards the application of both creativity and logic as important and sees the group as key to this. Learning is seen in terms of gaining better problem solving ability. She/he defers to wisdom and expertise and seeks agreement rather than obedience. Problems are addressed via the creation of a 'task group/team'.

The person culture

Here the focus is upon the individual. It is the culture for those who resist the concept of subordination to organization. Barristers' chambers, partnerships or commune type set-ups are where it is to be found. The aim is the minimal form of organization.

It is a culture sought by professionals where they can feel part of a structure yet not beholden to it. Management is seen as an undesirable chore and the actual term 'manager' does not symbolize any status – indeed it is often replaced by something like 'administrator'.

There are few sanctions and the members of the organization will insist on being consulted at all times. The lack of control and the resistance of the members to 'being managed' makes the culture a very frustrating one for those appointed to 'manage' it.

The culture survives because the individual talents of the members are in demand and will not deliver their skills through another form of organization.

A person in such a culture when asked what they do might say 'I am a (management consultant)'. She/he would resist being categorized. Learning is via experience and seeking out new experience once you know all about some area. She/he will only respect individuals not organizations. Management is thus a one-to-one activity.

The mix of cultures

Handy envisages that different cultures might be found in the same organization. He sees this happening because of the range of jobs required.

Cultural consistency

Handy argues that though there may be different cultures within the same organization there must be cultural consistency at the activity or unit level of the organization. Problems arise when the work requires one culture but the people involved subscribe to another.

The drift towards role cultures

Handy proposes that there is a natural tendency for organizations to move towards the role type of culture. This is a consequence of size (economies of scale) and the need for consistency (i.e. rules, systems, procedures associated with predictability).

However people resist such a drift. This arises because:

- organizations become too complex for them to manage
- specialist work roles become too alienating and constrictive
- people resist obedience and subordination (new value structures).

Handy suggests that new forms of organizational attachment will emerge. Organizations will still tend towards role cultures but the core staff will be smaller. Increasingly organizations will enter into different forms of work relationships (contracts, part time etc.).

He suggests the 'shamrock' model with a 'core' staff and part time/occasional staff and contracted out activities. There is a wealth of evidence which supports this model.

Thus the concept of the survival of the range of cultures despite the acknowledged tendency for role to emerge as the most durable and efficient organizational form.

Organizational structure

Structure is a key factor in the theory of organizations whether in the private, public or voluntary sector. Previously we have discussed bureaucracy and the concept has a lot of implications for structure. Henry Mintzberg is a widely respected management writer who has put forward a way of looking at organizational structure which has stood the test of time. He followed up his original work, *The Structuring of Organizations* (1979), with a later exposition, *Structuring in Fives* (1983). The views he developed in these books are used extensively in both the UK and the USA on management programmes.

One attraction of Mintzberg is summed up by the title of his second book. He suggests that organizations can be considered in terms of a succession of five factors.

There are five different co-ordinating mechanisms, five different parts of the organization and five different ways in which information flows and decisions are made or communicated. These are associated in turn with five different structural configurations. Mintzberg taken at a surface level is very easy to grasp. Naturally we would encourage you to consider the more detailed implications as set out in his books.

Figure 2.3 sets out in summary form how Mintzberg sees organizations in terms of 'structuring in fives'. We have found that public management students can easily identify aspects of the Mintzberg model which are relevant to both public and voluntary organizations.

Five co-ordinating mechanisms:
1 Mutual adjustment
2 Direct supervision
3 Standardization of work process
4 Standardization of outputs
5 Standardization of skills

Five basic parts of the organization:
1 Strategic apex
2 Middle line
3 Operating core
4 Technostructure
5 Support staff

Five 'flow systems' in the organization:
1 Formal hierarchy
2 Regulated work flow
3 Informal communication flows
4 As work 'constellations'
5 As ad hoc decision processes

These are associated with the following five different structural configurations:
1 Simple structure
2 Machine bureaucracy
3 Professional bureaucracy
4 Divisionalized form
5 Adhocracy

Figure 2.3 *Outline of Mintzberg's concept of organizational structure*

The traditional large local authority or health authority is typically viewed as a professional bureaucracy. As such the key co-ordinating mechanism is through standardization of skills. Thus a hospital relies upon the delivery of effective nursing care because the skills exercised by nurses are based upon professional standards. It is not necessary (or indeed possible) to directly supervise nurses in a hospital. The key part of the organization is the professional core. Hence the hospital would view the doctors, nurses and paramedical staff as the vital element of the organization.

A central government department (not necessarily a Next Steps Executive Agency!) would often resemble a machine bureaucracy. Co-ordination is by standardization of work and work processes. The old style Department of Health and Social Security Benefits Centres were cast very much in this mould. Those who have experienced working in this vast bureaucracy will recall the massive book of regulations for the administration of benefits known as the 'A code'. This enabled relatively junior staff who possessed only limited training to operate a quite complex benefits system. The key part of the organization was the technostructure which in days past was the codification of regulations.

Under Next Steps the focus moves towards standardization of outputs (as set out in the Agency Plans and Framework documents). Thus we would argue that Next Steps status would tend to move the structure towards a divisionalized form with the middle managers becoming increasingly important.

The greatest variety of organizational form is to be found in the voluntary sector. The enormous diversity of the size, age and scope of voluntary organizations means that it is conceivable to find all of the types of organizational structure envisaged by Mintzberg. Consider the difference between the following voluntary organizations:

- A small focused charity set up by an enthusiastic member of clergy (simple structure with direct supervision – the member of clergy as the strategic apex is the key).
- A large voluntary organization with a simple product, such as The British Legion and 'Poppy Day Appeal' (machine bureaucracy with standardization of work and the technostructure, making and distribution of poppy badges, as central).
- A voluntary organization with a research or health focus, such as the British Heart Foundation (professional bureaucracy with standardization of skills and the operating core of research and health professionals as dominant).
- A national voluntary organization with a range of operational activities including charity shops, such as Age Concern or SCOPE (divisionalized form with focus upon the managerial aspects).
- A strongly campaigning organization driven by quick response to issues, such as Greenpeace (adhocracy with mutual adjustment and the support staff as key).

Models of new public management

At the British Academy of Management Conference in 1994 Ewan Ferlie presented an interesting assessment of the variants he saw in new public management (NPM; Ferlie, 1994).

The first variant was prevalent throughout the 1980s and was characterized by a focus on efficiency and the adoption of business methods. It was inspired by Margaret Thatcher's view of the public sector as bureaucratic and inefficient.

The second variant is associated with delayering and downsizing which affected public and private sector alike. It is the move to markets as the determinant of organizational structures. Contracts rather than hierarchy are the basis for control.

The third variant stresses the importance of organizational culture in determining the nature of the organization. This might be top down as exemplified by such factors as charismatic leaders, mission statement, logos etc. Alternatively it might be bottom up as demonstrated by a stress upon organizational learning and decentralized responsibility.

The final version is demonstrated by the attempt to adapt private sector concepts to the public sector milieu. It is very much inherent in the approach of this book. It lays stress upon quality of service provision, user involvement and impact upon the way these services are shaped and the accountability of public managers.

The legal aspects

Legislation forms the basis of the world of the public manager. The route to the top in local government has strongly favoured lawyers in the past and indeed is significantly the case today. Neither is it mere coincidence that that so many senior politicians are lawyers. Margaret Thatcher trained as a barrister as did the late John Smith. Tony Blair, the current Labour leader and possible future Prime Minister, trained as a lawyer.

Therefore we view it as important that a public manager has a basic understanding of the legislative process; the way in which law is enacted and some key principles of interpretation which have a strong influence in the public management domain.

Before a proposed piece of legislation becomes law (an 'Act of Parliament') it is called a Bill. As such it comprises clauses, subclauses and paragraphs. After it has received the Royal Assent it becomes an Act with sections, subsections and paragraphs.

The Royal Assent does not in itself mean that the Act becomes law with immediate effect. Some Acts have a section which indicates when they come into effect. Otherwise the Act is usually brought into effect by something called a Statutory Instrument. This is an order the Secretary of State lays before Parliament to bring the Act (or section of the Act) into effect.

Legislation does not have to be made in Parliament. Parliament can 'delegate' its authority to another body or person. These include:

- Ministers of the Crown often make use of delegated powers through Statutory Instruments. The numbers of these greatly exceed the number of Acts of Parliament.
- Local Authorities are able to make by-laws through delegated powers under various Acts of Parliament.
- Public Corporations (a disappearing breed) are also able to make by-laws.

An important distinction between Acts of Parliament and Statutory Instruments is that the Courts can question the validity of the latter. The key concept here is that of 'ultra vires'. A court can hold that a Minister or Local Authority has exercised delegated legislative power in a way which was beyond the amount of delegation envisaged by the original Act of Parliament. This is an action which the courts have shown themselves willing to take as the Home Secretary and other Ministers have found out in recent years.

In interpreting Acts of Parliament the Courts have traditionally followed certain rules. Public managers who seek legal guidance over what Acts mean would benefit from an awareness of these rules.

The literal rule

This stated simply means that the court will give words in a statute their plain, ordinary literal meaning. If the words are clear they must be given that meaning even if the result would seem absurd. Thus in 1986 the House of Lords held that a person was not homeless within the meaning of the Housing (Homeless Persons) Act 1977 even though the place he or she occupied lacked cooking or washing facilities because they interpreted 'accommodation' in its literal sense. Many people would argue that the real intention of the Act was to regard such a person as homeless.

The golden rule

This can be used in one of two ways. On the one hand where there is some ambiguity in the words used it could be used to amend the literal rule to avoid absurdity. On the other hand it can supersede the literal rule where the court sees public policy considerations as taking precedence. Thus in 1981 an adopted person convicted of murder and detained as a mental patient was denied access to his birth records. He was entitled to such access under the Adoption Act 1976 but he was felt likely to be a danger to his natural mother.

The mischief rule

Here the court may look at the mischief which Parliament had intended to rectify when it passed the legislation. Thus in 1981 the House of Lords held that it was lawful for a nurse to participate in a procedure of medically induced abortion without a doctor present despite the fact that the Abortion Act 1967 provided that pregnancy could only be terminated by a registered medical practitioner. The House of Lords felt that the mischief that the Abortion Act sought to address was the unsatisfactory state of the law. So long as a doctor prescribed the treatment and accepted responsibility it did not matter if the doctor was not present when the pregnancy was actually terminated.

The statute must be read as a whole

The court must view the statute as a whole and not take a section out of context. If there is a conflict between provisions then the court must decide which is the leading provision.

Summary

This chapter has introduced you to some key theoretical concepts in understanding management in the public sector in the UK. There have been a major changes in the past twenty years. Managers must understand the elements of the philosophical basis for these changes.

The New Right has had an impact on the UK public sector manager. Though Margaret Thatcher has limited current impact upon government policy there is little doubt that the impact of successive Conservative Governments have changed the managerial environment for the public manager in the UK.

Some of the theoretical models used in the private sector are particularly applicable to the public sector. The approaches of writers such as Henry Mintzberg and Charles Handy have been discussed as part of this. We have also identified the more traditional bureaucratic model as a contrast. Domain theory is a useful way of understanding the especial pressures upon the manager who has to confront customer (or client) pressures, professional values systems and political priorities.

We have also briefly touched upon some legal aspects of the public sector which we feel it is helpful for a manager to grasp on a theoretical level, irrespective of the areas of responsibility that she or he may have.

Action points and discussion points

(Items in italics are intended to encourage the reader to develop a greater intellectual awareness, items in plain type are focused upon work-related activity.)

Review internal and external operating environments

Compare one private and one public sector organization. What do they have in common and what is different? What might explain the similarities and differences?

Provide information to support decision making

Gather editorials on a current public sector issue from several national newspapers which represent a range of political views. Analyse the different assumptions about the nature of the public sector that the articles make.

To what extent has new public management influenced your organization over the past five years or so? How is this demonstrated?

How has the power balance shifted in your organization over the last ten years? Which individuals or groups have changed their relative power positions, and why? What have been the structural consequences of these changes (as expressed in the rules, roles and goals of your organization)?

Further reading

Common, R., Flynn, N., and Mellon, E. (1992). *Managing Public Services: Competition and Decentralisation*. Butterworth.
The authors provide a thorough account of the evolution of the Next Steps Agencies.
Flynn N. (1994). *Public Sector* Management (2nd edn.). Harvester Wheatsheaf.
This is a readable and well-regarded book which addresses the main issues of the public sector in the UK.
Harrison, S., and Pollitt, C. (1994). *Controlling Health Professionals: The Future of Work and Organisation in the NHS*. Open University Press.
This book is written in an accessible style which makes it attractive to the non-expert. Many health service books presume upon the reader's knowledge of acronyms and terminology. Given the significance of professional groups in the NHS the focus of this book is useful and appropriate in understanding key aspects of the public sector.
Hudson, M. (1995). *Managing without Profit*. Penguin.
This is a recent book written by a practising management consultant who specializes in 'third sector' organizations.
Leach, S., Stewart, J., and Walsh, K. (1994). *The Changing Organisation and Management of Local Government*. Macmillan.
This is a recent and challenging book written by three well-regarded observers and writers of the local government scene.

3 What has changed in the public sector?

Aims and learning objectives

The aim of this chapter is to help you review the extent to which the 'New Right' thinking and the concept of the 'new public management' which we introduced in Chapter 2 are reflected in changes in the UK public sector. In doing so we will outline the major changes in the public sector at a national and local level so that you can consider the implications of these changes for your own area of managerial interest and responsibility.

At the end of this chapter, and associated activities and reading, you will be able to:

- describe the major changes taking place across the whole public sector
- place changes in your own organization in the context of these cross-sector changes
- discuss the managerial implications of these changes for your own area of responsibility.

The nature of change

What has changed in the public sector? We think that it would be fair to say – practically everything! As a manager you could be forgiven for thinking that your job entails responding to an unceasing progression of new statutory requirements, customer demands, codes of practice, pressures and problems. Obviously the pace of change in the UK public sector as it moves toward the model of a new public management is rapid, and the pace of change is increasing at an increasing rate. However your responsibilities as a manager also requires you to manage stability and consistency as well as change. Even, at times, to resist change if you feel that it is not really going to achieve its intended purpose or improve services to your customers and clients.

It is easy to characterize change in the public sector as resulting solely from top-down (i.e. government) pressure on managers. In our view this does an injustice to public sector managers and too easily conforms to the stereotype of public sector managers as bureaucrats (in the pejorative sense), unwilling and unable to change, and reliant on lessons and guidance from private sector managers if they are to change. Elcock (1995), amongst others, highlights the fallacies in these arguments. While clearly much of the change in the public sector has been a consequence of top-down government pressure and changes in legislation, much has also been achieved, through the initiative of particular public sector organizations, and individual managers.

In order to help you continue to make your own unique contribution to managing change and stability, it may be helpful to put changes in the public sector into their broad context by considering the impact of the new public management in the UK, firstly across the whole sector, and then area by area. In doing this we will be introducing many of the important themes that we will be exploring in greater detail in subsequent chapters.

Changes across the UK public sector

In the last chapter we considered some of the trends in public sector management from a largely UK perspective. It is probably important to note, as Hood (1991) suggests, that these can be regarded as a reflection of international 'mega-trends' in public administration and management. Clearly part of these changes entail the need to look, and manage, across national boundaries – indeed a move towards an 'international agenda' can be considered as one of the 'megatrends' of the new public management.

Building on the political philosophies outlined in the last chapter and the changing position of many organizations on the private/ public sector continuum and by reviewing the work of a number of leading authors on the public sector (for example, Ferlie, 1994; Hambleton, 1992; Stewart and Walsh, 1992; Winstanley et al., 1995) the following major trends and themes emerge across the whole public sector.

Decentralization and restructuring

This involves a number of processes, including a move from the tradition of political control through hierarchies to a separation of the political process from the management process, and from centralized management to the local management of service provision. One of the results of this restructuring has been the replacement of a relatively small number of large hierarchies with a more complex network of smaller organizations. At the same time direct hierarchical control is being replaced with arm's-length regulation.

An emphasis on the public as customers, and consumer power

An important aspect of this theme is the rise of 'Charters' for the customers, consumers and clients of public services.

Splitting the purchaser and provider roles

Involving the separation the task of deciding what type and level of services should be provided, from the task of providing them while also challenging the monopoly power of the 'provider' professions.

The creation of markets, or quasi-markets, and an emphasis on competition

Replacing single providers with a plurality of possible providers, extending the extent of charging for public services and reducing the extent of subsidization of these services.

A growth in privatization and contractual arrangements

Including the contracting-out of services, compulsory competitive tendering and a changing relationship between 'statutory' organizations and voluntary and private sector providers.

An emphasis on performance and accountability

Both a requirement for demonstrating 'value for money' and the achievement of Charter standards and a consequence of new contractual relationships and the need (or desire) to retain some control of decentralized management and service delivery.

Achieving increased flexibility

Decentralized services, 'closer to the customer', require flexibility in service delivery. This, in turn, is likely to require flexible patterns of organization, staffing, rewards, pay and conditions.

A change in the culture of public service

Moving away from perceptions of public services dominated by traditions of administration, hierarchy and professionalism to an approach based on the private sector culture of commercialism, market-driven, customer-led services.

Increased emphasis on management information and information technology

Particularly to ensure financial efficiency and service effectiveness.

These themes will provide much of the structure of subsequent chapters when we consider how the public sector is implementing them in detail, and the managerial implications of these processes in particular. But before we turn attention to this it is worth setting the scene by looking at the major changes over the last decade or so in each area of the public service of particular interest to this book, starting with the Civil Service.

Change in the Civil Service

In 1983 the Civil Service employed around 650 000 full-time equivalent (FTE) staff, by 1994 this number had fallen to about 533 000 (FTE).

These reductions reflect the considerable structural and cultural change which the Civil Service has undergone over the last fifteen years. Part of the change has been a response to a number of influential reports on the Civil Service, which we will briefly review.

In 1988 the Government's Efficiency Unit produced a report entitled *Improving Management in Government: The Next Steps*. This report, which became known as the Ibbs report, laid the foundations for a major restructuring of the Civil Service which resulted in the establishment of several government 'Agencies', often referred to as 'Next Step Agencies'.

In essence the Ibbs report was concerned that the traditions and culture of the Civil Service resulted in a slow and patchy pattern of managerial reform. In response to these concerns the report recommended the vigorous pursuit of three main priorities.

- The work of each department must be organized in a way that focuses on the job to be done; the systems and structures must enhance the effective delivery of policies and services.
- The management of each department must ensure that their staff have the relevant experience and skills needed to do the tasks that are essential to effective government.
- there must be a real and sustained pressure on and within each department for continuous improvement in the value for money obtained in the delivery of policies and services.

By 1994 102 executive agencies had been established, together with 31 executive units of HM Customs and Excise and 33 executive offices of the Inland Revenue.

A subsequent review of progress on the 'Next Steps' programme, the Next Steps Review of 1993, resulted in the scrutiny of any particular function being considered for agency function to see whether instead it should be abolished, privatized, contracted out, or 'market-tested'. Hence the introduction of 'market testing' into the Civil Service reflecting the themes of competition and the place of the market in the broader 'new right' thinking.

The radical changes being undertaken in the Civil Service at times highlighted a general lack of information about costs and outcomes. Without such information it is difficult to pursue objectives around improved performance and accountability. Two initiatives which were designed to deal with this issue are worthy of note – the Financial Management Initiative (FMI) and the 'Management Information System for Ministers', known as 'MINIS'.

The FMI can be regarded as an effort to reform the management of public spending, and in particular the growth of public spending, one of the 'megatrends' of the new public management. The FMI was launched in May 1982 and its objectives can be summarized as ensuring that each government department had a system whereby managers at all levels could achieve:

- a clear view of their objectives
- the means to assess and whenever possible measure their outputs and performance towards those objectives
- a well-defined responsibility for making the best use of resources and scrutinizing outputs for value for money
- the information, training and support that they need to exercise their responsibilities effectively.

These aims set the basic framework for a system of performance management, an issue to which we will be returning throughout this book.

Achieving improved performance management requires, amongst other things, the development of effective management information systems. MINIS is an example of one attempt to do this.

The broad pattern laid down at the inception of MINIS was the assembly of basic, but detailed, information about existing departmental activities and objectives, including who was responsible for what, and associated costs. The basis of the system was a series of statements prepared for each major section of the department by the responsible manager (under-secretary), which were considered by review meetings involving ministers and senior managers.

MINIS required the directorates, which formed the main subunits of government departments, to provide information on:

- their activities and objectives
- the priorities attached to these objectives
- the cost associated with them
- an assessment of the directorates' performance on each activity
- a forward look to set standards for future performance
- personnel budgeting
- the output of staff inspections and other scrutinies.

However, in practice, departments asserted their independence by producing their own information systems, hence illustrating some of the difficulties to be encountered when introducing major change into a large organization.

Change in local government

In 1988 there were 602 000 people employed in local government, with another 317 000 employed in justice, police and fire services. By 1994 local government employment reduced to 378 000 and justice, police and fire services to 315 000.

So in local government, as in the Civil Service, there have been significant structural, and cultural, changes.

In 1983 the Government which was re-elected with a manifesto which included a commitment to abolish the Greater London Council (GLC) and the metropolitan counties, introduced legislation abolishing these authorities in the 1984–85 session. This legislation became effective in April 1986, leaving London without an elected representative body for the first time in 100 years, and both London and all the metropolitan areas without a single authority responsible for strategic planning. This gap was, to an extent, filled by a number of special purpose authorities, such as the London Residual Body, and joint committees which increased the complexity of arrangements for local government.

The Inner London Education Authority (ILEA) was finally abolished in 1990 and its responsibilities transferred to the inner London boroughs.

In 1991 the Government announced that the structure of local government was to be reviewed again. In England this review was conducted by an independent Local Government Commission, established in July 1992. In Scotland and Wales the review was conducted within the relevant government departments. As Barnett (1994; pp. 127–28) notes:

> The ground rules for the reviews also differed. In both Scotland and Wales the case for a move to a unitary structure was taken as given and the reviews centred on the most appropriate form that such a unitary structure should take . . . In contrast, the Local Government Commission in England was given a wider remit, the arguments for a unitary system being balanced against those for a two-tier system.

In July 1994 the Local Government (Wales) Act was passed creating twenty-two unitary authorities to come into being on 1 April 1996, and in November 1994 the Local Government (Scotland) Act created thirty-two unitary authorities, also be established in April 1996.

Change in the health service

The NHS has undergone several restructurings over the last decade or so. A major impetus for these changes was a report prepared by a committee chaired by Sir Roy Griffiths, then managing director and deputy chairman of Sainsbury's, which introduced the concept of 'general management' into the NHS. The Griffiths report was highly critical of management at all levels in the NHS. At the centre it found that the Department of Health did not provide effective leadership; in the case of health authorities it criticized the system of consensus management through multidisciplinary teams for failing to deliver the drive and imagination needed in a modern health service; and the report also argued that within hospitals doctors should play a much bigger part in management (Ham, 1991).

The Griffiths report did not, however, result in a major restructuring of the NHS unlike the publication, in 1989, of the White Paper, *Working for Patients,* followed by the NHS and Community Care Act in 1990.

In essence the White Paper heralded the changes that have resulted in the separation of purchaser and provider roles; the creation of self-governing NHS trusts (including hospital, ambulance and community health care providers); the introduction of GP fundholding and contracts or service level agreements as the basis of an 'internal market' for health care.

Further reorganization of health care in London followed the publication, in 1992, of the report of an inquiry chaired by Professor Sir Bernard Tomlinson which advocated a shift of emphasis in London away from hospital-based provision to primary care and community health services.

In 1993 the Government announced a major review of the use of human resources in the NHS and subsequently published a report entitled *Management in the New NHS.* The prime concern of this report was reducing the cost of managing the NHS. As a consequence district health authorities and family health service authorities have merged into single health authorities and are responsible for purchasing or commissioning services from provider and regional health authorities have been abolished with their main functions being performed by the regional offices of the NHS Executive.

Change for voluntary and charitable organizations

While it is clear that the vast amount of change in the Civil Service, local government and the National Health Service outlined above have had a direct and significant effect on voluntary organizations and charities, it is less easy to chart these changes because, as Hind (1995) suggests, there is a lack of comprehensive data about this area of the public sector. However it is clearly a very important area with almost 300 000 registered charities and voluntary organizations (including friendly societies and grant maintained schools) in the United Kingdom employing an estimated 450 000 people, and millions of people involved as volunteers (Hind, 1995). This is clearly 'big business', with the gross annual income of all registered charities estimated at £12.8 billion in 1994 (Hind, 1995).

Adirondack (1992, p. vi) considers that 'voluntary organizations and community groups of all types and sizes are facing a bewildering range of new challenges, including:

- threats from changes in pattern of central and local government funding
- requirements to compete with other providers in the 'contract culture' for grants, or seek alternative sources of funding
- shifts in the emphasis of service delivery from statutory bodies such as local authorities and health authorities towards provision by a range of not-for-profit (and for-profit) organizations
- an increasing emphasis on what Adirondack terms a 'new philanthropy' (perhaps as a facet of 'new right' thinking) placing more onus on voluntary work and charitable fundraising
- new legislation, both domestic and European.

It is possible to chart a trend over the twentieth century from the provision of, especially, social services being largely in the hands of voluntary organizations, then this responsibility becoming primarily discharged by the 'Welfare State', to the late 1970s when the focus once again alighted on voluntary and charitable organizations as service providers.

While it is very difficult to find a comprehensive statement of the Government's policy on voluntary and charitable organizations individual statements by ministers and references in manifestos to an increasingly important role for these groups has been supported by tax concessions introduced throughout this period. Other government policies, such as arrangements for work experience and training for young unemployed people, compulsory competitive tendering under the 1988 Local Government Act and outsourcing of the provision of health services under the 1990 National Health Service and Community Care Act have had the result of increasing the supply of labour, and the opportunities available to, voluntary and charitable organizations. It could be argued that the rather ad hoc nature of these developments, without a coherent government policy in respect to voluntary and charitable organizations may have increased the opportunities, but it has also led to a complex and uncertain environment for those trying to manage and develop such organizations. As we will see later it has also placed more onus on voluntary and charitable organizations to manage service provision through contractual and quasi-contractual relationships, hence perhaps for the first time making organizations legally responsible for the quality and quantity of services they provide, and faced with dealing with lost income if the service does not fulfil the contractual obligations.

Given these changes it is possible to make a case for the advocacy function of voluntary organizations, supported by grant-aid, during the peak of the 'Welfare State' being superseded by a service-delivery function, funded by contractual relationships. If this is the case one challenge faced by voluntary and charitable organizations is how to continue to fund advocacy, advice and experimental work, should they wish to.

Structurally, there is significant movement from the statutory sector to voluntary, charitable or not-for-profit organizations; both of managers and other staff and whole organizations. According to Hudson (1995, p. 29):

> this trend will continue because the political philosophy that favours independence from the state has become well established . . . as providers are given greater independence, they are becoming managerially more sophisticated, require less support from centralized bureaucracies and place increasing value on their independence.

Summary

The public sector is a fast-moving environment, no matter in which area you are trying to manage. We will be returning to each of the themes and issues raised in this chapter in greater depth in the rest of the book. However as we do so it is important to keep the overview presented in this chapter in mind. Not only do the themes of say, contracting, closely interlink with each other but there are also important relationships between areas of the public sector over issues such as service delivery and inspection which we have not covered in this chapter. The ability to develop a 'helicopter mind', soaring down to deal with the detail and back-up to understand the overall picture is an important management competence which we will be attempting to help you develop further.

Action points and discussion points

(Items in italics are intended to encourage the reader to develop a greater intellectual awareness, items in plain type are focused upon work-related activity.)

Implement changes and improvements in organizational activities

Undertake a study comparing the way in which your organization is structured and sets about achieving its objectives with a similar organization in another country (or two!). What are the main implications of this comparative study for management in your organization?

Review internal and external operating environments

In what ways are national and local political influences reflected in your organization? Has the impact of these influences increased or decreased over the last two years? How? Why? How has your organization responded?

Secure resources for organizational plans

Prepare a forecast of the likely changes in the economic, political, social and technological environment of your part of the public sector. How do you anticipate your sector will change as a consequence? What are the implications of your analysis for the way in which your organization secures resources now, and in the medium term?

Manage activities to meet customer requirements/Establish organizational values and culture

What are the basic values underpinning your organization? To what extent are your organization's values a reflection of 'new right' thinking? How are these values reflected in your organization's service to its clients or customers? To what extent are your organization's values appropriate for meeting the demands or needs of its customers or clients?

Provide required personnel for activities

Rate the importance of each of the following general changes in the public sector for your organization by placing a 'X' on the appro-

	Not very important	Fairly important	Very important
1 Decentralization and restructuring	1.....2.....3.....4.....5.....6.....7.....8.....9.....10		
2 An emphasis on the public as customer, and consumer power	1.....2.....3.....4.....5.....6.....7.....8.....9.....10		
3 Splitting the purchaser and provider roles	1.....2.....3.....4.....5.....6.....7.....8.....9.....10		
4 The creation of markets, or quasi-markets, and an emphasis on competition	1.....2.....3.....4.....5.....6.....7.....8.....9.....10		
5 A growth in privatization and contractual arrangements	1.....2.....3.....4.....5.....6.....7.....8.....9.....10		
6 An emphasis on performance and accountability	1.....2.....3.....4.....5.....6.....7.....8.....9.....10		
7 Achieving increased flexibility	1.....2.....3.....4.....5.....6.....7.....8.....9.....10		
8 A change in the culture of public service	1.....2.....3.....4.....5.....6.....7.....8.....9.....10		
9 Increased emphasis on management information and information technology	1.....2.....3.....4.....5.....6.....7.....8.....9.....10		

priate point on the scale. What are the implications of your analysis for the skills required by staff and other people associated with your organization now and in the near future? How prepared is your organization to meet these changing requirements? How could your organization's planning in this area be improved?

Further reading

Hudson, M. (1995). *Managing without Profit: The Art of Managing Third-sector Organisations*. Penguin.
An accessible and structured review of the issues facing managers in not-for-profit organizations, with a bias towards practical managerial actions.

Hutton, W. (1995). *The State We're In*. Jonathan Cape.
While not focusing specifically on the public sector, this is a very readable and challenging review of the macro-economic and social position of Britain today. Excellent background reading.

McKevitt, D., and Lawton, A. (Eds.) (1994). *Public Sector Management: Theory, Critique and Practice*. Sage.
This is a fairly advanced text with a strong theoretical underpinning, but worth the effort if you want to achieve a real in-depth understanding of the context of change in the public sector, together with some of the practical managerial implications of these changes.

Robinson, R., and Le Grand, J. (Eds.) (1993). *Evaluating the NHS Reforms*. Policy Journals.
An interesting collection of empirical research testing the Government's claims for NHS reforms. Examines many of the important areas of reform such as NHS Trusts, GP fundholding and the NHS personnel function.

4 Competition and the contract culture

Aims and learning objectives

The aim of this chapter is to concentrate on what you need to do to manage in an environment where you are under pressure to be increasingly competitive in your service delivery, and respond to other organizations which are attempting to secure a share of the market for your services. This will involve you changing your approach to 'contracting', perhaps making the contract between you and your customers explicit, and even legally binding, for the first time.

At the end of this chapter, and associated activities and reading, you will be able to:

- explain the pressures from the external and internal operating environments of public sector organizations to become more commercially aware and oriented
- discuss the impact of new requirements for a more commercial approach to activities on the public sector in terms of improving organizational performance
- outline the managerial response required to increased competition, including establishing new organizational values and culture
- produce a draft business plan to secure, and determine the effective use of, resources
- identify and plan for the developments required in your own competence, that of your staff and of the team(s) you manage, to respond to these issues.

Managing in a competitive environment – the basics

In the previous two chapters we examined change in the public sector and began to identify some of the major themes and trends likely to require a response from you as a manager. You would expect any organization open to such environmental changes to adapt in some way, either by changing its structure, culture or both (although as we know some organizations try to ignore the changing environment, operating as if they are a 'closed system', and it is these organizations which quickly become unviable). An interesting question is the extent to which an organization adapts to the environment, and the extent to which it tries to influence the environment. For example in some local authorities the response to increasing pressure to privatize operations has been to place as much work as possible with external contractors; others have responded by restructuring the organization to include 'in-house' contractor units. Both cases have required a change in the culture of the organization, i.e. the underlying assumptions by which it works and makes sense of the world, for example a move towards a 'contract culture'.

As we saw in Chapter 3 concepts such as 'the internal market', 'competition' and 'consumer choice' have rapidly become prime concerns for managers in the public sector which have led to contractual and quasi contractual relationships being substituted for the tradition of direct service provision from public sector bodies to the public. According to Hind (1995, p. 284).

> contract, or agreement-based, fees paid to the voluntary sector increased by 154 per cent between 1990–91 and 1993–94, mainly for community care and other personal social services.

Hind goes on to chart the changing relationship between charities and local authorities over the last twenty or thirty years from cursory consultation, through more formalized partnership arrangements, to full contracting.

We have illustrated this emerging contractual relationship in the public sector in Figure 4.1.

The move towards increased competition has required the splitting of the provision of public services into two separate sets of roles: purchaser and supplier. Generally speaking the role of the purchaser is to assess need and demand for a service in their area of responsibility and then to contract with a service provider to deliver the

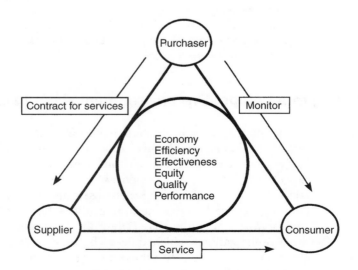

Figure 4.1 *The basic contracting relationship in the public sector*

service required to the consumers, i.e. the end-users. One consequence of these changes has been a redefinition of some of the terms used in organizations, for example the term 'client' used to normally refer to the recipient of the service. Now some organizations such as local authority housing services have split their operations between 'client' and 'contractor' departments. The client department specifies the service required, and the contractor department delivers it. Other organizations refer to the client role in this context as the 'commissioning' department or function. We have tried to simplify this in Figure 4.1 by referring to the *purchaser*, essentially the organization with the money to buy the service, the *supplier* as the organization who uses the money to provide the service, and the *consumer* as the person who uses the service. 'Consumers' can also be variously described as 'customers', 'clients', 'claimants', 'end-users', 'patients', 'passengers' and so on. One manifestation of the move towards the contract culture is a tendency to standardize on the term 'customer' to describe the service user.

'Purchasers' can include government departments and agencies, local authorities, health commissioners, community health trusts, local authority departments.

'Suppliers' can include contractor departments in statutory agencies such as those listed amongst the suppliers, voluntary organizations, not-for-profit organizations (which may include National Health Service Trust hospitals, 'floated-off' local authority strategic business units, and coalitions of service users and care organizations), and private sector (i.e. 'for-profit') organizations. As Best (1994) suggests each of these parties to the contract are likely to have their own agenda which they are pursuing in agreeing and operating the contract (for example purchasers may be concerned with value for money and risk management; suppliers with levels of service funding and freedom to exercise professional judgement; consumers with their own individual needs or community priorities), but in our opinion they are all likely to be concerned, albeit from different perspectives and with different emphases, on the issues at the centre of Figure 4.1. Purchasers and suppliers will both be concerned with achieving economical service delivery and most consumers would be unhappy if they saw resources being wasted in providing the services they were receiving. Similarly it is in everybody's interests to provide the maximum level of service output with the minimum level of resource input: to achieve efficiency and to ensure that the service is doing what it is supposed to (i.e. that it is effective), and in the context of public services that the services are being provided and distributed fairly (i.e. with equity). These factors taken together will determine to a large extent the overall quality of the service, which will be part of the assessment by each party of the service's performance.

We also think that it is important that the operation of the contractual relationship, and in particular the assessment of perfor-

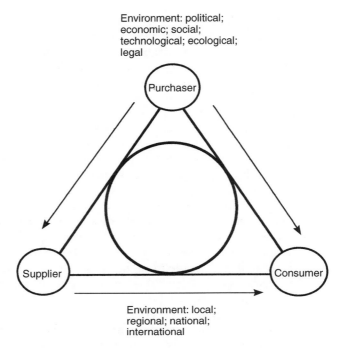

Figure 4.2 *The basic contracting relationship in its environment*

mance, is placed in the context of its relationship with factors in the wider environment (Figure 4.2). Macro-environmental issues, such as legal requirements and political imperatives, also need to be interpreted in accordance with the boundaries of the geographical environment in which you are managing. There are already signs that even managers whose prime focus is on a relatively small geographical area are having to enter into contracts with organizations (usually, but not always, from the private sector) who operate on a pan-European or international scale. We expect this trend to continue.

Mapping the managerial competencies required by competition and the contract culture

Identifying the main players in the contractual relationship, and highlighting the organization/environment interaction begins to delineate the competencies required of managers, irrespective of whether you are managing in a purchasing or supplier organization, or, perhaps, one representing the consumers or end-users. Within the broad framework of managing for economy, efficiency, effectiveness, equity, quality and performance (and drawing from the work of the Audit Commission, 1995a; Best, 1994; and Holtham, 1992) we believe that competition and contracting requires competence in the following areas:

- environmental scanning, including competitor/alternative-supplier analysis
- strategic planning
- financial management, including estimating and cost control, management accounting and management information systems
- establishing and managing trading accounts when computing rates of return
- tendering processes and contract negotiation
- service needs assessment
- information management
- the legal framework of contracting
- consumer consultation
- managing change, and negotiating new relationships between purchasers, suppliers and consumers
- performance management.

We will be dealing with many of these areas in subsequent chapters. In this chapter we will concentrate on competitor/alternative supplier analysis and the legal framework of contracting, before considering how these can be incorporated into a process of business planning.

Competitor/supplier analysis

These are two sides of the same coin: purchasers need to analyse the environment to identify potential suppliers, while suppliers need to be aware of the activities of their competitors if they are to build or maintain competitive advantage. According to the Audit Commission (1995a, p. 5) purchasers could do more to encourage potential suppliers to enter the market:

> A competitive market must be nurtured if the benefits of competition are to be achieved. This should result in tighter prices and greater efficiency and innovation. A critical part of the client role is to encourage competition by engaging in a proper dialogue with all potential tenders and packaging the contracts to attract bids.

Both purchasers and suppliers need to develop methods for gathering, collating, analysing and reporting 'market intelligence'. Such intelligence could include:

- The number, speed of growth, degree of differentiation, diversity, areas of service need/delivery competence of purchasers and suppliers in the marketplace.

- Opportunities for, and threat of new entrants into the market-place. This may require an analysis of capital requirements to become established, the existence of regulatory control and developed distribution channels, amongst others.
- The relative power of suppliers and purchaser: including the extent to which they dominate the marketplace, the absence of substitutes for service delivery, the degree of uniqueness or differentiation of product or service required or delivered, the volume or concentration of purchases made, the price sensitivity of the product/service, the quality of the product/service in relation to the consumers' requirements.
- The power of substitution for the service: its relative price performance, the costs of switching for the purchaser, the purchaser's willingness or propensity to substitute one service for another.
- Changing legal requirements, tendering conventions, funding decisions and shifts in central/local government priorities.

The legal framework

Competition and the contract culture in the public sector is obviously heavily influenced, if not determined, by legislative requirements. As we suggested earlier, individual bodies do have some degree of choice still about how they implement these legislative requirements. For the purposes of this chapter we will take these broad legislative requirements as a given and concentrate on some of the issues involved in entering into contracts between purchasers and suppliers.

It must be stressed from the outset that contract law is a complex and contentious issue, especially in the public sector where it is a relatively new arrangement in many areas and consequently not yet tested by the courts. As a manager we would strongly advise you not to enter into any potential contractual arrangement without seeking qualified legal advice. With this important caveat in mind this section is intended as a broad guide to some of the key issues and terms that you need to be familiar with, starting by differentiating between an 'agreement' and a 'contract'

An 'agreement' exists when two parties agree that one will provide goods and services and the other will pay for them. If both parties *intend* the agreement to be legally binding (i.e. if one side does not meet its part of the bargain the other side can sue for non-performance or breach of the agreement) then it becomes a contract. A 'contract' can therefore be defined as a legally enforceable agreement between two parties for the exchange of anything of material value (i.e. goods, services, money or the promise of any of those) with an unconditional offer and acceptance by both (or all) parties to the contract, with the intention to create a legally binding relationship.

Inherent in these definitions is an important distinction between a 'Service Level Agreement' (SLA) which is increasingly common between, but not exclusive to, two departments in the same organization and a Contract for Service. It would not be expected that if, for example, a finance department did not provide quarterly financial information to the personnel department within the time agreed in an SLA between the two that the personnel department would sue for damages! Similarly an agreement between a funding agency and a voluntary organization for the provision of services for a particular consumer group would not normally result in legal action if the target level of service provision was not achieved. However the situation might be different if, during negotiations, it was the intention of the funder to create a legally binding contract. Adirondack (1992, p. 82) advises voluntary organizations and community groups:

> Because of the uncertainty of the legal status of grant aid and service agreements, it is good practice to treat all funding arrangements as if they are legally binding, even if they are not . . . The important thing is that an organization should not enter into any agreement unless the committee and managers understand all of it and are very confident they will be able to meet all the conditions set out in the agreement.

We consider this to be very good advice for all managers.

Service level agreements and contracts

SLAs are often used by organizations as a preparatory stage towards full competitive tendering and contracting. Box 4.1 outlines some of the features of a good SLA while Box 4.2 shows an extract of a SLA prepared in the police service.

Box 4.1   Preparing service level agreements (SLAs)

The SLA should identify:

- the *service* to be provided, at a specified price, through a service statement or specification
- the *level* at which the service will be provided – its quality and quantity;
- the fact that an *agreement* has been made about the type of service and level of provision
- the mechanism for *charging* for the service, for *amending* the service or the level, for *dealing with disagreements*, and for *terminating* the agreement.

In preparing the SLA:

- the supplier should provide customers with a full description of the services currently available, hence increasing customers' awareness of the service they are receiving
- prices should be agreed for these services
- the supplier should initially draw up the SLA, with the involvement of the customer, who becomes increasingly proactive.

The SLA should:

- relate service descriptions to pricing arrangements
- be flexible in order to cope with likely changes in circumstances
- build in continuous goals over the period of the SLA
- clearly set out the content and operation of the agreement and mutual responsibilities
- form the basis for contract documentation for a contracted service.

The SLA should allow customers:

- to control the standards of service they can expect and to monitor their achievement
- to amend these standards in the light of experience
- to determine the volume and type of service they receive
- to control the costs of the service and processing SLA transactions through appropriate invoicing mechanisms.

Source: Adapted from Audit Commission (1994a).

Box 4.2   Extract from Surrey Police Service SLA

Service	Standard	Target	Customer obligation
Major crime support:			
Provision of Senior Investigating Officer (SIO)	To arrive at scene or other location as agreed within 90 minutes of receipt of call	90%	Provision of suitable accommodation
Provision of HOLMES equipment to incident room at request of SIO	To install onsite, fully operational within 4 hours of request	90%	Provision of major incident room

Maintenance of HOLMES equipment on site to ensure operability	To maintain uptime for 90% of required operating time	90%	Nil
Management of forensic examination of crime scene, at request of SIO or senior SOCO	Attendance at scene within 2 hours of request	90%	Provision of exhibits room
Assessment of scale of enquiry and resource implications	First: within 36 hours of appointment of SIO Second and subsequent assessments: after 28 days, at weekly intervals by ACPO-level officer	90%	To take active part in review process

Source: Audit Commission (1994a).

As suggested in Box 4.1, an effective SLA can form the basis of a contract; however as a contract is a legally enforceable document it will probably present even more detail about the nature of the agreement between the parties. In essence a contract should state:

- the parties to the contract
- the powers and responsibilities of these parties
- when and how the contract will come into effect
- how changes are to be made to the specification of services or other considerations in the contract
- the arrangements for making payments due under the contract
- what happens if things go wrong (including any arbitration arrangements)
- provisions for events outside the control of the parties
- arrangements for the termination of the contract.

Box 4.3 contains the major headings and subsections of a typical contract for services (just to remind you, these are offered as a guide and should not be used in drawing up a contract without qualified legal advice).

Box 4.3 Typical headings and subsections for a contract for services

- Introduction
    Parties to the contract
    Powers under which they are acting
    Start date and duration

- Service specification
  Description of service
  Service standards
  Customers/end-users
  Equality of opportunity
  Monitoring and evaluation
- Financial conditions
  Costs
  Payment
  Financial monitoring and review
- Other conditions (which could cover issues such as staffing, premises, equipment and insurance)
- Variation, renewal, termination
  Review and variation
  Breach
  Termination
  Notice
- Signatures and dates

Source: Adapted from Adirondack (1992).

It is important to note that, on its own, a contract will not guarantee that the consumer gets an effective service. This will only be achieved by ongoing monitoring and review of the contract, together with renegotiation if appropriate. Box 4.4 gives a case example to illustrate this point.

Box 4.4   Case example

South Yorkshire Metropolitan Ambulance Service (SYMAS)

SYMAS is a health service trust providing accident and emergency services, dedicated day transport and outpatient services throughout South Yorkshire. Amongst the purchasers of its services are the Doncaster Royal Infirmary and Montagu Hospital Trust. In 1993 SYMAS had two contracts running with the hospital trust: one for general outpatients and one for dedicated day transport to the trust's day hospitals for elderly people. For the day hospital transport service SYMAS provided staff dedicated to each of the day hospitals. The allocated crews usually work split-shifts and are specifically trained to care for elderly people. Importantly, this contract was put in place following discussions with the day hospitals about their particular requirements.

The outpatient's contract included transport for discharged patients and operated from 8 a.m. to 6 p.m., on five days per week. Forty-eight hours' notice was required under the contract for all bookings. Daily targets for the service were mutually agreed between the hospital trust and SYMAS based on dividing the projected annual level of activity by 251 (the number of working days per year), as neither party had experience of controlling demand to within contract limits. The issue of daily targets quickly became a subject of serious contention between the parties as 'targets' became 'limits'; the 48-hour booking condition became pointless as the service was regularly fully-booked (on the basis of the daily targets) 72 hours in advance. The problem was compounded because the basis of the agreed target was neither known or accepted within the hospital trust, and the SYMAS became to be characterized as inflexible.

To address these issues a 'user group' was established, drawing its membership from the clinics and departments who made use of the service on behalf of their patients, and SYMAS representatives. As neither purchasers or suppliers had a real understanding of the problems and constraints experienced by the other, time was needed to establish a working relationship, and set out and agree the hospital trust's requirements from the outpatients' transport service. Initially, while the issues of daily limits and notice periods were tackled, the hospital trust had to make use of private ambulances and taxi services. This led to expenditure above the contracted price paid to SYMAS, and caused some dissatisfaction amongst the consumer group.

The user group became the focus for renegotiating the outpatients contract, while the hospital trust decided that, whilst still committed to a joint problem-solving approach, it needed to set the agenda for the negotiations and clearly establish the level of service it required from SYMAS: no longer would clinics, discharges and so on be structured around what the supplier was willing to supply. The hospital trust, of course, had the option of testing the market for other suppliers of this service, a fact that was probably not lost on SYMAS. The group continued to address these issues, while a SYMAS Quality Assurance Officer, based at Doncaster Royal Infirmary, tackled the operational issues on a day-to-day basis. By the time the formal negotiations for the 1994–95 contract began the situation had improved dramatically. Amongst the factors leading to this improvement were the following:

- Hospital trust managers had identified their priorities for service delivery, and expressed a willingness to reinvest the money they were spending on private sector services into the basic contract with SYMAS.
- The pressure on beds and the requirements to shorten lengths of stay meant that discharge as soon as clinically possible was an imperative. The hospital trust decided that a

dedicated discharge service was the best option, and this has subsequently been achieved.

- SYMAS have based an ambulance at Doncaster Royal Infirmary for which the work is not pre-planned by SYMAS control room. SYMAS have based a liaison officer and assistant at the hospital who are responsible for allocating journeys to these resources. These vehicles undertake all the short notice or special journeys required by the hospital trust.
- Hospital trust managers set the criteria for the use of the service, for example, determining that appointments for special scans take precedence over routine discharges.

As a consequence improvements have been achieved in the general outpatient service, and a more flexible delivery of the service to the day hospitals has seen improvements in that area as well. Comments about the service's flexibility and responsiveness have replaced the accusations of inflexibility, and are likely to lead to further developments cementing the longer-term relationship between the SYMAS and the hospital trust.

Source: Adapted from Brand and Gill (1995).

We want to conclude this section by reinforcing Adirondack's earlier comment – you should not enter into an SLA, and certainly not a contract, without being able to assure yourself that you will be able to meet your obligations under the agreement, legally enforceable or otherwise. One way of ensuring that you will be able to do so is to prepare a business plan, before you enter into the agreement.

Business planning

Edmonstone and Havergal (1991) in their review of business planning in the health service plot a historical development of approaches to planning which reflect the prevailing economic and political environment at the time. In their analysis, before the 1950s past experience was a reliable guide to the future, managers could plan on the basis of 'familiar patterns or extrapolations of familiar trends'; after the 1950s however the pace of change became faster, more discontinuous and therefore less predictable. However the social and economic environment was relatively stable. The economy prospered and planning was characterized by 'investment planning'. The 1970s, with the oil crisis, saw a marginal increase in uncertainty and the emergence of 'normative' and 'bureaucratic' planning models. In the 1980s the environment became even more unpredictable especially in the public sector where, as we have seen, the underlying concept of 'public service' and its provision came under intense scrutiny. Edmonstone and Havergal characterize this as the era of 'performance planning', where managers attempted to avoid radical change in their services by demonstrating that the current structures and operations could deliver a high-performance service. Finally in the 1990s an even more uncertain environment required a move to 'competitive planning' with the use of competition as the driving force for change, with resources going to the 'best' service providers.

We think that it is probably important to note that each wave of change in Edmonstone and Havergal's model probably built upon, rather than completely replaced, the previous phase. So it is important still to plan for stability as well as change, and for performance as well as competition. However we would agree with Edmonstone and Havergal's suggestion that over this period there has been a move from an internal focus and direction in the 1950s to a situation in the 1990s where external environmental forces are a greater influence on the planning process. This obviously does not mean that as a manager you can be completely outwardly focused, you still face the managerial dilemma of planning for effectiveness (essentially outward looking) as well as economy and efficiency (essentially inwardly-focused).

Edmonstone and Havergal place business planning in a 'hierarchy of management activity' which we have summarized in Box 4.5.

Box 4.5   Business planning in the hierarchy of managerial activity

Mission statement
- What are we in business for?
- Who are our stakeholders and what do they expect of us?

Strategies
- What is to be done, over what time frame and with what, general, resource implications?

Business plans
- How is what needs to be done going to be done?
- What targets need to be established?
- How are the resources available (finance, personnel, plant, equipment and buildings) to be allocated?
- What are the priorities and key tasks?
- How will progress and quality be monitored and reviewed?

Tasks
- Specific actions, with time and resource constraints, forming the basis for performance review systems at the level of the group or individual.

Source: Adapted from Edmonstone and Havergal (1991).

Setting the process of business planning in a wider managerial context encourages us to recognize that, no matter how sophisticated the process of business planning may be, unless the organization has clarity about its overall mission and strategic direction the resultant business plans may be of little practical value (we return to these broad, strategic issues in Chapter 9). Assuming that your organization has provided you with this level of clarity you can proceed to develop a business plan, bearing in mind that your objective is to ensure the continued survival and prosperity of your area of responsibility in the context of the external environment and the needs of your purchasers and consumers.

The Audit Commission (1994b) has prepared a model for the contents of a business plan which we have reproduced in Box 4.6.

Box 4.6   What should be in a business plan

- Finance
  Budgets based on planned activity, funding sources, cost improvements
  A capital programme and related revenue effects (including capital charges)
- Analysis of current resources and workload
  Staffing and equipment
  Quality standards (e.g. waiting times)
- Market analysis
  Demographic trends, opportunities and threats, competitor analysis, customer analysis
  Pricing
  Marketing to new purchasers
- Links to corporate strategy
  Contribution to long-term objectives
- Risk analysis
  The major financial and (other) risks quantified
  Sensitivity analysis and contingency plans
- Service development priorities
  Planned activity levels and assessment against capacity including phasing details
  New service proposals (if any)

Source: Audit Commission (1994b).

According to the Audit Commission (1994b, p. 22), and on this occasion they are concentrating on the health service:

> Whereas business plans usually contain information on staffing levels and costs, most omit other areas such as market analysis and risk analysis. Risk analysis is particularly important.

In Box 4.7 we outline the business plan prepared by a NHS Trust which, you will see, does attempt to include an element of risk analysis.

Box 4.7   Case example

Kent Ambulance NHS Trust (KANHST) – Business Plan 1994/95

1994/95 was KANHST's first year as a trust. They set themselves the mission of providing the highest quality of ambulance care to the people they serve and to add value to the services they complement.

Their business plan was structured around four primary aims:

1 To continue to be the major provider of ambulance services to Kent.
2 To seek further opportunities to expand their core and subsidiary services.
3 To pursue all opportunities to improve quality, reduce risk and respond to the needs of the people they serve.
4 To meet their financial obligations.

Business objectives were established in the following areas:

● Staff. Including objectives around accelerated extended training, the provision of paramedic staff, enhancing customer care skills, management development and reviewing terms and conditions of employment.
● Vehicles and equipment. Including a five-year replacement programme and improved capital expenditure planning.
● Estate. Tackling a review of buildings, conditions, location and need, and a backlog of building maintenance.
● Resource management. Integrating financial, personnel, central resource office systems and risk management systems through a local area network (LAN).
● Quality and risk management. Putting risk management systems in place by April 1994, pursuing BS 5750 accreditation and introducing new complaints procedures.
● Finance. Achieving break-even by year end, ensuring a 6 per cent return on the trust's asset base, remaining within external financing limits, achieving a cost improvement programme.

- Activity. Comparison of 1994/95 projected activity with the preceding two years.
- Capital expenditure. Plan to achieve other business plan objectives.
- Income and costs analysis.

Source: Kent Ambulance NHS Trust (1994).

Summary

In promoting competition and the contract culture there may be an implication, as Metcalfe and Richards (1990, p. 155) suggest, that:

> the way to make government more businesslike is to make it more like business.

There are, in practice, likely to be significant limitations to the effectiveness of this approach although, as Metcalfe and Richards point out, the private sector experience does have a lot to offer the public sector including:

- not 'reinventing the wheel' by using solutions developed in the private sector to problems also faced by the public sector.
- recognizing that management is not a 'dull, low level routine', as perceived by some senior public sector officials and aspirants to these positions, but an innovative process, oriented to change.

Flynn (1994, p. 73) comments:

> Managers in many parts of the public sector are faced with the prospect of operating in ways which replicate management in markets. Even if those responsible for public services completely reject the simplistic 'new right' solutions, they are forced to respond to the challenge presented.

So, in essence, as a manager in the public sector you can choose to adopt and adapt private sector methods where they present tried and tested responses to the problems and opportunities you face. In fact the environmental pressures on you and your organization are such that a response will be required whether you choose to or not, always remembering as Lord Rayner commented (quoted in Metcalfe and Richards, 1990, p. 156):

> There is no risk whatsoever of my assuming that running government is like running Marks & Spencer either in content or execution. Government has to provide services which no sane business would undertake and whether it is more or less of government that the nation needs, a government will have to

deal with those issues which private enterprise and voluntary activities cannot handle.

Action points and discussion points

(Items in italics are intended to encourage the reader to develop a greater intellectual awareness, items in plain type are focused upon work-related activity.)

Implement change and improvements in organizational activities

Which 'private sector' concepts, methods and techniques has your organization adopted, and which has it adapted? How effective have these adoptions/adaptations proved in practice? How could their usefulness to your organization be improved?

Conduct a 'business risk analysis' for your area of managerial responsibility. How are you managing these risks? How could your risk management be improved?

Evaluate and improve organizational performance

Obtain a copy of a business plan prepared by an organization in the private sector (this may require a degree of ingenuity!) and critically analyse it. How could it be improved? To what extent is it likely to form the basis of effective managerial action? How would it have to be adapted to be of use to a public sector organization?

Manage self to optimize performance

Assess yourself against Holtham's competency model. Can you identify gaps in your own competence. If so, how will you work towards attaining these competencies. Are there any important competencies missing from the model in your opinion?

Provide required personnel for activities

To what extent are Holtham's competencies possessed by members of your team? Which team members have which competencies? Where are the gaps, either across the team or individual by individual? Prepare a plan with the individuals concerned, and the whole team, to develop the competencies required.

Establish organizational values and culture

Choose two or three private sector organizations, and two or three public sector organizations with which you are familiar and review their respective culture in terms of the contract between them and their customers. What are the implications of your analysis for the way in which the relationship between organization and customer is managed?

Review the 'contract culture' in your area of management responsibility. How would you describe it to a new member of your team? Look around your work area, does it reflect a 'contract culture'? For example are there documents readily available which describe your approach to contracting with your customers? Do you have information about your level of contract compliance, and are these figures widely publicized? Is your complaints procedure readily available to your customers? What underlying beliefs and values about contracting exist, and are they positively or negatively disposed towards contracting? Prepare an approach to developing your organization's contract culture.

Further reading

Adirondack, S. (1992). *Just About Managing: Effective Management for Voluntary Organisations and Community Groups*. London Voluntary Service Council.
An excellent, practical, wide-ranging management guide, with a chapter on managing in the contract culture.

Delderfield, J., Puffitt, R., and Watts, G. (1991). *Business Planning in Local Government*. Longman.
Although essentially a manual for business planning in local government drawing on practice in the private sector in their approach to constructing a business plan, this practical guide will be of interest to managers across the public sector. Those not in the local government area should not have too much difficulty adapting the models presented to their own practice.

Fenwick, J., Shaw, K., and Foreman, A. (1994). Managing Competition in UK Local Government. *International Journal of Public Sector Management*, 7(6), 4–14.
A concise review of the impact of compulsory competitive tendering (CCT) on the roles of managers in local government, the new skills required and the relationship between CCT and new public management.

Jones, J., and Bates, J. (1996). *Business Planning in the Health Service: A Guide for Managers*. Thompson Business Press.
Shows how the principles of business planning developed in the private sector can be tailored to meet the needs of health service managers.

Ranade, W. (1995). The Theory and Practice of Managed Competition in the National Health Service. *Public Administration*, **73**, 241–262.
This is a fairly demanding read as it draws on a number of theoretical concepts and approaches, but it relates the experience of four district health authorities in implementing managed competition, and identifies some of the key issues arising from writing, negotiating and monitoring contracts in practice.

Rathgeb, S. (1993). *Nonprofits for Hire: The Welfare State in the Age of Contracting*. Harvard University Press.
A detailed text reviewing some of the problems with, and unintended consequences of, contracts between governments and not-for-profit organizations. Tends towards a text on social policy, but with clear managerial implications for the way not-for-profit organizations are transforming in response to the growth of the contract culture.

Walsh, K. (1994). *Getting to Know the Competition*. Local Government Management Board.
Written for local authority managers entering markets for the first time, but of interest to all not-for-profit organizations concerned with appraising the competition and understanding markets.

Part Three   The Competent
Manager in the Public Sector

5 Managing people

Aims and learning objectives

The aim of this chapter is to help you review and develop the way you manage people, including ensuring that your organization has the correct number of people competent to perform well towards meeting the organization's objectives. We will also spend some time discussing the most effective way of managing people who are having difficulties at work, a situation which is bound to arise despite your best efforts, although this chapter also aims to help you prevent many problems arising in the first place.

At the end of this chapter, and associated activities and reading, you will be able to:

- provide a working definition of 'human resource management' and relate it to your own managerial and organizational experience
- outline the major elements of legislation relating to the management of people at work
- prepare a personnel plan for your own area of responsibility to ensure the provision of the required personnel for activities
- conduct a preliminary job analysis and prepare a personnel specification, job description and person specification
- outline the major elements of a systematic approach to recruitment and selection
- contribute to a selection process, including selection interviewing
- prepare, implement and evaluate a training and development plan for yourself and those staff for whom you are responsible, to develop teams and individuals to enhance performance
- contribute to your organization's performance management system, including responding effectively to poor performance of team members
- delegate authority for programmes of work
- take appropriate action, in consultation with others as necessary, in cases of redundancy.

Let us start by restating the obvious: the nature of work in the public sector, as in every other sector, is undergoing fundamental and profound change. We have already discussed many of these changes, and the increasing pace of change, which is making your job as a manager challenging, to say the least! In this chapter we will concentrate on your responsibilities for managing other people. It is important to note from the outset that these managerial tasks can now incorporate a broad range of people, in a variety of work situations. As Thomson and Mabey (1994, p. 6) suggest, an organization's 'human resources' include:

> all the individual employees who contribute to the operations of an organization, whether they are employed full time, part-time, on a temporary or permanent basis, centrally, in separate business units or from home.

As a manager in the public sector you are also likely to be involved in the 'management' of 'human resources' who are not employees of your organization in that they may be volunteers, governors or elected members. In many cases the selection, training and development, reward and monitoring of these human resources will be as important as that of employees.

Human resource management – a model for managing people

'Our employees are our most important asset' is a piece of managerial rhetoric espoused so often that it has become something of a cliché. It is often difficult to find evidence that this espoused theory has much impact on the reality of organizational life: attention is more likely to be paid to issues of meeting political objectives or ensuring financial efficiency than to really valuing people. However according to a number of management theorists and commentators this situation may really be changing at last. According to Pfeffer (1992, p. 11) for example:

> Traditional sources of success – product and process technology, protected or regulated markets, access to financial resources and economies of scale – can still provide competitive leverage, but to a lesser degree now than in the past, leaving organizational culture and capabilities, derived from how people are managed, as comparatively more vital.

The public sector has always tended to be labour, rather than capital, intensive and despite (one might also say because of) reductions in the overall number of people employed in the sector skilled management of this key resource is likely to become even more important in the future. These trends have been accompanied by what has been called by some (see, for example, Wright and Rudolph, 1994) a 'paradigm shift' from traditional, centralized Personnel Management to strategic, decentralized Human Resource Management (HRM). There are various models of HRM available and for this chapter we are

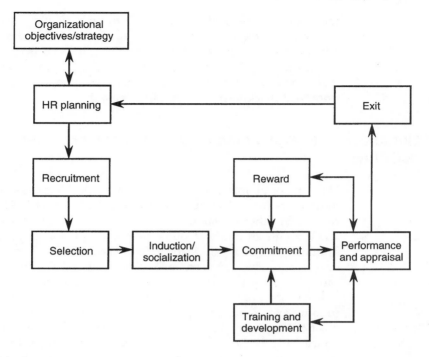

Figure 5.1 *A basic human resource management system*

adopting the basic model shown in Figure 5.1. This model suggests that an organization needs some sort of human resource plan, which may be more or less developed, bearing some relationship to the overall strategic objectives of the organization.

The plan should give an indication of the number and type of people that need to be recruited which, in turn, influences selection processes and methods. These should be designed to maximize the likelihood of achieving a match between the person selected and the job they have been recruited for. Once a person has been recruited and selected they need to be introduced to the organization, inducted and socialized, hopefully in a way that leads to them becoming committed to the organization and its objectives. It can be argued that without this sense of commitment being developed and maintained employees are unlikely to perform to their full potential, resulting, in turn, in a less than optimal level of organizational performance. Because, partly, of the increased emphasis in the public sector on performance and value-for-money more attention is being paid to staff appraisal and performance monitoring, which can (some would say should) link directly to reward and training and development outcomes. It is likely that someone who feels adequately rewarded for their efforts, and that they are being valued through training and development, will be more committed to the organization, and therefore more willing and able to perform well. Obviously part of training and development is concerned with career progression and advancement which will be one of the causes of people leaving the organization, which needs to be reflected in the human resource plan, thereby completing the human resource management system from 'exit' back to human resource planning.

Human resource planning – providing required personnel for activities

How many people will we need? What specific skills will be needed three years from now that are not currently required? The answers to these, and other questions crucial to the organization, can be addressed through an effective human resource planning system. An overestimate of need can lead to overstaffing which means that the organization has to carry excessive costs, whilst understaffing can cause the quality of the product or service to suffer.

Therefore human resources planning (HRP) is important in controlling costs while also providing a productive workforce. No organization can rely on obtaining highly skilled personnel at short notice. HRP is therefore essentially seeking to satisfy the objectives of the organization by ensuring the availability of people with the right types of skill, at the right quality, in the right quantities, in the right places at the right time. It is possible to envisage human resource planning taking place at a number of levels: from the macro organization-wide decisions about long-term needs to day-to-day decisions about recruiting a new member of staff or setting up a team for a specific project. Each entails management decisions about getting the best from the human resources available. In this section we will concentrate on the macro-level of human resource planning.

The obvious place to start the process of planning to meet an organization's need for staff is with the organization's overall objectives, which should be reflected in its strategic plan. This could be regarded as the 'demand' side of personnel planning. Managers also need to be aware of the 'supply' of people able to ensure the organization achieves its objectives. In reviewing the supply of people, managers should consider two sources – internal and external to the organization. As well as having an awareness of the external labour market, and the competences and potential of the current workforce, the issues we highlighted in Chapter 3 – decentralization and restructuring, an emphasis on the customer, splitting the purchaser and provider roles and the creation of markets, privatization, increased flexibility and so on – has made the task of personnel planning more complex. For example, a recent survey by an organization called New Ways to Work (1995) showed that while 'flexitime' arrangements have been established in local government for some time (85 per cent of the 249 local authorities who responded to the survey reported having a formal policy on flexible working hours) an increasing number reported either having in place, or planning to put in place, formal policies for a range of other flexible working patterns including job sharing (62 per cent in place: 19 per cent planned); career/employment breaks (22 per cent: 17 per cent); annualized hours (18 per cent: 16 per cent); term-time working (11 per cent: 13 per cent) and working from home (7 per cent: 14 per cent).

Box 5.1 provides details of one NHS Trust's approach to introducing annualized hours in an attempt to increase staff flexibility to cope with varying workloads.

Box 5.1 Case example

Annualized hours at Northallerton NHS Trust

Northallerton NHS Trust (NNHST) in North Yorkshire employs 1700 people (1100 full-time equivalent; FTE) and has an annual income of £31 million. As with other trusts, NNHST was faced with pressures both to control costs while also offering even more effective patient care and service.

In 1992 the trust's management was becoming increasingly concerned about exceptionally high unit labour costs in certain wards and a low level of productivity per employee. When investigating this situation it was discovered that the wards affected were characterized by a highly volatile and varying activity level. The grade/skill mix in these wards appeared to be appropriate, i.e. staff competence was not an issue, but rather the problem seemed to centre on staff deployment. A significant amount of staff time was being lost because of mismatches between required and actual staffing levels. Prior to this review rostering plans for nursing staff were planned a month in advance, while in practice up to 40 per cent of rosters were having to be changed to cope with the unpredictable and fluctuating patient needs. This meant that nursing managers were wasting considerable amounts of time in rearranging rosters and attempting to find part-time ('bank') staff to fill the needs. Heavy costs were also being incurred through 'on call' payments, overtime and time off in lieu of extra hours worked.

For a variety of reasons NNHST decided that the use of bank staff should be minimized, and that, instead, a more flexible approach to rostering be considered. The new approach would need to be more responsive to patient need and reduce costs through avoiding the 'inappropriate' use of bank staff, overtime and time-off in lieu.

In an attempt to find a more flexible way of working NNHST management began to investigate the 'annualized hours' system. Under such a system the number of hours at work are spread over a year, rather than a week or month. This system has the potential of providing a high degree of flexibility in meeting peaks and troughs in workloads, and therefore offers a more flexible approach to personnel planning.

Following a small pilot project involving a group of nurses in December 1992, the annualized hours system was extended to more nurses, and certain other staff, during the course of the next two years. At present around 10 per cent of NNHST nursing staff are working to annualized hours contracts, while on certain wards, where patient needs are more unpredictable, up to 40 per cent of nursing staff are on this type of contract.

Under the new system it is found that a much lower proportion of rosters need changing (as low as 5 per cent in some cases); management time is saved; staffing resources can be better matched to workload requirements; there is a reduced dependency on bank staff; and workforce productivity has increased and labour costs have been reduced.

Source: Adapted from IRS (1995a).

As the nature of 'work' in the public sector changes with a new mix of permanent, temporary, full-time, part-time, core, periphery and contract workers so the task of HRP is likely to become even more complex, albeit with the potential benefits of a diverse, flexible workforce more able to meet the needs of the organization and its customers. As in the Northallerton NHS Trust case, managers will need to carefully consider staffing options, in the context of employment, and other, legislation, equality of opportunity issues, and a range of constraints, with limited financial resources to meet all the needs presented being a major one. Figure 5.2 attempts to incorporate these, and other factors, into one integrated model of HRP.

Figure 5.2 starts with one of the major purposes of planning: trying to minimize shocks to the organization from its environment through careful investigation both inside and outside of organization. The best planning in the world will not eradicate shocks entirely, but a good plan, flexibly implemented, is probably one of the best tools the manager can have for dealing with the increasing level of environmental turbulence they face (it is fair to say that this view is far from uncontroversial but it represents one of our guiding principles). Once the needs of the organization and its environment have been investigated the supply of, and demand for, competent employees needs to be assessed before any imbalance can be addressed by the methods shown in the penultimate box. Putting these plans into action will result in a pattern of per-

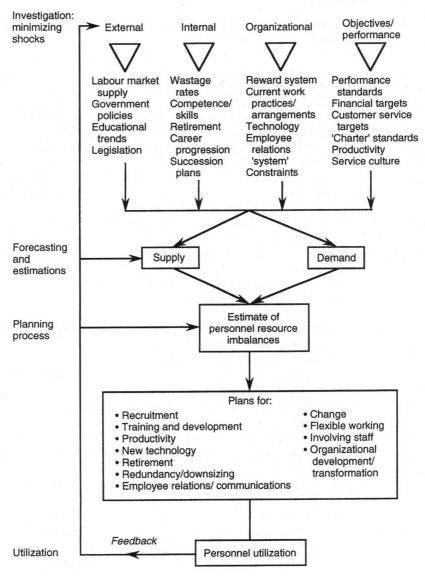

Figure 5.2 *A model of personnel planning*

Source: Adapted from Bramham (1989)

sonnel utilization, which feed back into each of the previous stages.

In putting the HRP into practice particular attention has to be paid to influences external to the organization, of these the legal framework around employment is of particular importance as it impacts on each stage of managing the employer–employee relationship, from recruitment to exit, so we will briefly review this framework next.

The legislative framework

There is now an extensive range of employment legislation regulating the relationship between employer and employee. Much of this, for example that relating to pensions or to self-employed people, is beyond the scope of this book. The purpose of this section is to alert you, as a manager, to the major elements of the legislative framework that you need to be aware of. We will not be pursuing these areas in great detail, and you are strongly advised either to seek advice from a professional legal or personnel practitioner, or to read some of the material suggested in Further Reading, if you think you are dealing with an issue at work which has legal implications (and most of them do!).

Employees have a number of statutory rights (and obligations), defined in Acts of Parliament such as:

- Employment Acts 1980, 1988, 1989 (EA 1980, 1988, 1989)
- Employment Protection (Consolidation) Act 1978 (EP[C]A 1978)
- Health and Safety at Work Act, 1974 (HSWA 1974)
- Sex Discrimination Acts, 1975, 1986 (SDA 1975, 1986)
- Race Relations Act, 1976 (RRA 1976)
- Disabled Persons (Employment) Acts 1944, 1958 (DP[E]A 1944, 1958)
- Equal Pay Act, 1970 (as amended) (EPA 1970)
- Trade Union and Labour Relations (Consolidation) Act 1992 (TULR[C]A 1992)
- Trade Union Reform and Employment Rights Act 1993 (TURERA 1993)
- Rehabilitation of Offenders Act, 1974 (ROA 1974)
- Social Security Contributions and Benefits Act, 1992 (SSCB 1992)
- Disability Discrimination Act, 1995 (DDA 1995).

This is not intended to be a comprehensive list of employment legislation, but does indicate the range of legislation you need to be aware of.

In essence this legislative framework, which is supported by a range of regulations and codes of practice, provides employees with various rights in the employment relationship. In some cases these rights only come into force after a 'qualifying period' of continuous service with an employer; others are available to the employee immediately. Box 5.2 shows some of these rights, the relevant Act and the qualifying period.

Box 5.2   Employment rights and qualifying periods

Statutory right	Act	Qualifying period
Not to be unfairly dismissed	EP(C)A	2 years
Not to be unfairly dismissed because of pregnancy	EP(C)A	None
Not to be dismissed for taking action on health and safety matters	EP(C)A	None
Not to be discriminated against on the grounds of sex	SDA	None
Not to be discriminated against on the grounds of race	RRA	None
Equal pay for women and men for work of equal value	EPA	None
Time off (with or without pay) for trade union duties	TULR(C)A	None
Time off work for ante-natal care with pay	EP(C)A	None
Statutory Sick Pay	SSCBA	None
Statutory Maternity Pay	SSA	26 weeks as at the 15th week before the expected week of childbirth
Maternity leave	TURERA	None
Written statement of terms of employment	TURERA	None
Itemized pay statement	EP(C)A	None
A healthy and safe working environment	HSWA	None

Source: Adapted from *The Personnel Manager's Factbook* (1996).

The law also gives certain rights to prospective employees during the recruitment and selection process. These include the right not to reveal a criminal conviction resulting in a sentence not exceeding thirty months in custody, after 'rehabilitation' (ROA 1974). The 'rehabilitation period' depends on the nature of the sentence, and some professions of particular importance to the public sector, such as teachers, doctors and accountants, *must* disclose previous convictions, as must those whose occupation brings them into contact with young people under the age of 18.

Employers also must not discriminate against women (or men) or married persons in the way in which they recruit or make selection decisions (SDA 1975, 1986) or discriminate against candidates on grounds of their race, colour, creed or ethnic origin (RRA 1976). When the provisions of the Disability Discrimination Act, 1995 (DDA 1995) come into effect at the end of 1996 it will also be illegal to treat a person with a disability less favourably than other people, unless there are justifiable reasons for doing so. DDA 1995 also scraps the quota system established under DP(E)A. 1944, 1958. It is important to note that DDA 1995 provides a statutory right of non-discrimination for people with a disability in employment *and* in the provision of services. DDA 1995 also requires employers to make reasonable adjustments to a workplace where this would overcome the practical effects of an individual's disability.

With this legislative framework in mind we can turn our attention to managing the recruitment and selection process.

Recruitment and selection

Job and person specification

The overall aim of the recruitment and selection process in an organization should be to obtain the quantity and quality of employees required by the Human Resource Plan, in accordance with organizational requirements and within the law.

The main stages of a systematic recruitment and selection process are shown in Figure 5.3.

The Human Resource Plan should provide the basis for a detailed definition of the type and number of jobs required to achieve the organization's strategic plans. The first stage in putting this broad HRP into action is Job Analysis. Job Analysis is the process of describing and recording aspects of the tasks required of a job holder successfully to contribute to organizational objectives. A good Job Analysis has the potential to clarify duties and related tasks; assist in determining a job's relative worth for effective reward management; and to provide applicants with realistic information regarding duties, working conditions and job requirements. Closely linking Job Analysis with Employee Training and Development can also contribute to career development programmes for employees.

The processes of Job Analysis is becoming increasingly complicated as the public sector strives to achieve flexibility in service delivery and, therefore, in the nature of jobs. The traditional approach to Job Analysis is describing what is happening now and trying to forecast how the job requirements will change in the future. In a traditionally structured organization there may be a tension between establishing equity between jobs and a responsiveness to changing work conditions. It is important when undertaking a job analysis to take into

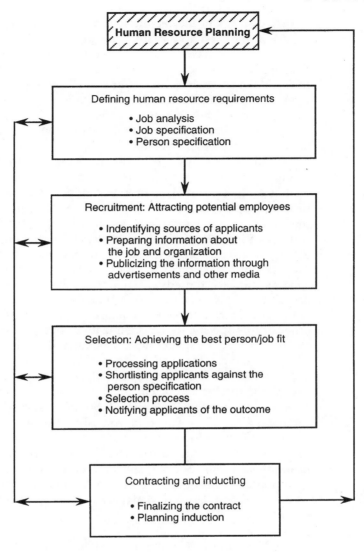

Figure 5.3   *The main stages of recruitment and selection*

account the views of all the relevant people. This is obviously likely to include the job holder(s) and their manager(s), but could also usefully extend to other people affected by the job holder's activities, including other employees and the recipients of the services provided by the job holder.

Once the requirements of a particular job have been analysed as clearly as possible, using the appropriate method for gathering information, or combination of methods, the resultant job analysis needs to be communicated concisely so that it can form the basis of the next two stages of the recruitment process: preparing the Job Specification (or Job Description) and Person Specification.

The Job Specification is the product of Job Analysis and is a detailed statement of the physical and mental activities involved in the 'job' and, when relevant, of social and physical environmental issues as well. The Person Specification is an interpretation of the job specification or description in terms of the kind of knowledge, skills, attributes, competencies or other factors a person needs in order to be likely to succeed in the job.

As with Job Analysis it is not surprising that traditional Job Specifications are more appropriate to stable circumstances. However as well as an important element in achieving a job-person fit a well-prepared Job Specification can help employees understand how and why the organization works. It is for this reason that in Figure 5.3 the process of induction and socialization is connected, via the feedback loops, to all the previous stages in the recruitment and selection process. For a newcomer to an organization their 'induction' starts as soon as they see the advertisement for the post. Therefore good Job and Person Specifications will emphasise not only the purpose of the job (and the job title, responsibilities, key objectives, competences and other details specific to the organization) but the importance of initiative and the need to respond to change and the job holder's relationship with the team as a whole. In a complex job (and most jobs in the public sector are increasing in complexity) it is unlikely that anybody ever meets the Person Specification completely. There is always likely to be some room for development. So, in most cases, when you select somebody to fill a vacancy you are also starting the important process of identifying their training and development needs.

Box 5.3 shows extracts from the Job Description and Person Specification (which the Society calls an 'employee specification' prepared by a not-for-profit organization, the National Autistic Society, for the post of Training Services Manager) as an example of good practice.

Box 5.3 Extracts from The National Autistic Society's Job Description and Employee Specification for a Training Services Manager

Job description

Reporting to: Chief Executive

Staff reporting to you: Training Administrator
                                     Clerk-Typist

Main purpose of post: Develop and manage strategies to deliver a range of external training and consultancy services provided by the NAS in conjunction with the Inge Wakehurst Trust.

1 Specific responsibilities

1.1 Training

    1.1.1 Ensure the provision of relevant, effective and efficient training and consultancy services as outlined in the NAS Mission Statement and Business Plan.

    1.1.2 Develop and maintain an annual programme of training and development opportunities for staff working with people with autism, incorporating appropriate, multi-disciplinary, modular and accredited approaches to training.

    1.1.3 Identify, commission, produce and deliver training initiatives to meet purchasers' needs.

    1.1.5 Develop strategies to monitor and evaluate the training provided.

(plus another seven items)

1.2 Consultancy

    1.2.1 In conjunction with the Development Officers, participate in detailed planning and marketing of consultancy with purchasing agencies.

    1.2.4 Develop contractual relationships with consultants.

1.3 Customer care and marketing

    1.3.1 Take a lead role in the marketing, income generation and customer care in all areas of external training and consultancy services.

    1.3.2 Development and manage clear contractual and collaborative planning relationships with purchasing organizations.

    1.3.3 Establish, promote and maintain relationships with and between different agencies and affiliated societies to achieve the business plan objectives.

1.4 Finance

    1.4.1 Draw up an annual budget for training and consultancy, adhere to it and meet all financial targets.

    1.4.2 Identify sources of funding for training development.

(plus another three items)

1.5 Management

1.5.1 Induct members of staff for whom there is managerial responsibility, supervise their work, and ensure opportunities for their career development.

(plus another five items)

2 General responsibilities

2.3 Ensure that your conduct within and outside Head Office does not conflict with professional expectations of the NAS, and the Inge Wakehurst Trust.

2.5 Maintain confidentiality for all areas of the job, its staff and its work and that of the Inge Wakefield Trust.

2.9 Carry out any other duties as are within the scope, spirit and purpose of the job, the title of the post and its grading as requested by your Line Manager or his/her higher level of authority.

(plus another six items)

Note: The job description reflects the present requirements of the post. As duties and responsibilities change and develop the job description will be reviewed and is subject to amendment in consultation with you.

Employee specification

Category	Essential	Desirable
A Qualifications		
Recognized training qualification		X
Management qualification		X
B Knowledge		
Knowledge of approaches to training	X	
Knowledge about autism		X
(plus one other item)		
C Skills		
Excellent verbal and written communication skills	X	
(plus another three items)		
D Work experience		
Working in training field (minimum three years)	X	
(plus another five items)		
E Personal qualities		
Self motivated	X	
Ability to work on own initiative	X	
(plus another three items)		

There are many points worth noting from the National Autistic Society example. In particular note the way in which the job is directly linked to the organization's objectives through mention of its Mission and Business Plan. Consider the way in which key relationships with other members of the Society, such as Development Officers and external agencies, are made explicit. Through establishing from the outset the standards of behaviour required, such as confidentiality, the Society is beginning the important process of induction/socialization *and* preparing itself to deal with any disciplinary and performance problems with the post holder, should they arise (we will be returning to these issues later in this chapter). We can also see in this example many of the changing emphases in the public sector in general, and not-for-profit organizations in particular, which we examined before including the increasing importance of contractual relationships, sources of funding and customer care.

In preparing these documents prospective candidates for the post have a clear picture of what is expected of them, both in terms of qualifications and experience and the major elements of the job. The National Autistic Society also includes a Job Specification covering issues such as travel, unsocial hours, the working environment and pressures inherent in the job and other information about the Society and its training programmes in an information pack for applicants. In preparing all this material the Society has not only prepared a powerful recruitment tool, but it has also taken the opportunity to publicize the work of the Society amongst people who may decide not to proceed with an application for the post on offer. Note also the important caveat to the Job Description about the changing demands on the post. It is important to keep Job Descriptions and Person Specifications under constant review, and not just to amend them when a vacancy arises. Changes in the requirements of the job, and the people doing it, need an ongoing, continuous management response, not just when the post becomes vacant.

Recruitment – attracting potential employees

Having analysed what the job entails and the qualities we are looking for in a person to do it, when a vacancy occurs the next stage in the process is recruitment.

Recruitment involves searching for and obtaining qualified job candidates in sufficient numbers so that the organization can select the most appropriate person to fulfil the needs of the job. Recruitment can therefore be defined as the set of activities used to obtain a pool of qualified job applicants. Throughout the recruitment process it is important to keep accurate records of the number of enquiries received, recruitment sources cited, application packs dispatched, applications received and similar information. Without these records it is not possible, for example, to compare the effectiveness of alternative advertising media.

Selection – achieving the best possible person/job fit

Once an appropriate field of applicants has been obtained for a vacant position a selection decision needs to be made about which candidate, or candidates, should be offered employment.

It is important to note that all selection is about making a prediction, predicting how a particular individual will perform in a job. Often the prediction will prove to have been incorrect and it will become apparent either the person selected is unsuitable for the job or vice versa. The consequences of a wrong prediction can be very expensive for the organization and disruptive for the individual concerned.

One of the reasons why selection predictions prove unreliable is that no systematic selection process was used, or the wrong selection techniques were chosen, or they were used and interpreted incorrectly. There are a number of selection assessment techniques available of which the selection interview is probably the most widely used. However research has shown distinct problems with the selection interview as a reliable, valid predictor of job success. This is particularly so of an unstructured interview. Here the danger is that assessments generated depend more upon the attitudes of the interviewer than the extent to which the interviewee meets the job criteria.

Interviews do, however, have a variety of positive characteristics which can be used by organizations to contribute towards effective selection and placement decisions. These include the opportunity to provide information to the applicant regarding the specific position in particular and the organization in general. A well-structured and managed interview can be important for wider public relations, leaving even rejected candidates feeling that they have been fairly treated (especially if they are offered feedback about their interview performance). Perhaps one of the most useful aspects of the interview as a selection technique is its flexibility. When used as part of a comprehensive selection package the interview provides an opportunity to fill in any gaps in the overall assessment of the candidate's fit with the selection criteria. Without complete information it is unlikely that an appropriate selection decision will be made. Interviews can also permit interviewers to make assessments of their compatibility with the applicant and this may be especially valuable if the interviewer will be the interviewee's immediate superior (although caution should be exercised here, there is an obvious danger of stereotyping or 'cloning' which may not be in the organization's best interests). Finally, the interview does have the advantage of being the selection method most candidates will be expecting. Where other methods are to be used as well candidates will need to be carefully prepared.

As we have suggested, interviews are likely to be most useful when they are part of a comprehensive selection package. In these

circumstances they can be used to review and explore the outcome of other selection techniques such as tests. A selection process which incorporates a number of selection methods is sometimes referred to as an 'assessment centre'. It is important to note that an assessment centre refers to the whole process rather than a physical site – you can hold an assessment centre anywhere! (The assessment centre process can also be adapted to help people review their training and development needs; under these circumstances the process is often referred to as a 'development centre'.)

Selection tests can have the advantages of being quick to administer (especially to a large group of applicants), inexpensive (compared, say, to the staff costs involved in using a panel of interviewers or a number of interviews) and relatively objective (according to the nature of the particular test). It is possible to design tests that predict job performance accurately, although these tend to be concerned with relatively restricted manual skills; it is less easy to design a test which can accurately predict effective performance for a more complex job such a management position.

Selection tests can be broadly classified into three categories: ability tests (covering both physical and mental ability); personality tests (which try to establish and measure stable behaviour patterns which are important for a particular job-profile); and tests of motivation or work preferences (which may relate to personality as well).

It is likely that a person's performance in an organization is determined jointly by a combination of the person's motivation, ability and personality. If this is the case then it reinforces the need for a selection process which is sensitive to a number of issues if it is to be the basis of effective decision making. Tests, when carefully constructed and validated, can aid in the assessment process. However it is important to note some important caveats. Perhaps one of the major problems with tests when used in selection is that they can appear more valid than they really are. It may be attractive for those making a selection decision to base it on the apparently 'objective' test results. On the other hand some selectors may disregard testing completely. Neither approach is likely to contribute to effective decision making. For these, and other reasons, it is important that tests are only used and interpreted by people who are carefully trained in the test concerned and understand its construction, application and limitations. These people also need to be competent in interpreting the test results to people who may be making the selection decision but are unaware of the detail of the test. They should also be willing, and able, to provide feedback to all the candidates on their performance in the tests.

While well-researched and constructed tests will normally include data on reliability and validity in the tester's handbook (in fact it is probably unwise to use any test which does not include this data for selection purposes) it is important that the capacity of any test to predict subsequent performance is systematically evaluated by the particular organization in which it is being used. This evaluation may be crucial in ensuring that the test is contributing to an equal opportunities approach, i.e. that the test is not unfairly discriminating between people. In addition organizations should determine whether a test adds anything to their ability to predict success over and above that provided by alternative methods.

Most organizations collect information from the candidate about their educational history and achievements, work experience, job related training, salary and similar biographical information (sometimes known as biodata). There is evidence that if this information is collected systematically, interpreted skilfully and validated in the context of a particular job it can be a useful predictor of subsequent job success. This method of selection also has the advantages of being available at a relatively low cost. This type of information is often contained within a curriculum vitae (CV) and it is worth considering asking applicants to include a CV in addition to, or instead of, an application form. One problem with CVs, however, is that they do not necessarily provide the information you want in a standardized format.

Whatever method, or combination of methods, you use we think that it is important that you view the selection process as one of collecting 'evidence' that you can cite when making a prediction of the person/job fit amongst the candidates. This evidence needs to be carefully collected. Irrelevant issues, in strict terms of the person's likely suitability for the job, need to be screened out and appropriate caution taken in dealing with 'first impressions' (either good or bad). Similarly caution needs to be exercised when you are collecting 'evidence' from other people, which is normally undertaken via a request for references. As with the selection interview a reference is likely to be more useful if you can focus your questions on elements of the job, rather than a more general request to the referee about the applicant's 'suitability' for the job. Obviously references need to be carefully interpreted, and the evidence they provide tested during other parts of the process. Although you will always provide truthful, fair references based on your knowledge of the person, you cannot always rely on others being so fair and principled!

Training and developing people to enhance performance

As a manager you have a prime responsibility for your own training and development as well as contributing to the training and development of your staff and the overall learning, development and growth of your organization. These responsibilities represent a considerable workload if they are to be met efficiently and effectively.

As with any workload management the clearer you are about what you are trying to achieve the easier it is to plan and work towards your objectives. One of the problems with 'training and development' is that the terms are often used as if they were interchangeable, or meant the same thing. Often 'training' will be used as a generic term for the training, development and education process. So let's start by trying to clarify these basic terms.

In general, training can be defined as a activity designed to meet the immediate skill needs of a person which they require in their present job. The emphasis is on a relatively short-term learning intervention, intended for immediate use. Examples might be a course designed to help a care assistant learn how to lift a client safely, a volunteer to prepare food in accordance with health regulations or a manager to understand basic financial information. In a training event the onus tends to be on an expert 'instructor' 'teaching' a relatively unskilled 'trainee'.

Development is concerned with the longer-term learning of an individual and can include activities which may not immediately be put into use. In development the emphasis is on the individual taking far more responsibility for their own learning.

Education is concerned with people's broader learning, often beyond their current work tasks and, perhaps, unlikely ever to be of direct use in their work career. In this respect 'education' can be seen as an extension of 'development'. In many organizations the importance of educational activity for young trainees and apprentices is recognized, but they are not the only groups who may benefit from educational opportunities.

In this chapter we will be using the term 'human resource development' to encompass training, development and education.

Figure 5.4 shows one approach to integrating human resource development with the needs of the organization by closely integrating it with human resource planning (which as we have already suggested should relate to organizational strategy and objectives).

The three major phases of any training, development and education programme should be:

- assessment, which determines training and development needs; assessment consists of organizational, job, and person needs analyses
- implementation (actual training, development and education)
- evaluation.

Assessment, sometimes referred to as 'training needs analysis' (TNA) is concerned with establishing training and development requirements. This phase can consist of organizational, team, job or individual needs analysis.

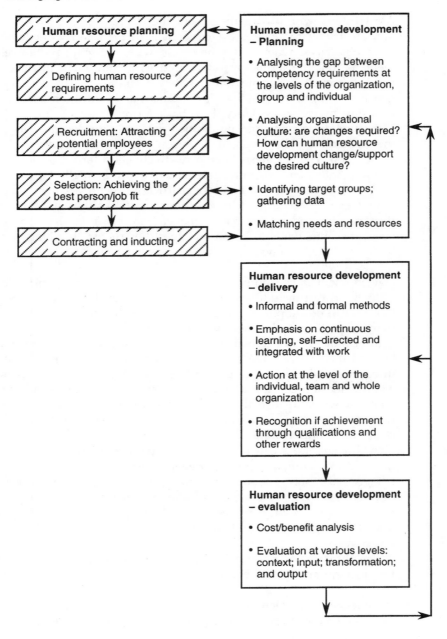

Figure 5.4 *An integrated approach to human resource development*

Once the need has been established attention can turn to planning ways of meeting the needs, ideally involving the employee or employees in every step of the process. There are a wide range of training, development and education techniques and resources avail-

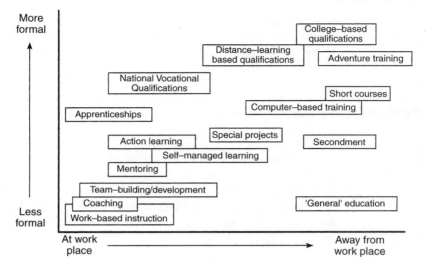

Figure 5.5   *Some approaches to human resource development*

able. Figure 5.5 shows a range of techniques positioned according to their degree of formality, and the extent to which they take place at work or away from work. Increasing concern with continuous development, especially, but not entirely, for employees with professional qualifications and the associated notion of the 'learning organization' means that more emphasis is being given to maximizing the opportunities for human resource development from normal work activities and integrating learning with work. This means that as a manager you are likely to be required to take even more responsibility for helping your staff to manage their own learning through offering coaching, counselling and other ways of helping people reflect on their experience and learn through experimentation.

The final stage, evaluation, tends to be the one often missed out, perhaps because it is rather difficult to perform well. In essence evaluation is concerned with assessing the benefits that have been derived for the individual, the job and the organization from the training, development or education undertaken and comparing this with costs (fixed, variable and opportunity) of the activity. Evaluation can take account of the context of the HRD activity (i.e. its match with organization culture, objectives and similar issues); the reaction of learners as they progressed through the learning experience; and the output of the learning activity at the levels of (a) immediate output (the learning gained by the end of the activity), (b) its intermediate outputs (the extent to which learning was transferred back to work in terms of improved effectiveness, cost reductions and so on) and (c) ultimate outputs (the impact of these changes on the organization and its objectives). It is easy to see that a 'good' training course, for example, may achieve a significant immediate output but if, for whatever reasons, the individual concerned is not able to transfer this learning into a direct organizational benefit the course cannot be evaluated as, ultimately, of much value to the organization.

Performance management

A major purpose of human resource development is to tackle performance deficiencies, either current or anticipated. A performance deficiency exists where an employee is unable to perform at the desired level. Beyond this we are also concerned with their continuous learning, development and achievement. Figure 5.6 integrates these elements of managing human resources, and includes another important element – that of reward.

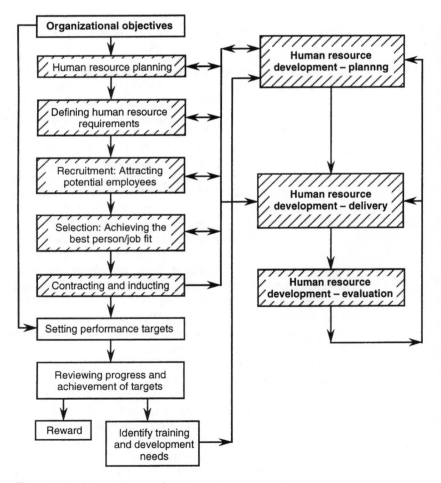

Figure 5.6 *Integrating performance management*

In a detailed study of managing people, performance and reward (in this case in the form of pay) the Audit Commission (1995b) suggests that some local authorities are hampered by traditional management structures which are inappropriate for managing in the current competitive environment. These structures can contribute to a number of problems facing such local authorities including a top-heavy management structure, poor match between staff skills and the requirements of the job, and low staff productivity. Other problems may include pay levels out of line with the market rate, or the size of any particular job and a mismanagement of pay progression. These problems can be compounded by inadequate information about the authority's paybill and the lack of an integrated system of pay management. In the view of the Audit Commission these problems, especially in the context of real cuts in resources available, can lead to higher costs, poorer service quality, reduced levels of service and dissatisfied staff. The Audit Commission offer a detailed 66-point action plan for dealing with, or avoiding, these problems and outcomes, the major elements of which are shown in Box 5.4. We deal with performance management in more detail in Chapter 10, but for the purposes of this chapter we will concentrate on the issues of appraising the performance of individual employees and relating these appraisals to reward, often in the form of performance-related pay, and training and development.

Box 5.4   Actions for improving the management of people, pay and performance – some key points.

- Develop a performance-led policy for managing people, pay and performance.
- Review the processes necessary to support this strategy.
- Define the separate responsibilities of members, chief officers, central service departments and managers.
- Senior managers to review overall performance.
- Involve front-line managers to build ownership: encourage them to review good practice in other organizations.
- Develop a tight-loose balance to maintain control.
- Develop a benchmarking policy for productivity targets and performance management.
- Develop workload indicators.
- Compare inputs and outputs.
- Develop policies for changing staff structures.
- Flatten management structures.
- Match staff and skills more closely with workload.
- Develop flexible working arrangements for individual staff.
- Review where functions may be suitable for outsourcing.
- Develop a pay policy that addresses key issues and reflects wider constraints.

- Develop information sources for tracking the pay market.
- Develop measures of workforce stability.
- Consider non-pay measures to secure workforce stability.
- Plan implementation of changes in pay to balance increased costs with savings.
- Link communication with staff regarding pay to the wider communications programme.
- Consider ways of linking pay progression with staff performance.
- Develop a performance management policy which addresses specification, communication and evaluation of objectives
- Develop performance indicators for each service area
- Develop a code of good practice for staff appraisal (to include all staff).
- Keep systems simple and eliminate duplication.
- Review the strengths and weaknesses of existing systems by using a range of measures.
- Set up periodic monitoring of progress.

Source: Adapted from Audit Commission (1995b, pp. 1.8–1.9).

Performance appraisal can be defined as measuring, evaluating and influencing an employee's job-related attributes, behaviours and outcomes to assess and enhance their contribution to the achievement of the organization's objectives. Our experience is that managers are often clear about the measurement and evaluation of employee performance through appraisal, but do not always explicitly recognize the 'influencing' role the process also plays.

Typically a developed, formal, performance appraisal system involves:

- Conducting a job analysis to identify job duties and responsibilities for which performance criteria need to be developed.
- Choosing an appropriate and valid performance appraisal method to assess job behaviours or outcomes.
- Developing a process for helping employees understand the job expectations prior to the appraisal period.
- Establishing a feedback system which reacts to job performance (i.e. by rewards, corrective action, training and development and other responses).
- Setting new performance criteria, measures and objectives for the next appraisal period.
- Evaluating how well the performance appraisal system is doing in relation to its stated objectives.

Box 5.5 gives two examples of approaches to performance appraisal linked to performance-related pay.

Box 5.5   Case example

The Valuation Office – Performance-related pay

The Valuation Office employs around 5000 people and is responsible for providing land and valuation services to government departments and other public bodies. The Valuation Office is an executive agency of the Inland Revenue and has had delegated responsibility for pay since 1994 when it agreed a new pay structure with trade unions as the basis for a performance-related pay system. The appraisal year runs from 1 April to 31 March, during which all staff are expected to meet at least quarterly with their line managers to discuss progress towards agreed targets. Performance is assessed and marked at the final meeting. To ensure a consistent approach to marking, managers from different offices meet and 'moderate' their assessments; however it is a feature of the agreement that there are no quotas for a particular performance rating and the overall pay bill is not taken into account when determining an individual's performance assessment. Based upon this performance assessment individuals can progress towards the top of their particular pay band via a number of pay steps varying from 3.5 per cent for high performers down to no increase at all for those assessed as not having achieved their performance targets.

Source: Adapted from IDS (1995b).

James Paget Hospital

James Paget Hospital is a 'third wave' trust general hospital employing over 2300 people in Great Yarmouth. New pay and grading arrangements were introduced into the hospital in 1995, replacing 112 separate grades with four broad occupational groups: clinical, diagnostic and therapy; direct patient care; services; and administration. Each of these groups has three salary scales, with the location of a particular post on the scale being determined by the knowledge, leadership, communication and problem-solving skills required in it. Pay progression, from 1997, will depends partly upon a general increase influenced by the labour market and other factors and a performance-related, or merit, element. Automatic annual increments will no longer be paid. Performance is rated in four bands with only those in the top two bands ('exceptional' and 'good') receiving a merit payment.

Source: Adapted from IRS (1995b).

If any element can be missed in practice it tends to be the last stage – the review of the whole system. It is possible for a system to be designed and implemented which, without review, loses sight of its original objectives and becomes largely irrelevant to the real needs of the organization and its employees. To avoid this managers need to have a clear picture of the purposes of performance appraisal. To be effective a performance appraisal system needs to impact on the efficiency, and effectiveness of service delivery or the achievement of other organizational objectives. The purposes of performance appraisal systems (outlined above) can be grouped into two broad categories: evaluative and developmental. The evaluative purposes include decisions on pay, promotion, demotion, layoff, and termination. The developmental purposes include feedback, management and career development, human resource planning, performance improvement and communications.

Many problems have been encountered with performance appraisal systems in practice, which have led to their review or even abandonment in some organizations. One of the major problems is encountered when a particular system is designed to achieve too many, potentially conflicting outcomes. There is evidence that performance appraisal systems are not good at achieving both evaluative and developmental outcomes at the same time. Employees are reluctant to discuss any problems they are having, which may indicate a training or development need, when they know that their rate of pay or other reward may be dependent on the outcome of the performance review. Generally speaking it is advisable to establish a performance appraisal system which tends to separate the evaluative and developmental outcomes, perhaps by dealing with them at different times in the appraisal period.

It is also suggested that performance appraisal based on the individual employee can be divisive and work against the development of strong teamwork which is increasingly crucial for organizational success. The problem can be dealt with, to an extent, by including the achievement of team goals in individual employee's targets, or operating a separate team performance appraisal.

In attempting to design a performance appraisal system which achieves its potential, and minimizes the undesired outcomes it is useful to consider the following criteria:

- Developmental. Will the system and the approach motivate employees to do well? Will it provide feedback, and aid human resource planning and career development?
- Evaluational. Does the approach make a valid contribution to decisions about promotion, discharge, layoff, pay and transfer and, therefore, allow for comparisons across employees and departments?
- Economical. How much does the system cost to develop, implement, maintain and review?

- Freedom from error. To what extent does the approach and/or system encourage halo, leniency and central tendency effects? How reliable and valid is it?
- Interpersonal. To what extent does it allow managers and employees to gather useful and valid appraisal data that can facilitate the appraisal interview?
- Practicality. How easy is the system to develop and implement? Can the cost-benefit advantages be clearly identified? Does the system have any dysfunctional, unintended, consequences?
- Integration. How well does the performance appraisal system integrate with other human resource and organization-wide systems such as financial planning and review?
- User acceptance. Do all users accept the appraisal format as being reliable, valid, and useful?

Delegation

One useful approach to developing staff, and their performance is to use carefully managed delegation. This also has the advantage of freeing up some of your time as well – as long as it *is* carefully managed, otherwise you may end up wasting time putting right problems caused by your delegation efforts (if you do it is important to note that any problems are a result of your management of the delegation, not the person whom you delegated to do something). Effective delegation is one element of a participative management style, the more that people are involved in the operation of a service, the more they will be able to accept delegated authority. Delegation without participation may be, at best, ineffective and, at worst, the 'dumping' by a manager of their responsibilities onto members of their team. In order to delegate you need to be able to assess the level of risk involved, and the competence of the person you are considering delegating to. However once you have made this assessment and decided that a member of your team is ready, willing and able to take more delegated responsibility you need to follow through your decision by supporting them, as far as is possible, in the way they exercise that delegated authority, i.e. they do not have to do it 'your way' to be effective.

Good delegation should be a positive learning experience for your staff, and for you.

Dealing with performance problems

Despite having a well-planned, implemented and integrated system of performance management and appropriate delegation, problems are obviously likely to occur from time to time. It has to be said that without an effective performance management system they are even more likely to occur. However assuming that you are managing within an effective system we will now turn our attention to managing people in difficult situations. Please note that we are choosing our words carefully here; it is not uncommon to hear a manager refer to a person with a performance-related problem as a 'problem employee'. We believe that problem people are very rare, but that people in problem situations are much more common. Dealing with a problem person is likely to be working from a position of prejudice; dealing with a person in a problem situation requires a far more reasoned, analytical response from you as a manager, together with a realization that you may be directly contributing to the problem situation! This is not to deny that during your career you may have to take people through formal disciplinary procedures, perhaps up to and including dismissal. This is obviously a very serious matter and you will want to assure yourself that you have done everything possible to respond to the problem before resorting to these actions (pragmatically it will also be likely to help you if you have to justify your actions before an internal appeal panel or an industrial tribunal).

The corollary of a formal discipline system is, of course, that employees should have the right to raise a formal grievance if they think that they are being unfairly treated or, perhaps, not being allowed to achieve the performance standards set. These rights and obligations are reflected in the EP(C)A 1978, as amended by TURERA 1993, where employers (with twenty or more employees) are under a legal obligation to provide written details of disciplinary and grievance procedures. We would argue that even in smaller organizations it is still good, and fair, managerial practice to inform employees of what might be regarded as a disciplinary matter, and what they should do if they feel aggrieved. The Advisory, Conciliation and Arbitration Service (ACAS) have produced a Code of Practice which may be regarded as the minimum standard attained by any organization in its disciplinary procedures. The main points from the ACAS code are given in Box 5.6.

Box 5.6 Essential features of the ACAS Code of Practice on Disciplinary Rules and Procedures

Disciplinary procedures should:

- be in writing
- specify to whom they apply
- provide for matters to be dealt with quickly
- indicate the disciplinary actions which may be taken
- specify the levels of management which have the authority to take the various forms of disciplinary action

- provide for individuals to be informed of the complaints against them and to be given an opportunity to state their case before decisions are reached
- give employees the right to be accompanied at disciplinary hearings
- ensure that, except in cases of gross misconduct, no employees are dismissed for a first breach of discipline
- ensure that individuals are given an explanation for any penalty imposed
- provide a right of appeal and specify the procedure to be followed.

Your organization is likely to have its own written procedures but, drawing on the ACAS Code, we would suggest the following, general, approach to dealing with performance problems.

1 Aim for prevention rather than cure. Take time to get to know your staff, in that way you may be more able to anticipate problems and take action to prevent them becoming serious issues of poor performance.

2 If performance problems arise try to deal with them firstly by using your skills as a coach and counsellor. Be aware when you may need to take advice from professional counsellors, such as your organization's employee welfare service, if it has one. As well as representing a humane approach to people in difficult situations you may also achieve a reputation for being a caring manager, with a resultant increase in morale and a direct impact on the overall performance of your team. You may also enhance your organization's reputation and increase its attractiveness in the job market.

3 If and when a disciplinary issue arises despite your best efforts, firstly establish the facts. As we suggested earlier this may also require you to confront your own prejudices. Under certain circumstances, in cases of a serious breach of discipline for example, you may need to take into account formal witness statements.

4 In the case of a serious disciplinary issue consideration should be given to suspending the person concerned from work while the matter is investigated. Any such suspension should be brief, and with pay.

5 Before a decision is made, especially one of dismissal, the employee should be interviewed and given the opportunity to state their case.

6 Following the decision the employee should be informed of their right to appeal and the appeals procedure.

As well as dismissal, which is obviously the most extreme type of disciplinary action, it is likely that your organization will also make provision for a verbal warning, a written warning and a final written warning. Gross misconduct, which you will see from the ACAS Code is the only category of disciplinary offence for which dismissal may be considered for the first, proven, incidence, is normally regarded as an offence so serious that is a fundamental breach of contract and totally unacceptable to the employer. The classification of gross misconduct will vary from employer to employer but should be clearly spelt out to the employee at their appointment. Examples of gross misconduct could include; theft, damage to equipment, assaulting another member of staff or a client, a serious breach of hygiene regulations, submission of false references. A clear distinction needs to be made between 'gross misconduct' and 'misconduct'. This distinction needs to be clearly communicated to, and understood by, all employees.

Similar procedures need to be followed for dealing with grievances, particularly an emphasis on preventing grievances arising through the practice of fair, consistent management.

Dealing with redundancy

As well as facing the possibility of dismissing someone for disciplinary reasons the processes of restructuring and reorganization in the public sector which we have considered earlier in this book, may also require you to deal with employees who are redundant. This is another complex area of employment law and practice for which your organization is likely to have its own procedures. We will only attempt to introduce you to some of the basic issues here, as a contribution to developing your underpinning knowledge and understanding.

Redundancy is defined in the EP(C)A as arising where:

- the employer ceases to carry on the business in which the employee was engaged, or closes the place where they were working
- the business ceases to require people with the particular skills of the employee or needs fewer of them to carry out the work.

The TURERA 1993 added a further provision, that the dismissal is for a reason not related to the individual concerned or for a number of reasons all of which are not so related. This was to protect workers who found themselves dismissed because of reorganization.

Remembering that employees have the right not to be unfairly dismissed, dismissal for redundancy will normally be fair as long as the following conditions are met:

- The redundancy is genuine. It is important not to fall into the trap of dismissing an employee because of incapability while claiming that the dismissal is on the grounds of redundancy, and then replacing them. This could lead to a claim for unfair dismissal.
- Redundancy has been effected in accordance with the organization's procedures.
- Elected employee representatives (not just recognized, independent trade unions) have been consulted.
- There is no suitable alternative work available.
- Redundancy selection must not contravene the Sex Discrimination or Race Relations Acts.

Summary

We have covered a lot of ground in this chapter. If there is one message in particular that we would like you to take away it would be that effective management of people involves getting to know them. If you are able to develop appropriate, professional, relationships with your staff you are much more likely to be able to assess their relative strengths and development needs. This means that you will be able effectively to delegate work to them, and help them manage their own performance and development. You are also more able to spot when a performance problem is arising and take preventative, proactive action, rather than reactive attempts to deal with the issue after it has arisen. This is not to say, however, that as a manager you will never be faced with taking difficult decisions and action such as those involved in redundancy. Even here knowing your staff well can help them, and you, deal with the pain often associated with dismissing someone.

Action points and discussion points

(Items in italics are intended to encourage the reader to develop a greater intellectual awareness, items in plain type are focused upon work-related activity.)

Implement change and improvements in organizational activities/
Respond effectively to poor performance of team members

Collect and review the following documents from your organization:

- a contract of employment
- the disciplinary procedure
- the grievance procedure
- the redundancy procedure.

To what extent do they conform to standards of good practice?

How might redundancy selection contravene the Sex Discrimination Act? (Clue – consider the case of employers who may wish to dismiss part-time employees before full-time employees at times of redundancy.)

Review internal and external operating environments

Evaluate the impact of the increased availability of electronic communications (e.g. the Internet, computer and video-conferencing) on your area of the public sector. Is it leading to the development of more flexible ways of working and a more flexible workforce? How is your role as a manager likely to change as a consequences of these developments? How can you prepare for these new ways of managing?

Establish strategies to guide the work of the organization

The Audit Commission (1995b) suggests developing a 'tight–loose balance to maintain control' of people, pay and performance. To what extent are the human resource policies and practices in your organization based on this principle?

Determine the effective use of resources

How could your organization make better use of its human resource budget? What factors are inhibiting these improvements? How could these inhibitions be overcome? What is your personal role as a manager in these processes?

Given that the public sector is experiencing significant 'environmental turbulence' what are the human resource management consequences of this? How should these consequences be managed? How are they being managed in your organization, and in others? How could this managerial response be improved?

Provide required personnel for activities/secure resources for organizational plans

Review your organization's recruitment and selection processes. Which parts work well, and why? Which require improvement, and why? How can you increase your contribution to effective recruitment and selection?

A number of organizations, especially elsewhere in Europe, are using novel selection procedures based on graphology and even astrology. Do some reading around this subject and consider why these techniques are being used. Under what circumstances do you think such approaches could be useful? What are their limitations?

Develop teams and individuals to enhance performance

The following is a list of some of the characteristics of an effective coach. How do you rate against these characteristics? How can you improve your performance as a coach? (It may also be a useful learning opportunity to ask your staff to give you their rating of your performance.)

An effective coach:

1 Is a good, active, listener.
2 Uses mistakes and errors made by staff as positive learning opportunities.
3 Takes time to help staff formally reflect on experience.
4 Actively promotes informal learning opportunities for staff
5 Involves staff in setting learning objectives.
6 Agrees clear standards with staff, and reviews their achievement.
7 Knows, and understands, the capabilities, interests and aspirations of their staff.
8 Is a good observer.
9 Adopts a non-judgemental attitude.
10 Models effective work behaviour.
11 Develops the confidence of staff, in both the coach and themselves.
12 Is committed to the learning of others, and themselves.

What factors encourage the transfer of learning from a training course away from work back to the workplace? What are the respective roles of the person being trained and their manager in ensuring an effective transfer of learning? How well do you perform these roles, both as a learner and as a manager? How could the workteam be involved in this process? Do you make good use of the team in this respect?

Determine the work of teams and individuals to achieve objectives

Collect examples of performance management systems and documentation from a range of other organizations in both the public and private sector. How do they compare? What theories of performance management appear to be underpinning the approach adopted? How do they cope (if at all) with the issue of individual versus team performance?

What techniques and approaches do you use to distribute work amongst your team members? Who assesses the extent to which they are achieving the objectives of the organization; is it you, the individuals concerned, the whole team or other people? How effective is this assessment process? To what extent is the work allocation system meeting the needs of the staff themselves? Put aside some time at your next team meeting to discuss these issues.

Delegate authority for programmes of work

You have been seconded to a government task force for three months. While you are way your post will not be covered. Therefore you need to delegate all your main duties to your staff (you are unable to 'delegate up' to your manager. Make a list of all your main duties and decide who in your team can have responsibility and authority for them while you are away. What training/preparation will they need to take on these new responsibilities? How will you ensure that they become competent to perform them? Once you have done that, what could you delegate *now*, and why don't you?

How does 'delegation' differ from the emergent concept of 'empowerment'. How empowered are you at work, and in other settings? Why does your apparent level of empowerment vary from situation to situation? To what extent do you think that people can really be empowered at work, and if they were, what would happen to the power of their managers? Based on your analysis, to what extent are you a 'delegator' or an 'empowerer'?

Further reading

Burchill, F., and Casey, A. (1996). *Human Resource Management. The NHS: a case study.* Macmillan.
An introductory text to HRM in the context of the NHS, but with relevance to other areas of the public sector as well.
Income Data Services (1995). Performance and Objectives. *IDS Focus*, **75**, July.
Reviews the implementation of performance-related pay and delegated decision-making across the public sector. Raises questions about the long-term future of performance pay in the public sector.
Local Government Management Board (1993). *People and Performance – the LGMB Guide to Performance Management.* LGMB.
Offers practical guidance to developing, implementing and reviewing approaches to making the best use of people.
Local Government Management Board (1994). *Performance Management and PRP – Local Government Practice.* LGMB.
Contains examples of good practice in performance management and performance-related pay.
Stewart, A. M. (1994). *Empowering People.* Pitman Publishing.
An interesting introduction to this topical subject, which takes a look at leading people beyond 'delegation'.
Thomson, R., and Mabey, C. (1994). *Developing Human Resources.* Oxford: Butterworth-Heinemann.
A broad review of strategic human resource management, recommended for managers seeking a general introduction to competent people management.
Wilkinson, A., Marchington, M., Redman, T., and Snape, E. (1996). *Total Quality Management: Organisational Change and Human Resource Management.* Macmillan.
A critical review of TQM, linking it to issues of HRM, culture and the changing role of managers.
Wright, P., and Rudolph, J. J. (1994). HRM Trends in the 1990s: Should Local Government Buy In? *International Journal of Public Sector Management*, **7**(3), 27–43.
Considers the changing HRM 'paradigm', the emergence of strategic HRM and relates it to changes in the public sector generally, and local government in particular.

6 Managing finance

Aims and learning objectives

The aims of this chapter are to introduce you to finance in the public sector. You should acquire an overview of how the public expenditure process operates both in terms of the central and local aspects. You should also develop an general understanding of the differences in how the finance process operates in different parts of the public sector.

This chapter does not make any assumptions that you are trained in financial management. Indeed our experience is that many managers in the public sector are profoundly nervous when they confront finance issues. Therefore in successive parts of the chapter we will introduce the concepts and practices relating to:

- Budgeting
- Costing
- Financial analysis
- Pricing in the public sector.

At the end of this chapter, and after associated activities and reading, you will be able to:

- understand the basics of the public finance process including audit
- appreciate the differences between various budgetary systems
- construct, monitor and control a budget
- apportion costs
- engage in simple financial project analysis
- appreciate the concept of value for money in monetary terms
- understand the basics of pricing.

Theoretical underpinnings

The nature of public sector finance

The Government tries to plan expenditure and the income to finance that expenditure well in advance. The government plans affect all parts of the public sector and indeed other sectors as well. Business looks carefully at what the Government intends to raise via taxation and the voluntary sector is concerned with the plans the Government has for expenditure in terms of grants. The whole process can be

Table 6.1 Public expenditure planning cycle

Date	Activity
November	Autumn Statement (expenditure plans for next three years)
January–March	Assessment of outcome of previous plans
March	Budget for current year
April–June	Government Departments prepare bids
July	Cabinet decides overall expenditure totals
September–November	Negotiations between Departments and the Treasury
	Disputes adjudicated by a 'star chamber' (a Cabinet Committee of senior ministers)
	Budget and expenditure plans for forthcoming year are published
January	Finance Bill published
February	Departmental Reports and budget statistical supplement to budget published
March	Detailed Estimates presented to Parliament

Source: Coombs and Jenkins (1994).

seen in terms of an ongoing cycle. This is illustrated by Table 6.1. This table sets out the chronological sequence of events. We would note that this process can change over time and the table should be regarded as indicating the current activities in the expenditure planning process rather than a precise prediction of what future activities will take place. It is important to grasp the principle of public sector planning which this process illustrates.

The nature of this cycle has implications for all who depend upon central government resources for a substantial part of their income. Though it is possible to plan on a contingency basis without the information from central government it is the published plans which give organizations and agencies a better understanding of what the Government's intentions are. Obviously these have sometimes been signalled in advance through legislation and government pronouncements.

Central government expenditure

In this section we will introduce you to the make-up of central government expenditure. You will be able to engage in some financial analysis both comparing expenditure between different categories and over time.

In government figures the term 'control total' was adopted from 1992. This replaced the previous 'planning total'.

The 'planning total' included:

- central government's own spending
- local government spending supported by central government
- the financial requirements of the nationalized industries and public corporations
- proceeds from privatization.

It excluded:

- local authority financed expenditure
- interest on central government debt.

The 'new control total' sought to deal with variation in the economic cycle particularly where social security payments were concerned. It therefore excluded cyclical social security payments such as unemployment benefit and income support to non-pensioners. It included expenditure by local authorities. This was a recognition that local government spending was now significantly determined by central government.

The summary of this can be seen in Table 6.2. The spending plans which the Government have made are laid out. You will notice that the Government plans to increase expenditure over the years 1994/95–1996/97 both in terms of central expenditure and in terms of local authority expenditure. However the amount in percentage terms is quite limited.

The bottom row looks at General Government Expenditure (GGE) as a percentage of Gross Domestic Product (GDP). Gross Domestic Product is defined as the value of the total output of the UK. Here you will notice that the proportion is projected to fall from 45 per cent to 42.5 per cent over the period 1993/94–1997/98. From this the astute reader will deduce that the Government expects the Gross Domestic Product to rise significantly faster than government expenditure rises over this period. These figure, we should note, are in *money terms* (i.e. the actual amounts of money budgeted).

It is also useful to look at the detail of where the Government is planning to spend its money. This is broken down by Department in Table 6.3. You will notice that some Departments are projected to spend proportionately more than others. In fact some Departments are projected to spend *less*. In particular Departments such as Defence, Trade and Industry, and Transport are, in Whitehall terms, clear losers in the projected spending plans up to 1997.

The Departments that are getting proportionately more are Education, Health, Social Security, and European Communities. Whilst the latter is probably outside the Government's control to determine it is

Table 6.2 UK general government expenditure

	Out-turn 1992–93 (£ billion)	Estimated out-turn 1993–94 (£ billion)	Projections 1994–95 (£ billion)	Projections 1995–96 (£ billion)	Projections 1997–98 (£ billion)	Percentage change 1994/95–1996/97 (%)
Central government expenditure	158.2	169.9	172.8	179.9	184.4	6.71
Local authority expenditure	69.4	70.2	71.8	73.8	75.6	5.29
Financing of nationalized industries	4.8	4.7	3.2	2.4	1.9	–40.62
Reserve			3.5	7.0	10.5	200.00
New control total	232.4	244.8	251.3	263.1	272.4	8.40
Cyclical Social Security	13.3	14.5	15.0	15.5	16.0	6.67
Central government debt interest	17.4	19.4	22.5	24.5	25.5	13.33
Accounting adjustments	6.0	7.9	9.0	10.0	11.0	22.22
Privatization proceeds	–8.2	–5.4	–5.5	–1.0	–1.0	–81.82
General government expenditure	260.9	281.2	292.3	312.1	323.9	10.81
General government expenditure as a percentage of Gross Domestic Product	44.75%	45.00%	43.75%	43.50%	42.50%	

Source: HMSO (1994).

Table 6.3 UK Government expenditure totals by selected Departments

	Out-turn 1992–93 (£ billion)	Estimated out-turn 1993–94 (£ billion)	1994–95 (£ billion)	Projections 1995–96 (£ billion)	1997–98 (£ billion)	Percentage change 1994/95–1996/97 (%)	Proportion of total 1992/93 (%)	Proportion of total 1997/98 (%)
Defence	23.6	23.4	23.5	22.7	22.8	–3	10	8
Employment	3.5	3.6	3.8	3.7	3.7	–3	2	1
Transport	6.6	6.2	5.9	5.6	5.4	–8	3	2
Trade & Industry	3.0	3.7	2.3	1.8	1.4	–39	1	1
Housing (Dept of Environment)	8.2	7.7	7.4	7.6	7.6	3	4	3
Local Authorities (Dept of Environment)	31.0	29.3	29.9	30.9	32.5	9	13	12
Home Office	5.8	6.0	6.3	6.4	6.4	2	2	2
Education	7.1	9.9	10.5	11.0	11.4	9	3	4
Health (& OPCS)	28.3	30.1	31.7	32.9	33.3	5	12	12
Social Security	61.7	67.6	68.8	72.9	76.2	11	27	28
Scotland	12.7	13.7	14.1	14.5	14.8	5	5	5
Wales	6.0	6.3	6.6	6.9	7.0	6	3	3
N. Ireland	6.6	7.1	7.4	7.7	7.9	7	3	3
Local authority (self financed)	10.2	10.5	11.0	11.1	11.2	2	4	4
European Communities	1.9	1.8	1.4	2.9	2.9	107	1	1
Total (including other departments)	232.3	244.5	251.3	263.0	272.3			

Source: HMSO (1994).

interesting to think about why the other Departments have been so favoured. Behind such spending plans lies not only the nature of the policy process in the public sector but also the political aspects of the Whitehall machine.

Clearly plans are subject to variation as a result of circumstances. One factor that was unlikely to have been taken into account when these plans were drawn up was any outcome of the peace process in Northern Ireland. There is little doubt that if this process took a positive direction then the assumptions which lie behind the spending plans for Northern Ireland will need to be revised. This may very well lead to money becoming available for other purposes than that for which it was intended.

You may have noted the use of the phrase 'money terms' a few paragraphs previously. It is important to understand the difference between 'money' and 'real' figures in budgets. It is linked to a very simple concept. If you were told that your pension was going to be 50 per cent of your *current* salary you might be concerned to know what it might actually buy when you retire – say in ten years. The value of £15 000 per year in 1996 is likely to be much less in 2006. The reason for this is inflation.

Therefore the Government also presents its spending plans in 'real terms' by allowing a factor for inflation. The apparently significant increases in Education, Social Security, and Health become much more modest in terms of the *actual projected spending power*. The only increase which still seems very significant in both money and *real* terms is that for the Economic Communities.

The local authority financial process

How the Government decides

The Government discusses financial issues with local government via the 'Consultative Council for Local Government Finance'. This consists of government ministers and secretaries of state of relevant departments and councillors representing the various local government bodies. These local government bodies include the Association of County Councils, Association of Metropolitan Authorities, Association of District Councils, London Boroughs Association and the Association of London Authorities.

The discussions include the level of local government spending, the distribution and level of government grants and policy relating to local government finance. If the two sides fail to agree central government may impose their proposals on local government. As in any consultation process of this size the consultative council has a number of offshoots in the form of working groups where much of the detailed work takes place.

The working groups will report on expenditure forecasts which may differ from the Standard Spending Assessments – the Government's own forecast of what local authorities would spend in order to furnish a standard level of service.

The current timetable for the consultative process is given in Table 6.4.

Table 6.4 Timetable for the consultative process

Period	Action
February/May 1995	Working groups look at expenditure pressures on local government for the subsequent years (1996/97)
February/March 1996	Secretary of State issues timetable, rules and work programme for the working groups
July 1996	Consultative Council considers working groups' reports on local government spending
September/October 1996	Consultative Council considers working group report on Standard Spending Assessments and Revenue Support Grant distribution options
December 1996	Secretary of State issues consultation paper on Revenue Support Grant proposals (after Chancellor of Exchequer's Budget Statement)
December 1996/January 1997	Revenue Support Grant consultation
January/February 1997	Revenue Support Grant settlement

Henley, Likerman, Perrin, Evans, Lapsey and Whiteoak (1992) identify a number of reasons why central government might want to furnish a grant to assist local government services:

- There is an issue of geographic equality. The aim is to enable the same level of service to be provided at the same level of council tax.
- It promotes accountability in that central government makes requirements of local authorities to meet certain identified needs. The finance of these is seen as appropriately met from central rather than local taxes.
- To promote a more progressive tax system because local taxes tend to bear down proportionally harder on those with lower incomes.
- Local taxation (such as the council tax/community charge) is highly visible. Central Government might decide to subsidize some of the costs of local government in order to reduce the size of the local tax.

What makes up local authority expenditure

The overall level of anticipated local authority expenditure in the UK is published by the Treasury each year.

The Government also analyses expenditure by type and here we must describe the difference between current and capital expenditure. This difference is also broadly applicable to other areas of the public and voluntary sector (the National Health Service and voluntary organizations). Current expenditure is defined by the Chartered Institute of Public Finance and Accountancy (CIPFA; 1994, p. 27) as:

> day to day spending needed to keep services running, but which does not create tangible assets. It includes, for example, the pay of local authority employees such as teachers, social workers, accountant and lawyers; stationery and materials used in schools; food for school meals; and the heating bills for children's homes ; and the fuel for the council's vehicles.

Capital expenditure creates a tangible asset or prolongs the useful life of an asset. An asset is something which the local authority owns. CIPFA (1994, p. 166) defines capital expenditure as:

> spending on the acquisition of assets . . . The nature of the expenditure may be acquisition of land or buildings, construction of buildings, improvement or 'enhancement' of assets. Assets include land, buildings, roads, plant or machinery. Expenditure which does not fall within the definition must be charged to a revenue account.

Allocation of expenditure

Local government expenditure is allocated according to function. Education is by far the largest component. This can help explain why there was so much concern over the funding of teachers' pay rises in early March 1995. The majority of Education expenditure is made up of teachers' salaries. Therefore a relatively small increase over budget on teachers' pay has a disproportionate effect on the budget.

Over the past ten years the proportion of local authority spending allocated to various functions has changed. Social security has consumed a higher proportion (going from just over 2 per cent to about 12 per cent) whilst Housing has gone down from over 6 per cent to under 3 per cent). Likely future changes include a higher proportion to Social Security as a result of community care.

It is also significant to note that the proportion of current to capital expenditure is not the same across various local authority functions. The vast majority of spending on Education and Social Security is current whilst a higher proportion of Housing expenditure is capital – this would not simply mean new houses but also improvement of properties already owned by the local authority.

The National Health Service financial process

There are similarities between aspects of funding for the NHS and for central and local government. The NHS funding is included in the annual Public Expenditure Survey. Also funding is divided into revenue and capital with the much the same distinction as we have described above.

Funding for the NHS can be divided into a number of categories.

- Hospital and Community Health Services. This encompasses funding via the Regional and District Health Authorities for both hospital-based and community services.
- Family Health Services (formerly called Family Practitioner Services). This relates to funding for General Practitioner (GP) services.
- Central Health and Miscellaneous Services. This covers a number of services which are provided centrally.
- NHS Trusts. This is an item which has grown as the number of NHS Trusts has increased.

Currently the Department of Health channels funds via the Regional Health Authorities (RHA). However this is likely to change as the current NHS reorganization leads to the reduction and disappearance of the RHAs.

The funding illustrates the 'purchaser–provider split' or internal market which currently operates within the NHS. The District Health Authorities and GP fund holders are viewed as 'purchasers' of health care on behalf of the patients (customers) for which they are responsible. The 'providers' might be either directly managed units of the District Health Authorities or NHS hospitals which have acquired 'trust' status.

Income is received by the Department of Health via capital charges from the directly managed units or dividends and interest from the NHS Trusts.

The allocation of funds to regions has, unlike the local government situation, undergone a number of major changes over time. Prior to 1970 allocations were largely based upon what had gone before. This is an illustration of 'incremental budgeting' which you may wish to recall when you look at budgeting further on.

For the period 1971–76 funds were allocated on a formula based upon population with certain adjustments.

In 1975 the Resource Allocation Working Party was set up with the intention of ensuring a more equitable distribution of NHS resources. This led to a formula being introduced in 1977 which led to a reduction in disparities between the worst and best regions from 26 per cent in 1977/78 to 11 per cent in 1988/99 (HfM/CIPFA, 1993, p. 6).

This reallocation formula (widely known in the NHS simply as

RAWP) came in for considerable criticism particularly since it involved redistributing resources from London hospitals which had long traditions (and strong interest groups lobbying on their behalf).

From 1990 there was another major change in funding allocation based upon a 'resident population'. The resident population for the region is adjusted by weighting it by age since certain age groups (the very old) place larger demands upon healthcare resources. There is also an awareness of social deprivation factors which can also adjust the formula. Finally there are adjustments which take account of the extra staff costs associated with the London or Thames areas and market forces.

Joint finance

This was brought in from 1976 to encourage health authorities and local authorities to develop initiatives particularly in the areas of mental illness, mental handicap and the elderly (over the age of seventy-five). Central government funding was allocated via the health side on the basis of a reducing 'taper' by which the proportion of the cost moved to the local provider (health authority, local authority or voluntary organization).

Joint finance was widely used particularly to promote community care. One of the authors chaired a Joint Care Planning Team in Mental Health and can attest to the focus that the prospect of joint finance gave to collaborative work between the local authority, health authority and voluntary organizations involved.

The Police Service

The Police and Magistrates Courts Act 1994 has significant implications for financial management. The Audit Commission in a major report (1994a, p. 8) notes:

> From April 1995 all provincial police authorities will be free standing, precepting bodies with their own standard spending assessment (SSA) and capping level. Police specific grants will in future be paid as a cash limited sum, not as a proportion of expenditure; the balance of funding will come from revenue support grant, national non-domestic rate and a precept on billing authorities for the proportion of the budget met by council tax.

The implications for these police authorities are that they will have to live within their budgets as the Metropolitan forces have had to do since 1986.

The introduction of cash limits and needs assessment is likely to have a very significant impact upon the police forces and the Audit Commission lays out in considerable detail the changes which it recommends should take place. It envisages that some police authorities will start off with financial difficulties; in some cases there will be an inheritance of high spending which will be hard to address.

In the figures the Audit Commission gathered, however, it indicated that most shire police forces spend below the Standard Spending Assessment (SSA). However the adverse report of the Inspector of Constabulary about at least one major shire force indicates that they might encounter problems.

The voluntary sector

Charities vary considerably in their sources of finance. Some would argue that with contracting out of services to the voluntary sector some charities are in effect largely funded directly by the Government. This is a concern to many in the voluntary sector as it is seen as representing a threat to their independence.

However charities will usually draw their finance from one or more of the following sources.

Voluntary income

This is acquired by a range of fundraising methods. Sometimes a charity can predict with some accuracy how much might be raised from the amount raised the previous year. Charities like Red Cross which operate a number of shops would be able to predict better than, for example, Band Aid. Legacies are a strong source of income for certain charities – particularly those relating to animals! However special appeals such as 'Poppy Day' are harder to predict (and adjust) than year-round appeals.

Statutory grants

These may be awarded in respect of particular projects or for certain purposes. Local authorities grant-aid a number of charities. However the grants are usually time limited and are vulnerable to external pressure upon the resources of the funding agency which may cause a loss of funding regardless of the strength of the case put up by the voluntary body.

Service agreements

This particularly relates to the area referred to previously where government (via health or local authority purchasers) contract with a voluntary organization to provide a service. Meals on Wheels for the housebound is a long-standing example. The funding may be on the basis of a block grant or a per capita (i.e. per person served) fee. These also are usually for a specified time and will usually be only renewed after a competitive tendering process.

Fee income

Some voluntary organizations are able to gain income from membership or usage fees. Though fees are often regarded as being associated with professional, sports and social organizations they are also charged to service users of, for example, Relate. Given a stable membership/clientèle a voluntary organization should be able to predict such fee income with some accuracy.

Income from investments

A number of voluntary organizations have considerable investment income. Indeed this is sometimes a source of some contention between 'investment rich' and 'investment poor' charities whereby the latter might claim that the former are not using their resources in accordance with their avowed aims.

The National Lottery

The apparent success of the National Lottery has, in our view, created a new category of funding for the charities and voluntary sector. At the time of writing it is unclear what effect this might have. Some claim that it will affect the funding activities of certain organizations. The success of the South Bank in getting National Lottery money has been criticized as the 'poor lottery ticket buyers' funding the 'rich concert goers'.

Budgeting

Principles of budgeting

Budgeting takes place for a number of reasons. Managers often feel unnecessarily threatened by a process which, if undertaken properly, helps them carry out their job effectively.

Tom Peters, a well-known management guru, once commented that his nightmare was to see his own gravestone with these words inscribed on it: 'Here lies Tom Peters, he always made budget'. Perhaps this implies that budgeting is not always regarded as demonstrating creativity or inspiration.

With this in mind we propose to introduce the concept in a very easy-to-follow fashion. For the moment forget about the notion of the organization. Rather consider budgeting on a personal level. Let's assume you have a regular income and you are seeking to work out whether you can afford a major expenditure – on an exotic summer holiday for example. How do you go about it?

Well one way would simply be to see how much money there is in your bank account. Let us assume that there is virtually nothing left in it. Is that the end of the story? Not if you apply some budgeting principles.

One step would be to see what your pattern of expenditure is over the year. Perhaps this month is February and you've just paid off the Christmas credit card bills. Quite possibly there may be more money left over in later months and you may have enough for the holiday by the summer.

Another step would be to look at what you currently spend your money on. Perhaps you eat out (expensively!) two or three times a week. If you reduced your spending on that (the budgetary term is 'control') then over about four–five months you might well have saved enough for that holiday. Furthermore in making such a saving you would be motivated by the reward of the holiday at the end of it.

For some people personal budgeting is an absorbing pastime which is a source of considerable pleasure. Other people spend with reckless abandon and worry afterwards about the consequences. We are not saying that managers in the public sector have to subscribe to the former (though some do). However if, as a manager, the latter model is how you behave then enjoy your career while it lasts – because it won't last long.

The principles of budgeting and budget preparation can be laid out as follows:

- It sets out the necessary income level that your part of the organization will need over the next year.
- It enables you to plan the level of expenditure.
- The budget itself (once agreed) is the authority to spend the money.
- The budget enables you to control the expenditure over the year.
- The budget also enables you to monitor expenditure – perhaps by budget holders who report to you.
- The budget, as a public document, communicates information to managers, staff and organizational stakeholders.
- To the extent that the budget is agreed, as opposed to being imposed, it is a motivational device.

Different types of budgeting process

Coombs and Jenkins (1994) offer a useful account of four different models of the budgetary process. They suggest that there is a continuum with 'incremental/departmental budgeting' at one end and 'rational–corporate budgeting' at the other.

There is a long established literature based in policymaking and decision science which has described incrementalism. Incremental budgeting in its essence is simplicity itself. You start with the current budget as a 'base' for preparing next year's budget. You then add on the amount appropriate for inflation and other factors such as new requirements. You then submit this as the projected budget for the next year.

Coombs and Jenkins offer two variants of 'incremental/departmental budgeting. The first they describe as the 'bid' system and set out the following stages in its operation.

1 Separate estimate preparation (the incremental budget setting described above).
2 Add up the various estimates and compare with the amount available.
3 Change (usually reduce!) the estimates to conform with available resources.
4 The departments make changes to the detail of their estimates.

The second system which Coombs and Jenkins describe is financial planning. Here the key factor is the period of time. The bid system is geared to annual budgets whereas financial planning operates over a longer time frame of several years. The figures in Tables 6.2 and 6.3 from the Government Public Expenditure plans are an example of this. A second key difference is that expenditure guidelines are given to each department. This may be a target or a limit and means that there is less likelihood of departments being forced to reconsider after submitting estimates. Thirdly capital and revenue estimates are looked at together. Thus the impact of capital proposals upon revenue budgets can be addressed.

Finally the formula for calculation is made more specific. Whilst the bid system simply takes an increment to base expenditure the typical budget formula reported by Coombs and Jenkins is:

Base expenditure (last year's budget)
+
Inflation (usually an amount set centrally)
−
Reductions (items not required/reduced)
+
Committed growth (effect of capital schemes from last year)
+
New growth (proposals/decision to expand services)

At the other end of the continuum offered by Coombs and Jenkins is Planning Programming Budgeting Systems, widely known as PPBS. This is not now generally used in the UK but is worthy of some discussion because it enjoyed a short period of popularity first in the USA then in the UK. It is not inconceivable that it may make inroads here again.

The aim of PPBS is to identify activities associated with the particular objectives and subobjectives of a programme. The activities may well cross department boundaries. Output measures are critical to measuring the success of activities in addressing the programme objectives.

Take as an example the prevention of reoffending by convicted people. We could compare the three alternative 'activities' of imprisonment, community service or probation. The usual 'output measure' used is reconviction rates (i.e. the proportion of offenders reconvicted of an offence within a particular period of time). The activities cross boundaries in that prisoners are usually in contact with probation after release and 'community service' is usually associated with some degree of supervision. Furthermore the more sophisticated reader could well argue the merits of regarding Housing and Supported Employment Schemes (which would possibly involve other agencies) as critical. PPBS would assess the cost and benefit of the various alternatives for resource allocation in order to achieve the reduction in reoffending.

Coombs and Jenkins offer several reasons for the lack of success of PPBS:

- Technical problems, particularly the way in which activities cross departmental boundaries make, for example, costs difficult to allocate.
- Accounting systems are set up on a department rather than a programme basis.
- The problem of reliable, valid and timely output measures (when and how, for example, would you measure the success of an adoption?).

We would add a further and in our view critical reason for the failure of PPBS. That is the political nature of the budget process. The failure of high rates of imprisonment to reduce reoffending has been known for a long time both in the UK and the USA. Yet on both sides of the Atlantic politicians are well aware that 'being seen to be tough on crime' is often crucial in elections. Indeed it has been argued that Michael Dukakis may have lost his chance at the Presidency on this issue. Budgets are political statements and politics is not necessarily a rational but rather an emotional process. Any public sector manager forgets this at her or his peril.

Costing

The nature of cost

Costs are the elements of the budget which are used up in the course of the operation of the organization. Mellett, Marriott and Harries (1993, p. 98) note that:

Resources are acquired and consumed as part of the process of undertaking a function or activity, or producing an output, to achieve a goal or aim. Costs measure the loss of monetary value of this acquisition/consumption.

Mellett et al. divide costs into three general categories. Though their comments are applied to the Health Service context they can equally well apply to other aspects of the public or voluntary sector.

- Costs can be seen as inputs. These are the resources which are acquired or used in order to deliver the service. Typically this might be the cost of a member of staff, furniture or rent of a building.
- The output might be costed. Here the cost is measured by reference to a unit of output delivered by the organization. In the public sector outputs are measured in a variety of ways depending upon the service. Thus transport might be measured in terms of cost per passenger mile. A Health Visitor Service output might be the cost of a family visit.
- The cost might be measured by considering the relevant manager or function in the organization. Therefore the cost of the personnel department might be measured. This is often used in order to make comparisons such as whether it is cheaper to 'contract out' a particular function. It is also used to monitor or control the actual responsible manager.

Cost behaviour – fixed, variable and 'sunk' costs

Two key elements in cost behaviour are time and activity. Management and cost accountants regard costs that do not change over a particular period (called the relevant period) as fixed. Therefore if you purchase a vehicle for the use of your organization then the actual cost of the vehicle is fixed. However the amount of use you make of the vehicle will affect how much fuel it uses. Hence the fuel is a variable cost which depends on the amount of use (or activity) associated with the vehicle.

In the long term all costs are variable with the exception of something called 'sunk costs'. Therefore, to continue using the example of a vehicle, eventually it will need replacement and at that point can be described as a variable cost because the organization might decide not to replace it.

A 'sunk cost' is a cost which cannot be retrieved. Therefore, using our vehicle example, if you decide to purchase a second-hand one then you might decide to have it checked out by the AA or RAC. If you then decide not to buy the vehicle then the cost of the AA or RAC check is a 'sunk cost' because you cannot get it back. 'Sunk costs' are quite important in the private sector because it is important to identify them to prevent them being taken into account in investment calculations. In the public sector 'sunk costs' are often investigated from the perspective of waste. Organizations such as the Audit Commission, the National Audit Office and the Public Accounts Committee of the House of Commons report on examples of wasted money which to a large extent represent 'sunk costs' because the money cannot be retrieved. However these investigations and reports are valuable because they can prevent the same mistakes being made again.

Variable costs change as the level of activity or service provided increases or decreases. If a local authority adds another ten meals on wheels to a round then it will have a number of variable cost implications. These might include:

- the actual cost of the meals themselves
- the additional cost for the vehicle in terms of petrol and other running expenses
- the staff and administrative costs *if* these were increased by the additional ten meals.

However variable costs often proceed in 'steps' as opposed to a straight line. Figure 6.1 illustrates the both the straight line and step progression of costs with increased activity. If we reconsider our vehicle example then fuel would be a 'straight line' relationship with activity. The more miles you drive the more fuel is used and the fuel consumption per litre is the same throughout. However if you consider the servicing and maintenance costs then you find a 'step progression' since vehicles are usually serviced at particular mileage intervals. Therefore the costs of driving the vehicle an additional 100 miles when it is close to a major service would involve the cost of the service.

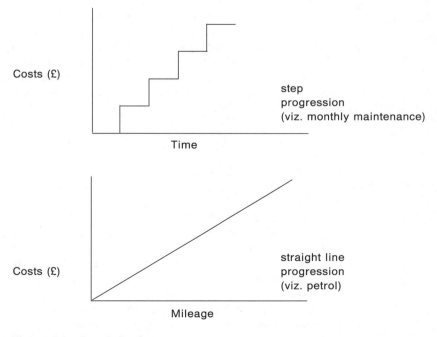

Figure 6.1 *Cost behaviour*

Some costs are 'semi-variable' where there is a fixed cost element and a usage element. A good example of this is a mobile telephone. The fixed cost element of the decision to purchase and use a mobile telephone is the cost of the telephone, the connection charge and the line rental contract. All these are incurred before you have made a single call. The variable cost is the costs related to how much you use the telephone. Most of this would be actual call charges. However a detailed statement of costs might also consider the electricity costs from keeping the batteries charged – and the replacement of the batteries themselves.

As public sector managers have become responsible for their own budgets so it is vital for such managers to understand the different types of cost. Also managers need to appreciate how costs behave in order to control and monitor them.

Apportionment of costs

Sometimes a cost is shared between several budget holders. In the private sector the apportionment of costs is a regular exercise. One of the authors was associated with the retail industry and was very aware of the care large shops take to carefully assess and allocate the costs of sales space. In the public sector such costs have been met centrally. With the growth of business units and cost centres cost apportionment has become crucial.

Cost apportionment is also described as 'allocation of overheads'. The principle is a simple one which most people practise in their everyday lives. If you have ever shared a house or flat with others then you will have almost certainly had to divide up bills between you. If the various bedrooms are of different sizes or desirability you may have had to devise a more sophisticated method than simply dividing the rent by the number of people. On the other hand something like the water rates would usually simply be divided by the number of people because there is not an easy way to divide it up by 'usage'.

Box 6.1 Case example of cost apportionment

The shared facility

Let's consider a situation where Social Services, a Community Health Centre and a voluntary organization share a building. They decide to divide up the building maintenance costs between them. One way to do this is to 'apportion' the costs according to the proportion of the building that each organization has.

Let us assume that the building has a total floor area of 400 square metres and that the annual maintenance cost is £5800. The apportionment of costs by floor area might look like this:

Social Services has 120 square metres
   120/400 is 0.3 (or 30 per cent)
   30% of £5800 is £1740

The Health Centre has 230 square metres
   230/400 is 0.575 (or 57.5 per cent)
   57.5 per cent of £5800 is £3335

The voluntary organization has 50 square metres
   50/400 is 0.125 (or 12.5 per cent)
   12.5 per cent of 5800 is £725

This approach is called 'absorption costing'. The various organizations absorb the overhead costs using an agreed formula based in this instance upon floor area.

The value of such a formula is its simplicity. However it may not be appropriate in all circumstances. Sometimes it is more important to look at the amount of 'activity' associated with the cost. If we look again at our shared building and assume that the three organizations (as part of customer service) decide jointly to provide subsidized coffee/tea to visitors. Though it is possible that the proportion of visitors to each organization will be the same as the proportion of floor space it is much more likely that this will not be the case.

Let us assume that the cost of the subsidized coffee/tea for the building is £150 and that the receptionist records that 1000 visitors took advantage of this. The cost per visitor is 150/1000 or £0.15 per visitor. The cost of the service can now be allocated according to the level of usage. The resulting figures might look like this:

	No. of visitors	*Cost per visitor*	*Allocated cost*
Social Services	200	0.15	£30
Health Centre	500	0.15	£75
Voluntary organization	300	0.15	£45
Total	1000	0.15	£150

Costing in the National Health Service

Costs in the National Health Service are apportioned in several different ways. This is important in that it affects pricing decisions in the Health Service because for the NHS the Department of Health guidance is that 'prices should be based on costs'. HfM/CIPFA (1993, p. 26) notes that:

In most cases, for contracts, the costs on which prices are based are unit speciality costs. Overhead costs, including capital charges, are added to these average speciality costs; and any other revenue . . . taken away to derive the appropriate 'quantum' of costs.

Control of costs and budget – an example

You might wish to try out your own knowledge on the example in Box 6.2. Obviously there are a wide range of budgets in the public sector but try to see if your analysis of this budget is similar to ours.

Box 6.2   Case example of budgeting and cost control

North-West Office budgetary monitoring report

We will illustrate cost monitoring and control by means of a fairly simple example. The following table is a budget monitoring report typical of what a cost centre manager in the public sector might receive. It states what the expected spend would be against the budget (here we have assumed it is halfway through the financial year) and indicated the actual spend. Subtracting the expected from actual spend gives any variance or difference from the expected spend. A negative figure means that the budget is spending more than the expected spend.

If we just consider the summary total then it seems that the budget is in fact within limits. There is an underspend of some

Month 6	Budget to date	Projected spend to date	Actual spend to date	Variance
Salaries	145 000	72 500	71 775	725
Agency	25 000	12 500	12 750	−250
Overtime	5 000	2 500	3 750	−1250
Rent	25 000	17 500	10 000	−2500
Electricity	5 000	2 500	1 750	750
Gas	7 500	3 750	3 187.5	562.5
Telephone	2 500	1 250	1 000	250
Postage	5 000	2 500	2 500	0
Travel	5 000	2 500	1 250	1250
Subsistence	5 000	2 500	3 250	−750
Training	20 000	10 000	8 000	2 000
Overall	250 000	125 000	119 212.5	787.5

£787. However it is important to not simply look at the total but to consider each figure. In particular to consider the implications of each figure. The four key factors to consider are:

- Is the budget item likely to be accurate?
- What type of cost is it: fixed, variable or semi-variable and is it a stepped cost?
- What are the likely future implications of any variance and how might the manager control these?
- What interrelationships are there between budget items?

Salaries: This item is indicating an underspend. The question which the manager must ask is whether there is a staff vacancy which accounts for this. If not then was the original budget in error. As a stepped budget salaries will change by significant amounts as staff are employed or leave.

Agency staff: This item is showing a variance which unless corrected would lead to an overspend. Possibly the agency spend is due to covering a staff vacancy.

Overtime: This item is clearly spending well over projections. The manager would need to consider carefully why this is happening. Was the original budget item unrealistic or is there a control issue emerging now? Overtime is a budget item which managers are expected to control carefully.

Rent: This item is showing an overspend. A number of factors might account for it such as rent being paid up front. Again the manager would need to assess whether this is the case. It is a large item and hence could have a significant impact on the overall budget out-turn.

Electricity: Though an underspend is shown here the manager would be aware that it is a semi-variable item with quarterly bills. Possibly the next quarter's bill just missed the budget report. Also there is an obvious seasonal factor here and the summer will be cheaper than the winter.

Gas: Similar comments to the electricity bill especially if the building has gas central heating.

Telephone: Telephone bills are also received quarterly and the apparent underspend does not necessarily mean that the item is on budget.

Postage: This is an item which is usually up to date unless there is a franking machine contract.

Travel: This item is significantly underspent. Depending upon the culture of the organization staff may be late in claiming travel. Car mileage sometimes comes in well after it has been incurred. It may also indicate a staff or work issue such as low morale or staff reluctance to undertake necessary travel associated with the workplace.

Subsistence: Here there is a significant overspend which the manager should investigate. The high spend on subsistence sits a little awkwardly with the underspend on travel. The manager should assess why these two items are varying so differently. Quite possibly there is a valid reason such as an appropriate change in work patterns.

Training: The underspend here should be checked. Training budgets are there for a reason. Again there may be invoicing delays which explain the apparent underspend. The overspend of overtime may be a factor in that if staff are having to work overtime then they may be unable (or unwilling) to take up training opportunities.

Financial analysis and audit

The tools of financial analysis

Managers in the public sector have to understand financial techniques which have previously been usually the preserve of the private sector. The private sector has developed a number of techniques to assess and decide between various alternative projects. Detailed discussion and comparison of all such techniques is beyond the remit of this book and we advise the interested reader to look at the Bibliography at the end of the book. But we will consider elements of some of the more common tools of financial analysis. We will consider Cost Benefit Analysis and Sensitivity Analysis in Chapter 7.

Rob Dixon (1994) offers some general words of caution in the application of financial analysis. He stresses the implication of the assumptions made by managers. Firstly he observes that not all the outcomes of an investment decision can be assessed in profit and loss terms. Here he is speaking primarily in terms of the private sector but his words are clearly applicable to the public sector. The range of stakeholders and issues of accountability make for a range of non-financial considerations.

Secondly he notes that frequently there is incomplete knowledge about the various available options and the outcomes arising from a decision. Therefore assumptions are made which may often prove, with hindsight, to have been wrong. Thirdly he suggests that the 'decision maker may lack the mental capacity, or may be unaware of the decision-making techniques, needed to evaluate, rank and compare the various options open to [her/him]'.

In the private sector an assumption is sometimes made that if a particular project is profitable then the market will provide the finance to enable the project to take place. So money is available if the returns are attractive enough. The money may come through company funds, the stock market (if the company needs to raise more money), banks or venture capitalists. There are a number of techniques used to indicate which projects are the most attractive in financial terms.

In the public sector the source of funds has traditionally been from government borrowing or taxation. But increasingly the government has encouraged public sector managers to use private sector techniques to appraise projects. These techniques were laid out by the Treasury in technical guidance to government departments (HM Treasury, 1990).

Discounted Cash Flow is one such technique which has been widely adopted in the public sector. The principle underlying it is very simple. It affects individuals in many everyday decisions about borrowing, spending and investing. The assumption which underpins it is that future costs or benefits should be presented from the perspective of what they are worth now.

The way this is illustrated is typically by example. If you were offered a choice of £100 today or £100 (guaranteed) in a year's time then you would naturally prefer the £100 now. However suppose the choice was between the £100 now or £110 (guaranteed) in one year. Then you might very well prefer to accept the money later.

The point of discounting cash flows is firstly to enable comparison between different options which have income and outgoings at different times. Secondly it enables income and outgoings to be compared against a 'cut-off' rate. In the private sector that is usually the expected rate of return for the particular organization or kind of project. In the public sector in the UK the government has also set expected rates of return for organizations based either on a return on the assets used or on a cost of capital.

These are not difficult principles to understand. The expected rate of return can be illustrated by the different interest rates you might expect for savings accounts depending upon the length of notice needed to withdraw your money. Cost of capital is demonstrated by a mortgage for house purchase. The rate of interest which you pay for your mortgage represents the cost of the capital.

The government has an impact upon the assumptions managers in the public sector can make over both the rate of return and cost of capital. The Local Authority Direct Labour Organizations were required to earn a rate of return of 5 per cent on the cost of capital employed under the Local Government Planning and Land Act (1980). HM Treasury sets a general discount rate of 6 per cent for central government departments (representing the cost of capital) in its *Technical Notes* published in 1991.

Capital project appraisal

Box 6.3   Case example

The sheltered workshop

In order to demonstrate the application of discounted cash flows we will take as an example an investment decision by a sheltered workshop for people with learning disabilities. The workshop is considering making printed T-shirts and for this purpose will need a machine to print the T-shirts. The workshop manager is considering the implications of the purchase. This is set out in the following table.

	Year 0	Year 1	Year 2	Year 3	Year 4
New machine	−1000				
Scrap value of machine					200
Maintenance contract		−100	−100	−100	
Electricity		−100	−100	−100	
Materials		−200	−200	−200	
Sales of T-shirts	700	700	700		
Total	−1000	300	300	300	200
Discount rate (6%)	1.0	0.943	0.89	0.84	0.792
Discounted total (total × discount rate)	−1000	282.9	267	252	158.4

The manager discovers that the new machine will cost £1000, is told it will last for three years and at the end of that time will be worth £200. The manager's estimated costs of running the machine are set out for the three years together with the anticipated income from producing T-shirts. The more astute reader might question the assumptions which underpin these figures and it is worth stating them.

Assumptions being made by the manager and possible questions we might ask:

1 The machine will last three years.
   What is the basis for this assumption? Does it depend upon how much the machine is used? If it is information provided by the manufacturer then can it be checked with previous purchasers of the machine?
2 The machine will be worth £200 after three years.
   Similar questions as for assumption 1, plus can it be verified by reference to trade publications, auction houses etc.?
3 The maintenance contract will cover all the maintenance costs.

What exclusion clauses might there be in the maintenance contract?

4 The machine will use the amount of electricity predicted.
  What evidence is there of this and how was the figure calculated?

5 The material costs will be as predicted.
  What is the basis for the material costs?

6 The sales of T-shirts will be as predicted.
  Has there been any market research or other evidence to suggest sales will be at this level?

7 There are no other relevant costs or income.
  What about the labour costs – will the machine involve any costs in addition to costs which would be incurred anyway? Is there any income obtainable from charging out the machine to voluntary organizations?

As you will note the actual cash flows when totalled up over the four years suggest that the project will show an overall surplus of £100. However if a discount rate of 6 per cent is applied then this surplus disappears and the discounted value of the project becomes negative (–£40). The reason this happens is because the project involves cash out initially followed by cash back later on.

Recently commentators on the voluntary sector have noted that charities need to consider carefully the implications of bidding for contracts. A local authority may contract with a voluntary organization for a particular service but pay *after* the charity has started (or even finished) delivering the contract. Thus the charity has to incur costs which may involve borrowing from the bank or using income which would otherwise have been getting interest for them. Using a technique such as discounted cash flow enables the charity to calculate the cost implications (and adjust its contract bid accordingly).

Value for money

Jonathan Bate (1993) observes that in the past ten years the phrase 'value for money' has become almost indelibly associated with public sector management and audit issues. He offers several popular reasons for why this has become the case. However in his opinion the underlying force is the challenge which Western democracies confront in trying to maintain or increase the achievement of public services whilst confronting a standstill or real reduction in expenditure.

Coombs and Jenkins (1994) describe value for money as achieving the three 'E's of Economy, Efficiency and Effectiveness. They go on to define these as follows:

- Economy is the practice of sound housekeeping which extols the virtue of thrift. As such it is cost focused.
- Efficiency is ensuring that the maximum useful output is achieved from the resources which are deployed.
- Effectiveness is measured in the extent the output of a particular activity fulfils the intended outcome.

The three 'E's can pull it different directions and a manager who focuses upon one of them can easily neglect the others. This can be illustrated by a story told to one of the authors about a contract for army boots. The focus was upon obtaining boots for the least cost. The contractor supplied the boots cheaply – but they were all the same size thus reducing their effectiveness. Osborne and Gaebler (1992) in their work identified many examples where the focus on achieving one of the 'E's inevitably led to absurd situations. Military aircraft could be rated as maximally efficient if they were never flown.

We must also distinguish between outputs and outcomes. Using the example of a residential or nursing home for elderly people the occupation level of the home is an output measure. But the local authority or health purchaser may seek an outcome which is not simply the highest possible occupancy level. With the focus upon care in the community this may be that residents are assisted to return to live in their own home, wherever possible. In order to achieve this outcome the output of the home (in terms of maximum level of occupancy or minimum cost per resident) may be adversely affected.

Audit in the public sector

There are two main public bodies responsible for auditing the public sector.

The National Audit Office was set up by the National Audit Act of 1983. It represented a review of the functions of the Comptroller and Auditor General who had been previously influenced by the Treasury in how he undertook his work.

The National Audit Office conducts audits of central government departments and various ad hoc bodies. The Comptroller and Auditor General is independent of the government of the day in that his (or her) appointment is made in consultation with the chairperson of the Public Accounts Committee of the House of Commons. This individual is by tradition an Opposition MP. Once appointed the Comptroller can only be removed by a vote of both the House of Commons and the House of Lords. The Comptroller is able to have considerable discretion over work objectives and staffing of the National Audit Office. However he/she has no power to disallow expenditure or give legal rulings.

The National Audit Office has also undertaken value for money studies in the Health Service but has no power to gain access to local authority accounts (where the Audit Commission has responsibility).

Nevertheless the National Audit Office has had a significant impact in identifying waste and mismanagement. The ill-fated Property Services Agency was demonstrated to have wasted money through poor planning. A report on the training of civil servants revealed that such training did not appear to be guided by any significant strategic planning. The discretion available in deciding where to direct investigations within central departments together with the direct reporting role to a major parliamentary committee furnish a significant weight.

As more of the central government functions move into Next Steps Agencies more significance will be attached to the drive for the three 'E's.

Local authorities, the Health Service and bodies such as the police and the fire service come under the auditing regime of the Audit Commission. There is a significant difference between the role of the Audit Commission in respect of the Health Service and local authorities.

Where the Health Service is concerned the Audit Commission reports any unlawful expenditure to the Secretary of State. However under the Local Government Act 1988 the auditor has powers to apply for judicial review of possible unlawful actions or to issue a prohibition order. These powers are not illusory as recent events have shown when the Auditor, Mr Magill, queried the actions of the City of Westminster and sought surcharges of a number of councillors. As we write the matter is yet to be finally resolved. But the weight of publicity attached to the Auditor's report and recommendations bears testimony to the effect that the Audit Commission has upon senior managers (and politicians).

The Audit Commission has also become adept at publicizing its work. National print and television media report regularly on its work. Discussions between the authors and senior staff of the Audit Commission suggest that the actual conduct of audits has a tendency to be rather limited and follows a constrained pro forma. The *Local Government Chronicle* regularly offers accounts from senior managers in local government which are also critical of the limited nature of the Audit Commission's interests.

Pricing issues

What is pricing?

Mellett, Marriott and Harries (1993) discuss pricing for the internal market in the NHS. Their analysis of price is particularly useful since it has a strong public sector focus. Public sector managers increasingly need to be aware of price issues but also need to be cautious about simply applying private sector models of price. The multiple stakeholders involved and the political dimension means that charging what the market would bear is not always acceptable. An obvious example might be suggestions that adopters seeking to adopt children from abroad should be charged a market price for home circumstance reports. Clearly if this was simply left to market forces then a high price could be obtained but only relatively wealthy individuals would come forward.

Mellett et al. (1993) offer the following definition of a price:

A price is the monetary value asked or paid for a specified activity or service.

They note that in the commercial world the price is not necessarily determined by the cost. Rather profit (or loss) is represented by the difference between price and cost.

Price and costs

In the NHS internal market pricing involves following Department of Health guidance. Mellett et al. (1993, p. 159) describe three principles which must be observed:

1 The price charged generally should equal the actual or anticipated revenue cost.
2 Costs should include depreciation, calculated on a straight line,
   current cost basis and an interest charge of 6 per cent on capital
   assets employed.
3 There should be no planned cross-subsidization of cost between
   contracts or purchasers.

This appears simple so long as the full cost of the service can be worked out. This would involve calculating both the fixed, variable and semi-variable costs. Depreciation on a straight line basis means spreading the cost of any assets used evenly across the whole life of the assets. The 6 per cent interest charge does not mean simply adding 6 per cent to the total costs. Rather it means establishing the value of the assets used to provide the service and then adding 6 per cent of the value of these assets.

Although it is not allowed by the principles there is a considerable potential for manipulation of the costing calculation. The provider may understate costs in order to get contracts and keep out the competition. Alternatively if the provider believes that there is a potential to get a premium price then costs might be exaggerated or potential usage (volume) underestimated.

Two approaches to pricing based upon costs

Bottom-up pricing

Here a service is costed for a particular delivery episode (e.g. the cost of providing one hip replacement) on the basis of the lowest practical cost. It is obviously quite time consuming and involves a considerable degree of 'time and motion' type of measurement. If undertaken properly it should give a high level of accuracy.

Mellett et al. (1993) comment that this is generally impractical in the NHS context because it needs accurate definition of treatments, measurements of how much of different resources the treatment consumes and then the conversion of all of this into costs. However it can be applied to low volume high cost contracts.

Top-down pricing

Here the all the costs in the budget are identified. They are then apportioned out to enable a calculation of the cost per treatment or service delivery. Obviously the cost will depend upon the number of treatment or service episodes which the budget is intended to cover. The more that fixed costs figure in the budget then the more that increasing the volume will reduce costs per treatment or service episode.

We can illustrate this by looking at the cost of providing a District Nursing Service shown in Table 6.5. (The example is simplified for demonstration purposes.)

Table 6.5 The District Nursing Service

	Year 1	Year 2	Year 3
Annual fixed costs:			
Office accommodation	£12 000		
Salaries	£26 000		
Vehicles	£3 000		
Total fixed costs (A)	£41 000		
Level of activity:			
Visits per week (B)	100	125	150
Annual variable costs:			
Materials	£2 500	£3 125	£3 750
Vehicle mileage	£1 000	£1 250	£1 500
Overtime	£0	£0	£100
Total variable costs (C)	£3 500	£4 375	£5 350
Total annual cost (A + C)	£44 500	£45 375	£46 350
Annual cost per visit/week ([A + C]/B)	£445	£363	£309

The fixed costs represent a large part of the budget. As the activity level is increased the fixed costs are spread out more thus reducing the cost per visit per week significantly. Therefore if charging is introduced which is priced at a level to cover the full cost of the service then the total level of activity is a consideration.

Summary

Understanding finance in the public sector involves, for the middle level and senior manager, more than simply keeping to budget and controlling costs. It also means being aware of the political process involved in planning and agreeing expenditure.

There are significant differences as well as similarities between different parts of the public and voluntary sector. The process of planning sends signals and, like the weather, it is possible to read these signals and anticipate the likely future turn of events. A skilled manager, especially at a more senior level, will know how and when to influence the budgetary process in an appropriate and effective fashion.

Skills in monitoring spending must be matched also with the willingness to control it. The reality of the public sector is frequently one of continual constraints upon financial resources. The concepts of efficiency, effectiveness and economy are closely associated with the overarching issue of demonstrating value for money.

The manager also has to be aware of pricing issues. In some cases – we give the example of the NHS – the price is closely linked to the recovery of cost. In other situations the question may be merely the need to identify a contribution towards a cost. Occasionally there may be a question of obtaining the maximum return possible – here we are coming close to the private sector market model.

Action points and discussion points

(Items in italics are intended to encourage the reader to develop a greater intellectual awareness, items in plain type are focused upon work-related activity.)

Determine the effective use of resources

Compare the way in which your organization decides how to spend money with that of another organization. Assess why there are similarities and differences. If there are differences then consider whether the practice of the other organization is more or less effective in resource allocation.

If you are responsible for making expenditure proposals or drawing up budgets then obtain feedback from the manager responsible for approving them upon the clarity, content and layout of your proposal or budget. In particular try and identify ways in which your proposals can be improved *even* if there is not any current problem over failing to gain resources.

Go through any budget for which you have responsibility and ensure that you fully understand the following:

- what the budget is for
- what the actual expenditure is against target
- what the projected out-turn will be
- how items on the budget impact upon each other
- what the historic pattern of expenditure of individual item is

Secure resources for organizational plans

Compare how your organization and its nearest rivals are resourced. How effective is your organization in securing resources and what useful lessons can be drawn from other similar organizations? How dependent is your organization upon one funding source?

Identify how you might be able to access alternative resources (financial, staff or other) in the event that your current resource became unavailable or was reduced.

Provide information to support decision making

Look at the information provided by your local authority about the way it spends its money (most provide this with the Council Tax bill). Using this information assess the extent to which your local authority spending coincides with the priorities which it has laid out in the literature it sends you.

Obtain (if you don't have it) a current and past budget for your organization. Then review the extent to which the decisions you and your colleagues have made over priorities are reflected in the changes in the budget. Where the changes in the budget and your priorities are out of step then analyse how you might have improved your financial case to obtain (or reduce!) the budget.

Further reading

Chartered Institute of Public Finance and Accountancy (1993). *Introductory Guide to NHS Finance in the UK. CIPFA.*
This is the companion produced by CIPFA for the NHS though in this case it is more focused upon the needs of finance managers than politicians. However it is concise and easy to follow. It is also regularly updated.

Chartered Institute of Public Finance and Accountancy (1994). *Councillors' Guide to Local Government Finance. CIPFA.*
This is, as its title suggests, a book aimed at councillors in local government. It is invaluable as a guide to senior managers in this area as well. It has the benefit of being drawn up under the guidance of the relevant accounting body, and is regularly updated.

Coombs, H., and Jenkins, D. (1994). *Public Sector Financial Management*. Chapman & Hall.
This is a well-established text which provides a solid grounding on public sector finance.
Henley, D., Likierman, A., Perrin, J., Evans, M., Lapsey, I., and Whiteoak, J. (1992). *Public Sector Expenditure and Financial Control* (4th edn.). Chapman & Hall.
A book which is authored by experts with a focus upon central government financial procedures and practice.
Manley, K. (1994). *Financial Management for Charities and Voluntary Organisations*. ICSA.
This is part of a new series on the charitable sector published by the Institute of Company Secretaries and Administrators (ICSA). It is easy to follow for managers conversant with basic principles without expecting the reader to be a specialist in finance.

7 Managing operations and activities

Aims and learning objectives

This chapter is focused on operations and information management. The manager in the public sector is usually service orientated. The following chapter (Chapter 8) is focused upon customer issues. Here we will look at aspects of bringing about change and improvement and how change (actual or proposed) can be evaluated. Increasingly the public manager is expected to be an agent of change rather than a guardian of the 'status quo'.

Information is vital to managers and it is not just the acquisition of information but the way in which you, as a manager, use and interpret it which counts. We will introduce you to elements of forecasting using data.

Finally we look at communication and we have chosen to focus upon the context of the meeting. In our experience as managers the ability to function effectively within meetings (whether as chair or participant) is vital in the public sector.

At the end of this chapter, and after associated activities and reading, you will be able to:

- assess the delivery of public services including aspects of quality assurance
- manage change in services, products and systems with particular reference to the use of several techniques of change management
- acquire, organize and assess managerial information and in particular use Cost Benefit Analysis and Sensitivity Analysis in public management settings
- effectively inform stakeholders
- achieve positive outcomes in meetings to resolve public sector management issues

Managing change and improvement

Identify opportunities

The public sector differs in a significant way from much of the private sector. In a private sector company such as 3M the culture of innovation is well established. Staff know that the company expects – indeed requires – that new products must be developed. The fact that the current products are profitable is not allowed to detract from innovation.

In the public sector a culture of innovation and new service development is constrained by the presence of:

- political constraints
- legislation which mandates certain activities (and by implication that which isn't legally required is often seen as low priority)
- multiple stakeholders
- a 'blame' (or risk) avoidance culture.

None the less managers and staff in public sector organizations have demonstrated an ability to be innovative. Recent concerns about developing 'learning organizations' (Pedlar, Burgoyne and Boydell, 1991) have fed through into the public sector. Geoff Mead and Sue Goss (1995, p. 19), writing in the *Local Government Chronicle*, comment on the implications in the the growth of the contract culture and the breakdown of unitary models of local government. They conclude that:

> As contract relationships proliferate, there is an urgent need to share experience and to explore ways in which local authorities can manage effectively through contract relationships to continue to achieve their goals. The rules and relationships around contracting are not 'fixed', and there is considerable scope to build on the innovations and good practice in many local authorities.

Examples of innovation are to be found in the public sector but all too frequently they are reactive rather than proactive. Willcocks and Harrow (1992, p. 52) note that:

> Innovation from within the public services, and particularly that based on professionally developed practices, may exist and be sought but gives the innovator a far lower managerial profile.

They go on to identify five attributes of innovation which impact upon the likelihood of the innovation being adopted (drawing on work by Rogers and Kim in 1985).

1 Relative advantage over preceding practices.
2 Degree of compatibility with potential adopters' needs and values.
3 Low complexity.
4 Potential to run on a trial basis.
5 Visibility of results to others.

Though the presence of these attributes arguably facilitate innovation, Willcocks and Harrow note that other factors might override. In particular Compulsory Competitive Tendering has taken place by legal requirement without the benefit of being run on a trial basis.

However the fraught experience of the Child Support Agency has been attributed in part to the failure to pilot the proposed changes. Indeed the Child Support Act arguably does not meet any of Rogers and Kim's attributes of successful innovation!

Edmunds and Bowler (1995) identified potential for innovation between primary health care teams in health services and leisure services in local government. They suggest that promoting physical activity represented an area of common interest for these two potential partners. Though some health care teams managed their own fitness projects, Edmunds and Bowler identified an increasing partnership with leisure centres whereby doctors and primary health care staff referred potential users to leisure centre programmes.

Using cost benefit analysis in evaluating advantages and disadvantages of proposed changes

Previously in the chapter looking at finance (Chapter 6) we examined the use of discounted cash flow techniques to assess projects. However in the public domain the goals of usually not simply measurable in monetary profit or loss. There are frequently quite complex issues associated with the introduction of change in the public sector.

One technique which is useful here is Cost Benefit Analysis. Cost benefit analysis endeavours to weigh up not just the tangible cost and benefits of a particular change or innovation but also attaches a value to the intangible costs or benefits.

Coombs and Jenkins (1994) offer a continuum of decisions in the public sector. At one end decisions are based upon purely political considerations and objectives. At the other end are everyday practical decisions over such matters as whether to lease or purchase equipment. These latter decisions can be based upon the cash flow techniques described in Chapter 6. But in between is where cost benefit analysis has a particular value.

Cost benefit analysis has been outlined by Dixon (1994) as follows:

Social benefit or private benefit + external effects

−

Social cost or private cost + external effects

=

Net social benefit

The evaluation will take account of costs or benefits which affect people who are not directly involved in the change or decision. The example often offered by authors is that of road-building decisions. However the recent public protests against road building (the proposals of which had gone through cost benefit studies) suggests a more suitable example should be offered in a text of this nature. We provide two, in Boxes 7.1 and 7.2.

Box 7.1   Case example

English Nature

In a Radio 4 series *Costing the Earth* Mark Whittaker looked at the application of Cost Benefit Analysis by English Nature to Pevensey Levels. This was an area which had been drained for agricultural purposes and as a result had lost much of its wild-life habitat. English Nature spent £130 000 to encourage local farmers to restore the wetland habitat.

   English Nature commissioned studies to look at the benefits accruing to local residents from the marsh improvements. Researchers initially asked local people to try to put a financial value to them personally on the benefits. This aroused considerable concerns amongst residents about nature becoming a 'commodity'. Nature could not be simply valued in monetary terms. Researchers then set up a series of focus groups to enable residents to contribute to the discussion over the importance of the environment.

Source: Radio 4, *Costing the Earth* (10 May 1995).

Box 7.2   Case example

Bolton Council

Bolton Council conducted a Cost Benefit Analysis to decide whether a company should be licensed to operate an incinerator. The analysis was based upon the company operating 'best available techniques' for disposal of waste products. Friends of the Earth challenged the way cost benefit analysis was being applied, claiming that the study should be broadened tq include examining all available ways of disposing of the waste products rather than simply the way the company in question intended to operate.

Source: Radio 4, *Costing the Earth* (10 May 1995).

Dixon (1994) outlines the following stages in conducting a Cost Benefit Analysis.

1 Deciding which costs or benefits to include

It is important to avoid double counting where one benefit or cost is the cause of another. Thus if a fire prevention scheme can lead to a reduction of firefighter staffing but the fire service decides to use the time for extra staff training then the analysis cannot count both as a benefit. Also some effects are relatively insignificant so need not be included, for example the fire prevention scheme may have an effect of reducing the environmental pollution associated with house fires.

2 Measuring and evaluating the costs and benefits

Tangible costs and benefits are easier to assess. Thus using the fire prevention scheme as an example the costs of time of fire service staff and provision of fire alarms is tangible. However if the scheme is assessed as likely to save X number of people from burns or smoke-related injuries how do you assess the value of this? Often the answer involves using a shadow price such as the notional cost of treating X number of burns and the cost of lost income for those afflicted.

3 Timings and flows of the costs and benefits.

As the previous chapter has shown, a higher value is attached to costs or benefits that occur sooner than to those that occur later. In order to adjust the value of differently timed costs and benefits a discount rate is used.

Negotiating and agreeing introduction of change

The public sector, because of the political dimensions, is vulnerable to the charge of introducing largely cosmetic change as electoral window dressing. In local government in particular most experienced managers will have many recollections of changes which were introduced just before an election in order to give the political party in power something to trumpet as an achievement. It was truly a wonder to see how 'beautifying' municipal parks and gardens and rubbish collection received political support as election dates drew near.

Managers who work in the public domain must accept political caprice as part of their territory. Good managers see it as representing an opportunity. One of the authors, in his role as a senior manager, adopted the tactic of having a range of 'politically desirable' projects of changes costing varying amounts of money 'on file' and ready to go. The key factors which guided the selection of such projects were:

- They must be visible and preferably photogenic.
- They did not involve long-term resource implications – especially in terms of staffing.
- They had the potential to make good press.

An example of such a project was adding a parents' room to a children's day nursery.

In the public sector the political dimension is often crucial. Without active political support (or at the bare minimum the absence of major political opposition) change will be an uphill struggle.

One of the most comprehensive studies of change in the UK public service sector was that undertaken of the National Health Service by Andrew Pettigrew and his colleagues (Pettigrew, Ferlie and McKee, 1992).

Pettigrew and his colleagues looked at making change in the NHS. He previously had looked at other large organizations in the private sector (such as ICI) as well as the NHS.

The work they engaged in was empirical – that means that they went out and interviewed people and gathered data from a wide range of documentary sources. The breadth of the research (eight regions) and the duration (1987–90), together with the fact that it was supported at a very high level in the NHS, makes it particularly significant.

The timing of the project was also significant coming as it did after the Griffiths Report and the introduction of a management ethos into the NHS.

The focus of the research strategy was case study based and particularly sought to examine whether the 'top down' management approach to change was effective.

The research found that the pattern and pace of change differed between authorities. Pettigrew et al. argued that there were differences in the receptivity to change dependent upon context. They identified eight factors which were derived from the research they conducted.

Quality and coherence of policy

Here they found that simply taking central policy and implementing it locally was not always enough. A vision was important even if that vision was imprecise. An absence of such a vision could promote inertia. Policy also had to be broken down into actionable 'chunks' and they commented on the tendency of short termism to push aside long-term issues.

Availability of key people to lead

This means the ability to gain continuity and a degree of stability. The research did not support rotation of managers to maintain change. The loss of key people was associated with a draining of energy and could even put the change process further back than its original start point.

Long-term environmental pressure

Environmental pressure can also drain energy and impede the change process. Financial crisis produced a range of reactions such as delay and denial. It was often seen as a threat rather than an opportunity. However in some cases management were able to use the crisis to accelerate the rationalization process.

Supportive organizational culture

They found a great deal of effort was required to change culture. This was attempted in a range of ways. One was to set up a 'management cadre' as opposed to simply general managers. The NHS was not seen as one culture but rather as a set of sub-cultures. Factors associated with a change culture at district level included:

- flexible working across boundaries (skill rather than rank focus)
- an open risk-taking approach
- openness to research and evaluation
- a strong value base
- a strong positive self image.

Effective managerial clinical relations

These were easier where negative stereotypes had broken down. It was important for managers to understand what clinicians (doctors) valued. Also clinicians with managerial perspectives played an important role and considerable advantage could be gained from alliances. They found that relationships were slow to build up but quick to sour.

Co-operative interorganizational networks

There were a number of agencies (i.e. Departments of Social Services and voluntary bodies) where the NHS District Health Authority had only power to influence and not to control. The impact of individuals who 'spanned boundaries' was critical. Effective networks were those which were informal and purposive. However they were also fragile and vulnerable to staff changes.

Simplicity and clarity of goals and priorities

Managers varied greatly in their ability to narrow and focus the agenda down to a limited number of priorities and to protect these from short-term pressures. The risk was constant escalation of priorities until they became individually meaningless. Persistence and patience in pursuing a limited number of priorities over a long period bore fruit.

The fit between District Health Authority change agenda and its locale

The sort of factors which had a bearing on this were:

- degree to which Health Authorities shared Social Services Department boundaries
- one large population centre
- teaching hospital
- strength and nature of local culture
- nature of local NHS staff.

Pettigrew et al.'s findings had five significant implications:

Turning problems and panics into sustainable action

The NHS tends to be 'panic driven' yet few of these panic situations are life threatening. The challenge is to separate the urgent from the important. If all things are crucial few get done.

The origin of this 'panic culture' may be political or possibly from the importance attached to 'symbolic decision making' rather than action. The authors suggested a focus upon simplicity of goals and priorities as a way forward together with greater skill in environmental assessment.

Managing incoherence

The NHS is enormous and segmented in many ways:

- political–managerial
- professional–managerial
- professional–professional
- regional, district and local
- geography
- care group.

Segmentation such as this is linked to inertia, and factors such as structural complexity and poor communication linkages create challenges to management of change.

Incentives and politics

These are critical in mobilizing energy for change. Labelling what you call change is often important–'closure' becomes 'redevelopment' and 'crisis' becomes 'opportunity'.

Combining top-down pressure and bottom-up concerns

There is a debate as to how much of the Thatcherite era has survived her. Is public management in the NHS context more 'action orientated'? Has a new culture of public management emerged?

Top-down pressures were apparent at District Health Authority level. Often pressures were interlocking with 'Care in the Community' local issues adding to central pressures.

Dualities and dilemmas in managing change

- issues of micro and macro aspects of implementation (the authors stressed the need in creating central policy to leave room for local manoeuvre)
- raising and sustaining energy to generate momentum
- conceptualizing change as an opportunity rather than as a threat
- maintaining continuity whilst also promoting change
- building commitment from hierarchies and networks.

Implementing and evaluating changes

The public sector often takes pride in its expertise in the actual planning of change. First Division Civil Servants and top managers, especially in the Health Service, are very familiar with planning exercises. The implementation of the changes envisaged by plans and the subsequent evaluation of the change activity is, however, less well established as a public sector skill. In part this is linked to the political nature of the public arena. Politicians react to events and their senior managers know that when media attention moves away from the issue then the political will to carry through promised change can easily evaporate.

However a key skill for a public manager is to possess the skills to carry through necessary and desirable changes. In a key work Rosabeth Moss Kanter (1983) talked of the power skills associated with carrying through change in the face of resistance and apathy.

As organizations become flatter then spans of control become larger. The control mechanisms familiar to bureaucracy (see Chapter 2) have less impact in flatter, leaner and more organic organizations which are increasingly typical of the public sector.

Therefore the effective change manager has to be able to make use of a range of sources of power other than simple position power. Charles Handy (1993) has identified a large number of sources of power which can be mobilized by a manager seeking to bring about change. Effective implementation of change will usually involve using more than one source of power or influence. Sources of power include:

- Position power which is derived from the level you occupy in the hierarchy.
- Expert power based upon actual knowledge (such as a doctor might exercise).
- Referent power which involves using a connection to a person possessing another power base (such as a personal assistant in respect of their boss).

- Resource power derived from being able to facilitate access to material, human or financial resources.
- Charismatic or personal power such as possessed by great leaders. This is seen as less applicable in public sector organizations such as local government or the health service. However its importance should not be underestimated. The appointment of relatively young chief executives and senior managers suggests that the role of charisma may be increasing.

In the public sector in order to secure change it is often essential to make use of a wide range of power or influence bases. This is because of diversity of stakeholders, the political dimension and the frequent lack of clarity over outcomes or conflicting targets. A private sector manager can use the lever of enhancing company profit to drive through change (and can subsequently be judged upon her/his effectiveness by reference to company profits).

Resistance to change is not a purely public sector phenomenon. Much has been written about it and a manager seeking to effect change must understand the factors which lie behind such resistance.

David Buchanan and David Boddy (1992) comment in detail upon this and cite the work of M. Lynne Markus who sees four broad areas of resistance:

- People. Individuals in the organization might resist change for a number of reasons associated with their own experience, personality, attitudes etc.
- System. The actual system or technology involved in carrying out the work may be ill able to accommodate change.
- Organization. The culture of the organization may be impervious to change
- Politics. The way power is distributed in the organization may mean that change is hard to bring about.

One way to try to overcome resistance is to ensure that the proposal for change is presented in a positive fashion. Rosabeth Moss Kanter (1983) suggests the following:

- Pilotable. If a proposal for change can be tried out on a smaller scale then this helps to overcome opposition.
- Reversible. If the proposed change can be changed back to how things were before the change then people are more willing to agree to it.
- Divisible. A proposal which can be divided into separate parts then a problem affecting one aspect would not jeopardize the whole proposal.
- Concrete. The more tangible the proposal is then the more people can get a feel for it. Intangible or abstract proposals are more easily deflected or put off.

- Familiar. The proposal should be expressed in a way which people can understand and appreciate. The vision should be within the grasp of the recipients.
- Congruent. If possible the change should fit with the policies and practice of the organization.
- Sexy. A project which generates favourable publicity either inside or outside the organization is more likely to find favour.

Box 7.3   Case example

The challenge of Lambeth

Heather Rabbatts, Chief Executive of the London Borough of Lambeth, took on what was advertised as the worst management job in local government. Changing the culture of this local authority had challenged previous chief executives. In particular the consistent negative press coverage had been a problem. Ms Rabbatts identified the area of housing as particularly crucial. She instituted competence tests for housing staff which led to a number of staff failing on grounds of literacy and losing their jobs. She commented that, whilst she did not regard it as the fault of the staff themselves that they were not able to do the job, the needs of tenants to receive a proper service must be addressed. Lighting on housing estates was also identified as a problem. Rather than going through layers of hierarchy to address this she visited the estates herself and directly empowered staff to resolve the problems.

When the government announced that all schools in Lambeth were to be inspected Ms Rabbatts responded by issuing a public statement that the local authority would welcome such inspections. Some headteachers felt that this statement was not helpful and Ms Rabbatts pointed out that it had stopped the government proposal becoming a media issue. However she also indicated that any problems identified in Lambeth schools would have to be addressed.

Source: Various print and media reports.

Quality assurance

A rich jargon has grown up around the issue of 'quality'. The impact in the public sector has been considerable. One journal (*The International Journal of Health Care Quality Assurance*) is devoted to quality issues. Perhaps significantly its previous title suggested that it had a management focus. The replacement of the word 'management' with 'quality assurance' does not imply that it no longer is aimed at managers but rather that quality issues have become central to health service managers.

A recent book focused upon applying quality management in the UK public sector; Morgan and Murgatroyd (1994) notes problems associated with introducing Total Quality Management (TQM) into the public sector in the UK.

Firstly TQM is manufacturing based and thus orientated towards physical products rather than services. Secondly it is marketing driven whereas much of the public sector services is delivered to people who are not necessarily in a position of exercising a full consumer choice. Finally concepts such as 'right first time, every time' are less applicable to services in the public sector such as community care.

Morgan and Murgatroyd then proceed to identify a number of reasons why the public sector in the UK is resistant to TQM concepts. They list such factors as:

- general resistance to change
- lack of a performance focus
- professional work cultures
- status hierarchies
- the diversity of customers and stakeholders
- conflicting goals.

Perhaps significantly when one of the authors presented these factors to a diverse group of public sector managers the overwhelming response was the view that they represented a perception of the public sector that was already out of date. Quality, in the view of the group of managers, was a highly visible issue which they were expected to address. To adapt a cliche from *The Hitchhikers' Guide to the Galaxy* their view was the 'resistance to quality is useless'.

The link between quality and the contracting culture has been discussed by Trevor Colling (1995). He notes that whereas contracting was introduced with the intention of reducing costs it is now seen by many as fostering customer responsiveness and service improvement. The concept in local government of 'the enabling authority' suggests the withdrawal from direct service provision. Yet the Government White Paper extending CCT to professional services was entitled *'Competing for Quality'* (Colling, 1995).

Colling (1995, p. 40) concludes after assessing the local government situation that:

> contrary to the proponents of competitive contracting, however, the long term relationship between service quality and competition may prove to be an inverse one.

However in the same issue of *Local Government Policy Making* Adrienne Curry and Claire Monaghan (1995) identify the importance of BS5750 for local authorities. They comment that:

The dynamic environment in which local authorities now operate, demands not only continuous improvement which is based upon a position of strength and commitment, but a skilled motivated workforce and organizational coherence. A quality system based upon BS5750/ISO9000 provides the infrastructure upon which the strategies relating to human resources and a total quality culture can be built.

The impact of TQM in the National Health Service has been quite significant despite the pace of structural reorganization. Richard Joss (1994. p. 4), reporting on a major study by Brunel University, noted that:

After three years of observation and analysis we now feel reasonably confident that the factors we originally identified do indeed predict more TQM movement. We should stress, however, that successful implementation of TQM is not *necessarily* correlated with high quality of services.

Monitoring, maintaining and improving service and product delivery

The supply of resources

Recently one of the authors received a request from a Danish health manager who wished to visit the UK and learn about aspects of the NHS. He contacted an NHS manager to arrange an appointment. The NHS manager remarked that she hoped there wouldn't be a repeat of a previous overseas visit when the visitors had asked about purchasing. She had launched into a long account of the NHS internal market and the 'purchaser–provider' split. The visitors listened with furrowed brows. After a while they interrupted the manager to clarify that what they wished to know was how the hospital resourced bandages and cleaning materials.

The significance of this story is that terminology changes and ten years previously there would have been much less likelihood of such a misunderstanding.

The move towards compulsory competitive tendering has set up situations within both local government and the Health Service where managers 'enter into contracts' to either purchase or supply resources. Martin Willis (1995) comments (in Stewart and Stoker, 1995, p. 135), in respect of community care, that:

The Government's argument is that a purchaser/provider split is necessary to ensure that there is a functional distinction between the assessment of a user's needs and the provision of services to meet those needs.

Deakin and Gaster (1995, p. 21) observe that:

> The ultimate rationale for these changes lies in the belief that market values and procedures are the best means to empower users of the service and provide them with new remedies against inefficiency, insensitivity and the abuse of authority by the state.

Yet arguably the implications of this policy is also that in some respects public sector managers have more freedom in the choice of supplier than had been the case in the past. One of the authors recalls the limited choice available to him as a social worker seeking to obtain care for an elderly person. Budgetary constraints notwithstanding he was required to use the local authority managed resources unless an exception could be made out (usually on religious grounds). Now the social worker has in principle become a 'care manager' who has a budget to purchase the necessary care – which may not be local authority managed or owned. The budget may not be adequate to allow purchasing freedom . . . but that is a different point.

However Willis (1995) comments that the trend under this new purchasing regime is moving towards 'block contracts' which tend to be negotiated at a more senior level in the organization. Thus the supply decision has moved away from the user and local authority staff closest to the user.

In the health service context researchers are reporting an emerging pattern whereby as the purchaser/provider divide becomes more established purchasers are entering into alliances with each other. Hunter and O'Toole (1995) describe the example of the West Yorkshire Initiative which was set up by the four health authorities in the area. They looked at a range of strategic issues and entered into collaborative purchasing for such services as renal and cardiac services.

Chris Ham and Jonathan Shapiro (1995) note a similar trend towards what they describe as 'integrated purchasing'. Links evolved between the health authority and general practitioners (GPs) over decisions concerning where to place contracts. They comment that:

> In parallel the role of the FHSAs (Family Health Service Authorities) in commissioning family health services has come to resemble the role of the HAs (Health Authorities) in commissioning hospital and community health services. So many HAs and FHSAs have decided to plan jointly the development of secondary and primary care services in their areas (pp. 22–3).

They report a range of examples of changes in service as a result of this but note that they found that insufficient recognition was paid to involving junior and middle level managers. This implies that the user and health authority staff closest to the user might become distanced by such a development.

Pat Oakley writing in the *Health Service Journal* and in discussion with one of the authors (Oakley and Greaves, 1995) reports a growing pattern for GP fundholders to enter into joint purchasing arrangements in order to obtain more leverage with suppliers.

Agreeing customer requirements

The concept of the customer has been both explicitly and implicitly imported from the private sector. Citizen's charters, a major plank of government policy, are a manifestation of the aim to 'empower the consumer'. However as David Prior notes (in Stewart and Stoker, 1995, p. 91):

> Throughout local government generally, a new emphasis on making the process and the outcomes of local government activities more relevant and more accountable to consumers and citizens was apparent.

The Local Government Training Board (LGTB) distinguishes between providing services *to* the public and providing services *for* the public. In a key publication (Local Government Training Board, 1987, p. 5) they note:

> If councillors and officers see themselves as providing services *to* the public, then their basic focus of interest is likely to be the 'nuts and bolts' of the particular services offered rather than the customers and citizens who take up these services.

Providing an efficient service which fits within the organizational structure *to* the public would count as satisfactory – even if the recipients did not need or wish for the service. Providing services *for* the public involves identifying and responding to a change in the recipients' needs or wishes for the service.

Maintaining and improving operations

Getting Closer to the Public, the Local Government Training Board publication mentioned above, stresses the key importance of asking questions in order to understand both what the customer or public want and how they perceive the service provided.

It suggests that managers should be able to know (or find out) the answers to questions such as the following.

- Do all members of the public want the same kind of service?
- Are some customers' needs being met better than others?
- How well are 'difficult' customers handled?
- Does the public know what the intended standard of service is?
- Do you, the manager, know what standard of service the public think they are getting?
- Do all customers have equal information about the services on

offer and have equal access to them?
- How long do customers wait for answers to enquiries?
- Do customers understand the procedures they have to follow?

Information to answer these and other questions can be found through using devices such as surveys and records of complaints. Some question may require specialists to answer them. The question of disabled access, for example, may need a specialist adviser. In one local authority conversion work was undertaken to make the building accessible for blind people. The buttons on the lift were changed in order to make them readable by touch. Unfortunately the local authority initially overlooked the fact that the blind user would not know when the lift had arrived at the correct floor. After some further consultation a voice announcement was incorporated into the lift to inform users which floor the lift was on (and when doors were opening and closing).

Information

Forecasting trends from information

Managers do not simply operate in the here and now. A vital part of the role is to anticipate future events and plan accordingly. This involves using information about what has happened in the past (and is happening in the present). Some information is 'hard data' in that it is numeric such as budgets or numbers of staff/clients etc. Other information is 'soft' or non-numerical such as consumer attitudes, staff morale or rate of change.

The are a number of forecasting techniques which managers can use. Chapter 6 on finance has already opened up this subject because the whole process of setting up a budget is in effect a forecasting one. Therefore here we will focus on techniques which are not directly covered in that chapter.

The average MBA student or stock market investor is familiar with techniques used to try to predict the movement of share prices. These involve taking a series of figures and using various mathematical techniques to predict what the next figure might be. Some of the simpler of these techniques can be useful in the public sector.

As an example let us consider the figures for an Advice Centre (Table 7.1). The manager has records of monthly requests for advice over the past five years. The problem which the manager confronts is predicting the likely future demand upon the centre over the next year. The Advice Centre uses a lot of part-timers and volunteers so it is important to try to plan for likely future work pressures.

A simple method is to just take the total number of enquiries for

Table 7.1 Dunshire Advice Centre

| | Requests for advice | | | | | A % change | B % change | Prediction for 1996 | |
	1991	1992	1993	1994	1995	1991–94	1994–95	Using 'A'	Using 'B'
January	100	90	80	75	70	-30	-7	65	65
February	40	80	97	110	155	288	41	223	218
March	90	110	115	120	160	78	33	173	213
April	50	60	75	100	120	140	20	150	144
May	130	140	160	156	180	38	15	189	208
June	125	120	175	165	190	52	15	205	219
July	101	100	95	124	140	39	13	148	158
August	107	110	150	178	200	87	12	233	225
September	110	120	145	178	190	73	7	219	203
October	100	118	167	190	220	120	16	270	255
November	80	82	85	90	60	-25	-33	62	40
December	83	82	80	76	70	-16	-8	69	64
Annual total	1116	1212	1424	1562	1755	70	10	1930	1972

1995 and project the increase from 1994 to 1996. This will suggest that the Centre will see a 12 per cent increase in 1996.

However the manager possesses more detailed data both for each month and for previous years. When the comparison is made between 1994 and 1995 in terms of months it becomes apparent that there are some quite significant differences over the course of the year. November, December and January are in fact showing a pronounced decline in inquiries whilst February, March and April are well over the average increase.

If the manager looks back to previous years it is possible to improve the forecast for 1996 by identifying whether the earlier data supports the evidence of a trend for more inquiries overall but falling inquiries in November, December and January. The evidence confirms the trend for December and January but not for November.

The production of numeric predictions is only one type of forecasting. Much of the forecasting activities in the public sector cannot be based upon the use of a calculator. If we take the Advice Centre example again we can see the manager wondering what might impact upon future demand for advice services. Possibly the government policy may be to favour the Advice Centre and offer the possibility of more work. There may be local alternative sources of advice which have either just started up or closed thus having an impact upon the demand for the services of the advice centre.

One way of trying to forecast the future is to ask a range of experts to try to predict what might happen at different time intervals into the future (one year, five years, ten years etc.). This is often called Delphic Prediction from the Ancient Greek legend of an oracle that predicted the future. That oracle was famous for giving ambiguous messages – much like the fortune teller at the fun-fair.

One use of the technique we have seen was in the mid-1970s when academics were asked to predict when particular events might occur in higher education. One such event was the requirement for university lecturers to undertake teacher training. The reaction of the 'experts' was clear and unequivocal: 'not in my lifetime' was one of the milder responses. South Bank University has required all new lecturers to undertake teacher training since 1994 and many now predict that this trend is likely to continue.

Box 7.4   Case example

Forecasting and use of information in the NHS

An interesting forecasting dilemma for the NHS relates to the demand for beds. The challenge is to manage hospital beds in order to balance booked-in patients and emergency admissions in order to avoid too many empty beds or the absence of emergency beds. This used to be handled by using a blend of past experience and common sense together with an element of straight guesswork.

However the power of the computer has now been harnessed to assist in bed planning. Ormskirk Hospital in Lancashire has been trying out such a program. London hospitals are having to deal with problems of a loss of beds but no significant reduction in demand. If there is no bed available for an emergency admission then staff must often spend a great deal of time calling other hospitals to locate a bed. Recently this meant that a critically ill patient was flown by helicopter half way across England – the patient died and questions were asked in the Press.

St Thomas' Hospital adopted a computer program some five years ago. It involved the manager predicting how many beds would be available each day. Unfortunately the uncertainties of emergency admissions was a major problem in accurate prediction. They found that forecasting demand was not simply a matter of pressing computer keys but rather involved an element of intuition. The Joint Medical Director commented: 'Optimum use of beds is an art form; by using computer technology you're trying to convert nous and experience into software.'

However, intuition is not sufficient. The Ormskirk Hospital manager noted that accurate forecasting relies on real information. When West Lancashire NHS Trust opened a new District General Hospital they reduced the number of emergency beds and soon found that they had a bed shortage problem. The problem was in part occasioned by the way they had calculated the figures. The use of 'average length of stay' had concealed the trend for some patients to stay longer in hospital because other patients were coming in for quick turn-around operations using keyhole surgery. When the hospital looked at the number and duration of admissions as opposed to the 'average length of stay' they realized the reason for the failure to forecast the shortfall in beds. The use of more powerful computer software can enable more data to be evaluated. Ormskirk (and other hospitals) need to build new information into their forecasts – in particular such factors as the developments in community care and changing population demographics.

Source: *The Times*, 30 June 1994.

Recording and storing information

The example of bed forecasting in the NHS demonstrates the importance of both recording and storing information. However collecting information which guides positive and effective management decision making is not achieved by simply recording every available item of data. The public sector is awash with data which is either of little practical value to managers or worse still serves actually to impede managers.

When John Harvey Jones visited South Yorkshire police during the *Troubleshooter* series he was given large amounts of documentation and information. His comment (1992, p. 163) was that:

> very long documents are easy to produce but tend to give people excuses for lack of sharpness in their decision taking. Very frequently they are not read properly, and people take different views about which key points they should be reacting to.

Sir John's comments about South Yorkshire police would sound a familiar note with most public sector managers and those whom they serve. A key difference between the not-for-profit sector and the profit sector is in the focus upon key information variables that the profit motive provides.

The Government has sought to furnish a proxy for the sales and profitability data found in private companies by publishing statistics linked to 'performance indicators' in the public sector. In some instances such as school league tables, these are held to offer fairly direct comparison with the private sector. Significantly perhaps the Government is keener to stress comparisons in terms of examination results and national curriculum attainments rather than comparing, for example, average class size.

In areas such as health care the focus has been on statistics such as waiting list length. Here comparisons are often rendered difficult because of varying practices in how (and more significantly, when) such information is recorded. If a person is not admitted to the waiting list until they have seen a particular hospital consultant then it is obviously possible to manipulate the waiting list length simply by controlling access to that consultant.

Nationally gathered data such as unemployment rates have been widely criticized because of changes in the criteria over what constitutes being unemployed. Similarly it can be argued that crime statistics are unreliable on account of the fact that they only record 'officially reported crime'. In America an experiment of introducing more intense policing in certain areas was associated with an apparent *increase* in crime in those areas. This was explained by the fact that people were more likely to report offences when there were more police around.

Information is increasingly being held in computerized format and this raises major issues. Such electronically held information is regulated by the Data Protection Act 1984 and managers have a legal responsibility to ensure that information is only held for the declared purpose and that proper care is taken to ensure that information is both accurate and secure.

Health care is one of the most complex information systems in the public sector. A number of publications have sought both to describe the way such systems are set up and to offer guidance to setting up an information system. We will offer a model based upon the work of Sheaff and Peel (1995).

Sheaff and Peel provide a model of the typical life cycle associated with the introduction of a health service information system. We have simplified this for illustrative purposes. There are several phases:

1 Preselection

- Decide what information you wish the system to give you.
- Prioritize and cost these.
- Link the information needs to the objectives of the organization, in particular to any requirements of outside bodies.
- Agree a strategy for introducing the new system.
- Decide how it should be managed.
- Agree standards and definitions.
- Undertake a systems analysis (this usually involves looking at the current system to identify any shortfall and weakness).

2 Selection

This frequently might involve a system design, and here the steps might encompass:

- Review objectives.
- Evaluate constraints.
- Design output.
- Design a model to produce the output.
- Design an input into the system.
- Design the controls.
- Plan the installation.
- Cost the system.

3 Acquisition

Here the system is acquired often by a competitive tendering process which may in itself have various substages.

4 Installation

This involves several activities including:

- Setting up the system.
- Training users in its operation.

5 Handover

Here the managers in the organization take over the system from the supplier. Activities such as adapting building systems and staff (re)training and recruitment would need to take place.

6 First use

This involves several activities including:

- Testing the system.
- Training users in its operation.
- Parallel running the new system with the previous system (especially important when any system failure has a high consequence).
- Demonstrating the benefits to users.

7 Problem identification

All new information systems are likely to present initial teething problems.

- People need time to adjust to new technology especially if it is unfamiliar and requires new skills.
- Rates of work will often be lower at first on an automated system which has replaced a manual system.

8 Problem resolution

This will continue over the life of the system. If the system has been contracted out under a facilities management agreement then there is likely to be an ongoing interaction with the contractor over a range of issues.

9 Routine operation

Once the major initial issues have been dealt with then the system will function under normal conditions. This will usually be characterized by managers having less need to become involved in day-to-day issues and a pronounced decline in 'fire fighting' and system down time.

10 Review and updating/replacement (preselection?)

As the information needs of the organization change or as contracts come up for renewal or review then the decision process begins again.

Exchanging information

Leading meetings

During one author's time working in social services there was a discussion as to what a social worker's bumper sticker might read. One suggestion which attracted general agreement was 'Social workers do it in meetings'. However the description could just as easily apply to managers in general and public sector managers in particular. The need to follow process and to consult with various stakeholders is especially critical in the public domain.

Therefore the ability to manage meetings is a core attribute of an effective public sector manager. The expansion of the 'contract culture' and the growth of part-time work in the public sector means that managers have to be more skilled in meetings. In the old stable hierarchies the chair of a meeting had a position of power and was almost invariably the most senior person present. Nowadays with organizations taking a more dynamic and matrix form the person chairing the meeting may often not have line authority over those present. In such situations any weakness in chairing skills is likely to present a major problem to a manager.

Phil and Jane Hodgson (1992) identified the skill factors which made for competent chairing of meetings.

Purpose

A good chair would know the *purpose* of the particular meeting. Meetings may have a range of purposes. A basic classification is as follows:

- Decision making
- Problem solving
- Information (seeking or providing)
- Influencing
- Ideas or option generation
- Team or consensus building
- Conflict resolution
- Confrontation.

We would stress that most – perhaps all – meetings fall into more than one of the above categories. A good chair will identify beforehand which purposes are applicable. The arrangement of the seating for example would be very different for a disciplinary meeting as compared to an annual appraisal interview. Yet often managers simply leave the office furniture set out in exactly the same way irrespective of the type of meeting taking place.

Planning

Knowledge of the purpose will enable a good chair to plan the meeting. The majority of meetings most managers attend are informal in nature. However the public sector's stress upon accountability often leads to a need for a record to be kept of even relatively informal encounters.

A manager will need to plan who needs to be invited, what information needs to be provided in advance to participants and what the participants themselves need to be requested to bring.

A key element to any meeting is an agenda. This need not necessarily be typed but it must be communicated. Indeed in one authority one of the authors worked for it was a clear rule that every meeting scheduled had to have an agenda. This created some problems for a group of professional staff who had met as a mutual support group. Their meetings had customarily had no set agenda. The chief officer informed them that the group could meet at lunchtime (i.e. outside work time) – otherwise they had to circulate an agenda in advance.

Opening the meeting

Hodgson and Hodgson (1992) comment that you can set the tone of a meeting by the way in which you introduce it. You can ensure a positive, brisk, purposeful meeting, or a dull, tedious, frustrating one. This statement seems obvious common sense but most managers view a significant number of the meetings they attend with dread expecting them to be dull, tedious and frustrating. We offer the following advice on opening meetings drawn in part on Hodgson and Hodgson:

1　Adopt a positive tone of voice and body language. Actions such as speaking clearly and succinctly, leaning forward and holding good eye contact with colleagues all promote this.
2　Make sure that you state the purpose of the meeting and indicate the way you intend to structure the discussion.
3　Make sure that the duration of the meeting is made clear and people present are agreeable. Going over time allocated for a meeting should be exceptional.
4　Start on time. Starting late for late arrivals in effect penalizes those who turn up promptly. A manager who gets into a habit of starting late soon finds that people get used to it and turn up late. Often the reaction of the manager is to then blame those attending. Starting a meeting and then taking time out to furnish lengthy summaries to late-comers is equally frustrating to those who came on time. A better tactic is simply to wait till a convenient point to summarize the progress of the discussion for *all* those present.

During the meeting

1 Keep the meeting on track. It is all too easy, especially in large meetings, for the agenda to be hijacked or for the discussion to 'wander off course'. The degree of leeway for digression will depend upon the purpose of the meeting, the culture of the organization and the style of the chair. However as a general rule meetings which are not kept on track generally fail to reach any conclusion – and the chair is almost always blamed either overtly or covertly for this failure.

2 Encourage participation. Communication is usually a two-way street. There are few meetings where those present have nothing to offer to the discussion. Part of the skill of chairing a meeting is to ensure everyone with something to contribute is given the opportunity to do so. This can be done in a number of ways:

- Each person can be asked in turn to contribute.
- Non-verbal communication (eye contact, smiling, nodding) is vital in helping the shy person to contribute by displaying 'active listening'.
- A good chair will use a range of questions (open ended, probing and focused) to bring out valid information from people such as technical experts.
- Contributions should be acknowledged by thanking the person and by summarizing what they have said.

3 Keep an eye on the time. Few meetings are open ended in time and one of the unforgivable sins of a poor chair is to fail to realize this. A good chair will demonstrate an awareness of the passage of time and the cost of time to those present. Scheduling (and disposing of) quick items at the beginning of a meeting can often create a good impression of progress. When a meeting is deadlocked over something a good chair will quickly recognize this and either move on to another item or refocus the discussion to untangle the blockage.

4 Summarize. Summarize both at the end of each item on the agenda and at appropriate intervals during the meeting. Summaries of progress (or lack of it) should be given by the chair:

- when an item has been discussed and a decision point has been reached
- when a decision has been made and needs to be recorded
- when discussion has become bogged down and/or is going round in circles
- to clarify a complex issue or point
- to identify several options from information provided
- when there is conflict in the meeting and tempers are rising.

In workshops with managers the authors have found that summarizing is a key activity which distinguishes effective from ineffective chairs. Effective chairs summarize a lot.

Contributing to meetings

The nature of the contribution you make to a meeting is shaped by several factors. Effective participation is not simply a matter of being assertive. A good chair would ensure that a non-assertive person was able to make a contribution.

The essential key to effectiveness is to know why you have been invited to attend the meeting. A manager in the public sector will attend a wide range of meetings – probably far more than most of her or his private sector counterparts. Senior managers (at chief or deputy chief officer level) will usually have a secretary or assistant who runs their diary for them. Such a manager will normally delegate authority to that individual to make an initial assessment regarding what sort of contribution the manager is expected to make at a meeting.

However the growth of information technology and the pressure on staff resources means that most managers now have to manage their own diaries and prepare for meetings with only limited administrative support.

A useful guide to meeting preparation is to remember to ask the following questions of yourself:

- Why have I been asked to contribute to the meeting? Is it in my capacity as a manager? If so am I there simply to lend authority to the proceedings? Possibly one of your subordinates could cover the meeting – and it would be good experience for her or him.
- What sort of expertise or knowledge will the meeting require of me? A high proportion of public sector managers are also professionals and a meeting may draw upon the manager's professional knowledge. Sometimes this is actually an inappropriate use of the manager. A doctor who has moved into health management may be less professionally up to date than one of his or her colleagues who spends their time practising medicine. It would be better to ask one of those colleagues to a meeting where it is a professional rather than a managerial contribution that is required.
- Who else will be attending the meeting? Sometimes this is crucial. One of the authors as a chair of child abuse case conferences had to spend much time negotiating with police officers to ensure that they attended case conferences where parents of the child would also be present. The initial reaction of the police was to refuse to attend at all unless the parents would not be present.

- Where and when will the meeting take place? Few things can more successfully undermine your contribution than failing to attend because you have not checked out the time and venue. Being late because you got lost is a familiar but flimsy excuse which you can usually only get away with once. If the meeting is at an unfamiliar venue then it is essential to allow time for finding your way there.
- What is the purpose of the meeting? Here we refer you to the previous section. Obviously there is a significant difference in how you would prepare for a meeting which is to share information as opposed to one intended to make key decisions.

The political dimension of meetings is highly significant in the public sector. Some meetings are held publicly because it is an expected part of the process of conducting business. In the private sector the only public meeting most organizations hold is the annual general meeting for their shareholders. However both in local government and in central government a considerable part of the debate takes place publicly. We would note that some writers have expressed concern about a move towards secrecy and less representativeness as shown by the expansion of quangos and National Health Service Trusts.

The political dimension raises the question of meetings as a form of theatre. Roles are played out on a public stage by politicians and public stakeholders. As many managers are well aware the real decisions were frequently made in small and private meetings held beforehand. Managers, if they are senior officers of the public organization, may have to attend the public meeting where the decision is put through a public process of agreement and ratification. In some public organizations these meetings can be emotionally highly charged.

Summary

In a chapter such as this it is difficult to effect the coverage of all operational and information issues given the broad range of the public sector itself. A key ability is to manage the ongoing work process whilst being alert to signals suggesting areas for improvement. Hence we have laid considerable stress upon aspects of innovation and the use of a particular technique (cost benefit analysis) to assess change options. We have also examined quality management in some detail.

The ongoing implementation and evaluation of change is equally important. Indeed the level of manager we hope is reading this book is likely to spend an appreciable proportion of his/her time and efforts in change management. In the old public administration hierarchy and role-based organization change took place in a slower and often almost routine fashion. However in the current and possibly future models of the public sector organization change is likely to take place in a more rapid and less predictable way.

We have spent some time focusing upon the one venue in which we feel any public sector manager must be competent – the meeting. Meetings are an important part of the life of most managers but for the public (and particularly the voluntary) sector manager they are the life blood. In our experience a high level of competence in managing meetings characterizes almost all effective public managers.

Action points and discussion points

(Items in italics are intended to encourage the reader to develop a greater intellectual awareness, items in plain type are focused upon work-related activity.)

Implement change or improvements in organizational activities

Identify a current public concern over a shortfall or failing in a product or service. Follow the progress of the concern and examine how the organization tries to resolve the problem. Consider to what extent the key people in the organization are 'managing' the change process as opposed to merely reacting to events.

Identify two attempts to manage a change in your organization, one successful and the other not. Compare the two and draw out what distinguished the 'successfully managed' change from the unsuccessful one. Write these factors down in your desk diary for future reference.

Facilitate meetings and group discussions

List the meetings you attend and group them in terms of the purpose of the meeting and the role you have in it. Then consider the others who attend the meetings and whether they share your view of the purpose and the reasons they might have for attending.

In meetings that you chair ask a trusted colleague to give you feedback afterwards on the way in which you exercise your role.

Ensure that regular meetings for which you are responsible start (and finish) on time, have agreed agendas and, where appropriate, a formal record of outcomes and discussion.

Provide information to support decision making

Identify the sources of information that your organization uses to improve decision making. Group it into categories (numeric, non-numeric) and rank it in terms of importance. Are there any sources which are under (or over) used?

What are your own main sources of information in making decisions as a manager? To what extent are they reliable and appropriate? Are there any ways in which you can cross-check one source of information against another?

Establish communication and information systems

What is the policy and practice of your organization over the obtaining, storage and retrieval of information? How does it compare to other similar organizations?

Review the way in which you store information necessary for your work. Do you have information duplicated? How much of your information is archival in that it is never used but kept 'just in case'.

What back-up is there particularly of electronically stored data? How inconvenienced would you be if:

- your computer was stolen
- your secretary/assistant's computer was stolen
- you lost your diary.

Do you know how to access your data held on your assistant's or secretary's computer?

How easily could you direct a colleague, by phone, to locate a key piece of information in your own office?

Further reading

Common, R., Flynn, N., and Mellon, E. (1993). *Managing Public Services. Butterworth-Heinemann.*
This is a readable and accessible book which examines the managerial aspects of the Whitehall reforms. It is particularly useful to help managers understand the customer and market orientation which has driven change in the past decade.

Gaster, L. (1995). *Quality in Public Services: Managers' Choices.* Open University Press.
This is a well-written and well-regarded book which tackles the quality and customer issues which are impacting upon the public manager. It offers some clear and useful guidance upon implementation.

Hind, A. (1995). *The Governance and Management of Charities.* Voluntary Sector Press.
This is an enormously informative and well-received book. It is certainly valuable for a senior manager in the charity sector. It may be rather expensive for the casual reader though – the book by Mike Hudson (1995) mentioned in Chapter 2 provides a good introduction to managing charities at a paperback Penguin price.

Sheaf, R., and Peel, V. (1995). *Managing Health Service Information Systems: An Introduction.* Open University Press.
This book provides an enormous amount of information on the subject. It will tend to appeal more to the information specialist.

Willcocks, L., and Harrow, J. (Eds.) (1992). *Rediscovering Public Services Management.* McGraw-Hill.
This is a book which furnishes some very valuable material on systems and information issues. One author (Willcocks) is an expert on technology and information systems in the public sector. A number of the authors are experienced managers who blend their experience with a rigorous intellectual approach.

8 Customer issues

Aims and learning objectives

In this chapter our intention is to help you review the way in which you ensure that you are managing resources to meet the real needs and expectations of your customers. In Chapter 7 we introduced the concepts of quality and agreeing customer requirements in the context of managing systems. In this chapter we are developing these important issues further. We are taking a wide definition of 'customer' in this chapter to include anybody who relies on you to produce something. So a customer may be the user of your organization's services, such as a client, a patient or a tenant, or it may be someone inside your own organization, such as a colleague, someone in another department, your manager or a member of your staff. It is important, therefore, to recognize that even if you are not in a 'customer-facing' role in terms of your organization's external customers, you are part of an important internal 'customer–supplier chain'. If any link in this chain breaks then the service to the external customer is likely to suffer.

At the end of this chapter, and associated activities and reading, you will be able to:

- manage activities to meet customers' agreed requirements
- identify your major customers and assess their needs
- evaluate you organization's approach to customers with reference to examples of best practice in the public sector and implement changes and improvements to levels of customer care
- prepare and implement a plan for improving levels of customer satisfaction
- outline the requirements for the award of a 'Charter Mark' and establish a strategy to work towards its achievement in your organization
- outline the requirements of a quality assurance system for your area of management responsibility

The changing nature of the customer role in the public sector

[We are] . . . moving away from the amorphous all-purpose local authority that determines what services it wants to provide and then provides them. This traditional local authority model rapidly descends into a conspiracy against the public – the council's customers. At the first sign of financial difficulties or cuts, traditionally many local authorities have closed offices, reduced opening hours, delayed in responding to correspondence while working parties have been established to navel gaze and think how the 'organization' can cope. The customers have been betrayed in the process.

This strident assertion from Brent Council reflects many of the elements of the move towards recognizing the changing role of the 'customer' or 'consumer' in public sector organizations.

Faced with increasing competition and heightened consumer expectations managers in all sectors of the economy are paying more attention to service quality and customer care. Public-sector managers share these concerns and many attempts are being made to apply the principles of managing for quality, sometimes known as 'Total Quality Management' or TQM, to their particular setting.

Approaches to managing for quality find their roots largely in manufacturing industry and this will obviously have implications for their implementation in the public sector. The public sector can primarily be regarded as a service industry whose 'product' or 'output' does not have the same features as a manufactured product. It is easier to define 'quality' in manufactured goods than in the provision of services. Manufacturers, and other private sector organizations, can more easily define their customer(s) – they are the people they sell things to. Public sector organizations are often not involved in 'selling' and even the immediate recipients of a public service (such as clients, service users, householders, patients etc.) are not the only people involved with, or affected by, the service. Similarly not all recipients of public services actually want the service, some 'services' are compulsory or enforced. In the context of the 'public purpose', central to the public sector, quality may be determined by the extent to which the service meets public purposes, as well as the requirements of particular users.

A systematic approach to meeting customer needs and expectations

Figure 8.1 relates a basic 'quality improvement cycle', designed to analyse, assess and plan to meet customer requirements, to other organizational systems which are dealt with elsewhere in this book. For the purposes of this chapter we will consider each element of the basic quality-improvement cycle in turn.

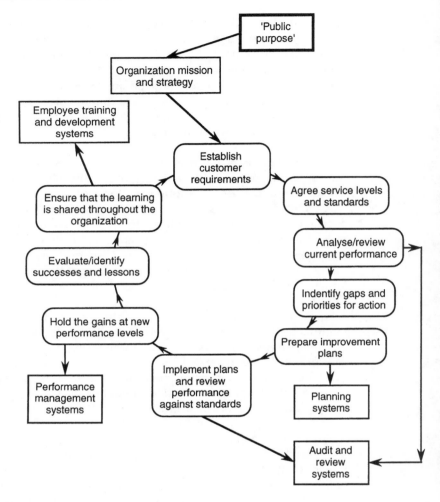

Figure 8.1 *A systematic approach to quality management and some of the links to other management systems*

Establish customer requirements

The model starts by connecting the process of establishing customer requirements to the organization's overall mission and strategy. This could be shown as a two-way process, for while the mission and strategy is likely to delineate the broad range of customers the organization is trying to serve (e.g. young people at risk of offending, patients referred for psychiatric care, other departments in the case of an in-house service such as Legal Services) it is also likely that the changing customer requirements discovered by an effective process will influence the overall mission and strategy. The evolving role of some charities concerned with child care illustrates this process. Consider the moves they have made from offering traditional institutional care to community-based preventative services. As well as the immediate needs of their clients this change in the emphasis of the services provided also reflects changing perceptions of the 'public purpose' of the charities, i.e. the wider expectations of people beyond the immediate client group. This concept of 'public purpose' can both provide an impetus to, and a constraint on, the process of establishing customer requirements. Take, for example, the Prison Service where, it could be argued, the conceptualization of the 'needs' of its prisoner 'customers' will reflect broader political and societal expectations about the balance, say, between punishment and rehabilitation.

However potential complications such as this obviously do not negate the value of ensuring that the voice of the user is heard in planning services and monitoring and evaluating their delivery. There is a wide range of opportunities and methods available to you in establishing customer requirements. These include:

1 Developing 'customer intelligence' systems. By this we mean systematically using the information your organization already gathers. Your customer-facing staff are an obvious source of information and there may be considerable benefit in making this explicit through, for example, team meetings designed solely to share and collate data on customer requirements. Similarly, as we mentioned in Chapter 1 local media such as newspapers can be important sources of trends and developments in customer perceptions.

2 Monitoring customer complaints. Perhaps better seen as a way of discovering what customers do not want rather than what they do! However establishing and using an effective complaints procedure can help you determine recurring problems and indicate any weakness in your service delivery. You need to pay attention to customer compliments as well, partly because it gives you the opportunity to be seen by your staff as just as ready to recognize good work as to investigate potential problems. As well as having an accessible and easy to understand complaints procedure available at the point of service delivery, you could also consider a customer-suggestion scheme to encourage both positive, and negative, feedback.

3 Listening to representative groups. In most service areas there are likely to be local and national bodies representing the interests of your customer group and/or putting pressure on for service improvements. If such a body does not exist for your particular service or locality perhaps you should consider facilitating the establishment of one (we carefully use the term 'facilitate' here because you are more likely to elicit customer information and suggestions from a group that is independent of your organization, and seen as such).

4   There may be occasions when it would be useful to establish temporary representative groups, sometimes known as 'focus groups'. With the support of a good chairperson or facilitator you can convene a meeting of customers to address a focal question, such as 'To what extent is (your organization) meeting the real needs of its customers' or 'How have your requirements as customers changed over the last two years and to what extent have our services responded effectively?' The output from the ensuing discussion needs to be carefully recorded and analysed before proposals for service improvement are made, and perhaps fed back to a reconvened focus group for comment.

5   A more informal variation on the focus group theme is to hold an open day where customers are invited to attend and contribute their ideas through one-to-one discussions with members of your staff or unstructured group discussions. You could also consider going out to meet your customers rather than expecting them to come to you.

6   Using discussions, customer representatives, focus groups and similar methods is likely to provide you with good in-depth qualitative information on customer requirements. You may decide to augment this with a broader survey of customers to check that the information you are gathering and the perceptions of customer requirements which are beginning to form are valid across your customer base. A well-constructed, reliable, survey can provide useful quantitative data to support, or challenge, your more qualitative data. It is possible, for example, that a particular group of customers who have formed themselves into a pressure group are more concerned with pursuing their own, more limited agenda, than representing the broader interests of customers. That is not to say that you should ignore their views, but rather that you should test them out on a larger 'population' of customers.

Agree service levels and standards

It is not unusual to find that customers articulate requirements (wants) which are beyond the capabilities of the supplier to meet within the timescale, financial resources or staffing levels available. This is likely to be as true for a motor manufacturer as a supplier of hospital care. In both cases the supplier needs to negotiate an agreed standard of product or service, for an *agreed* price or within a particular set of resource constraints. Hence the generally accepted definition of a 'quality' product or service is one which meets customers' agreed requirements right first time, every time. The agreed requirement then becomes the basic standard for service delivery. Clearly it is in the interest of both supplier and customer to state the standard as precisely as possible in terms that are measurable, observable, realistic and achievable.

Analyse/review current performance

This stage involves profiling the current level of service or product delivery and comparing it with the agreed standards. As the standards have been expressed in measurable, observable terms it should be relatively easy to construe a set of performance measures or indicators as the basis of this profile. We will return to performance measures in Chapter 10. You will see that Figure 8.1 links this stage of the systematic approach to other audit and review systems, which means that you may be able to draw on other internal and external, relatively objective, investigations of your service when completing your service profile.

Identify gaps and priorities for action

Comparing the current service profile with that necessary to meet customers' agreed requirements will probably identify some areas where standards are falling below expectations. This is to be expected, for one of the tensions in managing to meet customer expectations is that these expectations are constantly rising. Once a customer sees that you can reduce a response time from two weeks to two days their expectation becomes that it should be available in two hours! Hence the notion that improving quality and customer care is a journey rather than a destination. Just as gaps will continue to emerge you will not be able to fill all of them at once, which means that priorities have to be established. This will be easier to do if, from the first stage of this process, you are clear about your customers' priorities, this avoids you having to guess what they might be. It is also important to ensure that you get to the root causes of any identified gap so that you can move to planning ways of dealing with these important, underlying factors.

Prepare improvement plans

Having analysed the gap and agreed priorities for improvement you can establish objectives, standards, targets and an action plan for the next period of development. This needs to link in with your organization's other planning systems, such as its human resource plan (as discussed in Chapter 5) and budgetary process (see Chapter 6), which are all framed by, and contribute to, its overall strategic plan (see Chapter 9). An effective improvement plan will include:

- Clear ownership for the overall plan and its elements, that is everybody involved will know the part they are required to play, and how this relates to other peoples' responsibilities.
- Clear statement of the objectives of the plan and each of its elements.

- The measurements required to ensure that the objectives are being met.
- Overall timescale, interim targets and significant milestones towards achieving the plan.
- An estimate of the costs involved in implementing the plan (which requires a schedule of resource requirements) and the anticipated benefits (also costed).
- A contingency plan to deal with any potential barriers to the successful implementation of the plan.
- A procedure for communicating the plan and ensuring that everybody involved is trained and competent to play their part in its implementation.

Implement plans and review performance against standards

Time spent in effective planning will pay dividends during implementation, but the implementation needs to be managed in a flexible manner rather than with slavish adherence to every element as initially conceived. Despite your best efforts and contingency planning the unexpected will arise, including unintended consequences, and these will require appropriate amendments to the original plan. Because you have put a performance review process into your plan, measuring achievements against predetermined standards (and looping back into other audit and review systems), you will be quickly aware of any deviations from the plan and decide whether corrective action is required to get the implementation process back on track, or whether it is the plan itself that requires modification.

Hold the gains at new performance levels

There are many reasons why having achieved a new standard of service delivery there is a tendency to revert to previous, less satisfactory levels. These include the general resistance to change present in all social systems; the tendency for people to respond to, and concentrate on, the current concerns of management (and having achieved a service improvement it is very possible that you will turn your attention to the next pressing issue); a degree of inertia in organizations which tends to encourage a regression to the previous level of status quo. As you can anticipate these forces you can also take proactive steps to ensure that improvements in standards of quality are maintained. This involves continuing to take a managerial interest in the particular service area; rewarding people for sustaining the new standards of service and ensuring that the process of measurement and the publication of the results actively reinforces the gains made. Integrating the new standards into your organization's performance management and monitoring system is also important to ensure that the gains achieved become part of 'business as usual'.

Evaluate/identify successes and lessons

Having progressed this far through the process of change and development learning will have occurred at the levels of the individuals involved (including yourself of course) and the team, for there can be no change without learning. Part of holding the gains involves making this learning explicit through evaluating what has been achieved, how it was achieved and what has been learnt which will be of value to the next change programme. As change and transformation will become a regular part of your managerial experience, if they are not already, you have the opportunity to become very skilled at this part of your role! Making the lessons learnt explicit also allows you to recognize the achievement of your team, and yourself. Helping people become skilled at change in this way means that they will feel less threatened by the process, more competent and empowered in handling change and, therefore, less resistant to change.

Ensure that learning is shared throughout the organization

Once you have made your own learning, and that of your team, explicit you can take steps to share it with others in the organization, hence contributing to a wider process of 'organizational learning'. The opportunities for you to do this will depend on your particular organization, but they could include:

- preparing a report for the senior management team or governing body
- writing an item for the organization's staff magazine or newsletter
- hosting an in-house seminar where you and your team invite others from the organization to meet with you and discuss your learning and compare it with their own
- with your manager's support, preparing an article for wider dissemination in a professional journal or to a training organization responsible for your area of the public sector.

Through this process of actively learning from the change process you can both contribute to, and be supported by, your organization's approach to employee training and development.

Examples of good practice

Let's look at a couple of practical examples of quality and service improvements. We mentioned the London Borough of Brent in the introduction to this chapter. In Box 8.1 you can see an overview of the Brent approach to quality. Box 8.2 provides an example from the Civil Service – the Benefits Agency.

Box 8.1   Case example

London Borough of Brent

Brent Council has set itself the mission 'to be simply the best local authority in the country. A local authority in which the community we represent and serve, and the staff we employ, have pride, concentrating on achieving excellence through Total Quality.'
    The Council's mission is supported by four core values:

- Serving our customers.
- Valuing and empowering our staff.
- A quality service.
- An efficient organization.

In this case example we will be focusing on Brent Council's approach to the first core value, although in practice all four are closely linked. Indeed Brent now recognizes that commitment to customers and staff are the principal values, and that through achieving these two quality services an efficient organization will be delivered.
    The key elements of Brent's approach to its customer orientation are:

1 Developing and publishing a wide range of 'customer charters' which set out performance standards. Brent presents a 'customer pledge' in which the Council aims, at all times, to give customers a warm and friendly welcome, clear and quick answers to questions, a quality service which meets the customer's individual needs, to give honest information about what the Council can or cannot do and to give a sincere apology if they do make a mistake and action to put things right.
2 Identifying the behaviours and attitudes that will build effective partnerships across the whole organization and encourage everyone to play their part to provide the best possible services. These are reflected, for example, in a draft 'Management Style Audit', designed to be part of a 360-degree feedback system, which invites employees to rate managers according to a number of criteria, including the extent to which the manager encourages each employee to participate in the development and maintenance of high quality services to customers and rewards employees according to their contribution in the development and maintenance of high quality services.

3 Expecting its senior management to lead by example, giving a consistent and clear sense of direction, and reflecting these attributes in the senior management appraisal scheme, which makes explicit mention of the need to collect information from customers and the wider community as part of the appraisal process.

4 A fundamental reorganization which reduced the number of departments from ten to five, reduced the number of senior managers by one-third, radically slimmed down central departments, established the role and functions of devolved business units, hence stressing the themes of maximum devolution and a purchaser/provider split.

5 Developing a set of 'corporate standards' that replaced previous centralized policies and procedures, thereby providing a regulatory framework for management within the Council, without any indication of *how* they should be applied.

6 Introducing its own internal quality assessment standard, the 'Brent Mark'.

7 Designing training packs that address customer relations issues, such as telephone skills, simple written communications, handling difficult situations and face-to-face customer care.

8 Undertaking over seventy customer surveys, and acting on the results.

Brent's efforts have been recognized in a plethora of awards, including a number of 'Charter Marks', a SOLACE/PA Consulting Group Total Quality Award and a SOCPO Innovation Award. It has also been recognized by the Audit Commission as an 'exemplar' for performance management and for customer relations.

The Council's own monitoring statistics include achievements such as a 120 per cent increase in the number of planning applications processed within eight weeks, a 60 per cent reduction in the waiting list for occupational therapy, Social Services opening hours up by 15 per cent and a 25 per cent increase in library stock issues.

Brent commissioned MORI to conduct two borough-wide residents' attitude surveys, which showed, amongst other improvements, an 18 per cent increase in residents' satisfaction with the way the council is running the borough, and with contact with Council staff, between 1990 and 1993. A separate survey conducted by the Library Service over the same period showed an increase in users' satisfaction with the way the service was run from 54 per cent to 80 per cent.

It is worth noting that these improvements have been

achieved along with a *reduction* of 60 per cent in average council tax bills.

Source: London Borough of Brent publications.

Box 8.2   Case example

The Benefits Agency

The Benefits Agency, which is responsible for the delivery of Social Security benefits, has established four core values:

- Customer service.
- Caring for staff.
- Bias for action.
- Value for money.

These core values form the basis of twelve criteria which individual Benefits Agency business units are encouraged to use to self-assess their performance in quality improvement. It is a feature of the Benefits Agency approach that while the Agency's director chairs a Quality Management Project Team at corporate level, business unit managers are free to adopt their own approach to quality improvement, guided by a pack produced by the Agency called 'Quality Framework'. Support is also available, if required, from a central Quality Education and Support team. There was, however, an expectation that all units would have completed an initial assessment and have plans in place for quality improvement.

Units can also apply for a 'quality award' which subjects their self-assessment to verification by both internal and external validators.

The Agency's approach to quality improvement was formally launched in 1993, and a number of successes were claimed during its first year of implementation. These include halving absence rates, through encouraging staff to take more control and responsibility for their work, resulting in an estimated saving of £100 000 per year; and a 2 per cent increase in customer satisfaction, from 82 per cent in 1992 to 84 per cent in 1993. Local staff surveys also suggest that units which introduced the Quality Framework approach quickly achieve high assessment ratings and also have improved staff morale.

Source: IDS (1994).

Customer care

Once embarked upon a systematic approach to continuous quality improvement as we have suggested, you will, as a matter of course, improve your standards of 'customer care' because you have directly addressed customer expectations. Some organizations have approached this the other way round, that is from a concern to improve relationships with their customers as a priority, which has led to a broader review of standards of services. According to Gaster (1995, p. 77–78) there is little information about the origins and form of customer care programmes but:

> They seem mainly to concentrate on the immediate impression that a service provider makes on the 'customer'. In this sense they could be a contribution to improving the interpersonal or non-technical dimension of quality . . . So it could be argued that customer care programmes provide a useful counterbalance to an approach that might otherwise overemphasize the role of the professionals and bureaucrats, to the detriment of those receiving or potentially receiving the services in question.

This notion of a counterbalance to the professional or bureaucrat sets customer care firmly in the context of the move towards consumerism and consumer choice in the public sector that we reviewed in earlier chapters. Harrow and Shaw (1992) point out that the relationship with a customer of a public service can be strongly influenced by external contextual factors and the personal traits of the individual customer and service provider. Amongst the contextual factors they include:

- Legal framework.
- Customers' social status.
- Public service ethic.
- Professional autonomy.
- Political climate.
- Service resource allocation.
- Competency of service staff.

We have seen how the legal framework, public service ethic and political climate have moved towards a more customer-centred approach, while professional autonomy has been seriously challenged in many areas. This makes the competency of service staff in managing customer relations and customer care an increasingly important concern (although one could argue that this is countered by reductions in the resources available for service delivery). Focusing on staff competency leads us to the second of Harrow and Shaw's (1992) influences on the customer/supplier relationship: the personal traits of the customer and service provider. Amongst the clusters of user characteristics affecting the customer/supplier relationship they include:

- Regular/Irregular
- Fee-paying/non-fee paying
- Voluntary/Involuntary
- 'Grateful'
- Persistent
- Knowledgeable
- Abuser.

Perhaps this helps us identify the essence of a customer care programme, that is helping staff to develop their competence in providing a customer-focused service *despite*, rather than being influenced by, these types of user characteristics. How can this be achieved? It probably requires a quality improvement programme in its own right with three key objectives:

1 Developing a positive attitude in staff towards customers
2 Developing staff skills in customer care
3 Improving the flow of information between the organization, staff and customers.

We know that attitudes are largely developed and changed through experience. If, for example, staff experience a positive change in the way they are treated as the 'customers' of their managers, they are more likely to change their behaviour towards their customers in turn. This points to the importance of senior management commitment to any customer care programme, and the importance of managers, trainers and other change agents 'modelling' (that is acting out) the behaviour towards customers which they are trying to encourage. This may help to avoid the situation reported by Gaster (1995, p. 78) where:

> many customer care programmes appear (but this is anecdotal evidence) to have been introduced in a very top-down way as a substitute for thinking deeply about quality as a whole. Such programmes have tended to put the front-line staff under the spotlight, while the systems and back-up to enable those staff to provide a better service have not been attended to . . . Assumptions are made by senior managers as to the desired staff behaviours that might minimize trouble from the public, rather than creating a culture where public needs and demands are both listened to and responded to.

Here Gaster is alerting us to the fact that a really effective approach to customer care is likely to involve a wide-ranging change programme which will, and should, impact on organizational culture, strategy and structure. Senior managers need to be aware of the scale of the change required and be prepared to support, champion and resource it.

Once this senior management commitment has been achieved we can progress through a 'normal' quality improvement process involving the following, or similar stages:

- Assess and audit the current level of customer care (taking care to involve the customers in this process).
- Identify the gaps and set clear objectives for the customer care programme.
- Address the required attitudinal change in managers and staff and develop their competence. This may be achieved through a process of formal training and development, followed up in the workplace. Typically customer-care skills programmes may include developing written and oral skills, including handling telephone calls from customers; assertiveness and dealing with aggression; complaints procedures and ways of preventing problems arising in the first place.
- Measure and evaluate the programme against targets.
- Review and plan for continuous improvement.

Box 8.3 gives one example of a customer care programme in practice.

Box 8.3   Case example

London Underground Limited (LUL)

The LUL approach to customer care is particularly interesting because it highlights some of the tensions between local responsiveness and corporate standards. Attempts in the late 1980s to delegate responsibility for customer care policies, along with other issues, to individual tube lines (i.e. Northern Line, District Line etc.) resulted in overlaps and duplications in services and a waste of some resources. Importantly LUL customers saw the Underground as one network rather than a collection of autonomous lines and, therefore, tended to demand consistency across the whole system, In the light of these customer requirements LUL decided that the obvious way forward was to find out what its customers wanted and to attempt to satisfy these requirements across the network as a whole.

In 1992 LUL started work on an integrated customer care policy, which became known as 'Right Time, Right Place'. The process started by interviewing some 3000 customers, and a smaller number of staff. This survey concentrated on four main areas:

- pre-journey information
- passenger arrival at the station
- the Underground travel itself
- leaving the station.

The research resulted in a report which made some 180 detailed recommendations. The major findings were that customers wanted a significant staff presence on stations to provide information and a feeling of safety. Indeed customers felt that staff often appeared to be hiding, and had little concept of what customer service meant. Staff also accepted that customer care could be improved. Customers also said that the public address system on stations was difficult to hear. LUL investigated this and concluded that the problem was caused by a combination of unsuitable equipment, poor staff training and difficulties with station acoustics. This illustrates how perceptions of customer service and care can rely on an interrelationship between technical and human factors. The survey also confirmed managers' suspicion that over half of LUL's customers used two or more lines regularly and regarded it as a network which, therefore, required consistent standards of customer care across all the lines.

In response to these findings LUL established a Customer Strategy Information Team to consider the report's recommendations in detail. This team drew its membership from all parts of the organization and, importantly, reported to a steering group chaired by the Director of Passenger Services, hence demonstrating senior management commitment to its work.

Of the 180 or so recommendations, 70 per cent fell into three major areas covering the 'soft' issues of customer care training, public address training and recruitment and selection policies. 'Harder' issues related to things such as the need for electronic signs and telephone information lines on platforms. Guidelines were also produced on how public information should be displayed at stations.

To support these changes LUL has introduced an extensive package of customer care training, targeted at the needs of individual staff via a series of training modules, hence consciously avoiding a 'sheep-dip' approach to training. In addition all training courses run by LUL now include an element of customer care training, because of the belief that there are customer care implications in virtually everything that LUL does.

To support the recruitment and selection of customer aware staff with appropriate communication and interpersonal skills LUL has developed a behaviourally anchored rating scheme which centres on a prospective employee's customer and commercial orientation and teamwork skills, amongst other things. It is anticipated that these factors will eventually be reflected in LUL's performance management system.

Customer satisfaction is now included as one of LUL's key performance indicators and measured by a mystery shopping index and a customer satisfaction index. Both the reports by the mystery shoppers and the customer satisfaction index are based on five criteria:

- cleanliness of stations
- information supplied at stations
- station service
- safety
- security.

The results of the monitoring exercises are fed back to line managers every four weeks, and they are expected to make improvements where necessary.

As well as the work of the Customer Information Strategy Team customer care at LUL is also the concern of the Customer Charter, which covers issues such as train regularity and escalator services.

Source: IDS (1995a).

The benefits of an effective customer care programme may include a strengthening of *internal* customer–supplier relationships as even staff who are not usually customer-facing come to realize their part in providing a high standard of service to the end-user or ultimate customer.

The Charter Mark

We will be examining the Citizen's Charter programme in more detail in Chapter 10, however the 'Charter Mark' is directly related to meeting customers' needs and customer care, so it is worth spending some time on it here.

According to the guide for applicants for the Charter Mark Awards (Cabinet Office, 1996, p. 6):

The Charter Mark is an award for organizations which provide an excellent service to the public. It is a sign of excellence. A Charter Mark means an organization has shown that it puts its users first.

If this is the case then, potentially, the requirements of the award and the process of achieving it could provide a useful model for managers concerned with managing customer relationships. One slight problem with the Charter Mark in the context of this book is that it is not available to charities and voluntary organizations (apart from housing associations), however this does not mean that the model is irrelevant for managers in these organizations.

In order to be considered for the award, which lasts for three years before a winning organization needs to reapply, it is necessary to prove that you and your organization:

- set clear, tough and meaningful performance standards (we consider this issue further in Chapter 10)
- tell users what those standards are and how you perform against them
- tell users in a clear, straightforward way about all the services and help available and how to get the most out of them
- consult people on what services they need and how services can be improved, and make good use of their ideas
- give people choices whenever possible.
- have polite and helpful staff, and a user-friendly approach to things like opening hours, answering the phone and any special needs of the people who use the service
- make it easy for people to say when they are not happy with the service and act swiftly to put mistakes right
- give value for money by budgeting carefully and using resources efficiently and effectively.
- continually make improvements in the quality of service you provide and have new ideas for value-for-money improvements in the future.

For each of these areas further guidance is available on the type of evidence that needs to be submitted as part of an application. Under 'standards' for example the judging panel for the award will expect to see evidence that standards are precise: measurable and meaningful to users; brought clearly to the attention of the service users; genuine, specific, user service standards and not just general standards of service or promises of service; and have been set following user consultation and that they reflect what the user considers to be important. Evidence required to support a claim for offering 'value-for-money' includes proof: of savings already made; that you are improving value for money; that your claims are supported by independent assessment (for example, audit reports); and that you consult users about value for money and service priorities.

It is easy to see the manifestations of the 'New Public Management' in this list of requirements.

Box 8.4 gives some examples of Charter Mark winners from recent years.

Box 8.4 Case examples

HM Prison, Porterfield, Inverness

Employing 105 people Porterfield Prison caters for men and women prisoners and young offenders with the mission to provide 'security, good order, prisoner opportunity, care with humanity and value for money'. It was decided to apply for a Charter Mark because an opportunity was seen for the scheme to provide a framework for improving service quality. A cross-area team was established to pursue the application, which they supported with a portfolio of evidence. This included a video of the prison's Prisoner Induction Programme and documents detailing improvements and innovations introduced into the prison. The real benefit of applying for the award is seen as help in developing the prison in a positive way, raising the standing of the prison in the Scottish Prison Service, enhancing the prison's profile in the local community and involving all the staff in continuous improvement in the quality of services.

Belfast City Council – Building Control Service

Faced, in common with other local authority building control services, with having to compete with other providers Belfast City Council Building Control Service decided to spend even more time focusing on the needs of its customers. By 1992 the service had reorganized, begun a process of user-consultation, introduced performance standards, instituted a formal complaints system and produced a range of information leaflets. Having decided that they were offering an excellent service which was worthy of formal recognition through the Charter Mark the service involved its forty-six professional and support staff in working towards making an application. Making contact with other building control services enabled them to undertake some comparative analysis of their performance which they used to fine-tune areas requiring improvement. They consider that winning the Charter Mark has provided marketing and publicity benefits together with recognition for the staff of their efforts and commitment.

King Edward's Medical Centre, Ruislip, Middlesex

This case example is of particular interest because of the relatively small size of the organization – a two-doctor practice providing primary care for 3000 patients. Following their nomination for a Charter Mark by one of their patients (to be followed later by another fourteen nominations) the Centre decided that it was a worthwhile award and worth pursuing. Drawing support from their local Health Agency who provided statistical information on the Centre's performance and other help, the Centre completed the application form. They updated their practice booklet and made their complaints procedure more formal (even though they did not have any complaints!). Following the assessment visit they were told of their success which they consider has been good for staff morale and given them added impetus for further improvements to the service they offer patients.

Source: Cabinet Office (1996).

Summary

Managing resources to ensure that they are meeting customer requirements as economically, efficiently and effectively as possible requires, first of all, a clear picture of what customers' real requirements are. It is therefore important for you and your staff to get 'closer to the customer'. This is particularly important if your service is dealing directly with the end-user or external customer, although it is not possible to provide a high quality service to the end user without all the internal customer–supplier links being in place and working well. So, as with many aspects of management, excellent customer service requires you to be able to look, Janus-like, both out from your organization to its environment and inwards to assess its performance. There are many opportunities and methods available to you to identify the requirements of internal and external customers, identify opportunities for improvement and plan an appropriate response. Improvement plans need to be prepared in consultation with all the key stakeholders, especially customers and staff, effectively communicated and closely monitored. Once you have achieved gains in service quality your job has by no means ended and you will also need to expend a fair amount of effort in ensuring that the gains are held. Planning, managing and reviewing the changes required present excellent opportunities for learning at the levels of the individual, team and organization. Actively seizing these opportunities and exploiting them to the full means that all involved will be more able to meet the challenge of the next change effort as the organization transforms itself in pursuit of continuous improvement in the quality of its services and levels of customer care. Once this process is established in your organization you may wish to consider having your achievement recognized through an award such as the Charter Mark.

Action points and discussion points

(Items in italics are intended to encourage the reader to develop a greater intellectual awareness, items in plain type are focused upon work-related activity.)

Manage activities to meet customer requirements

Using your own experience as a customer think of occasions when you have been impressed by examples of good service, and annoyed by bad service. What criteria are you using when you define 'good' and 'bad' in this context? Do you find yourself using different criteria for different types of organization, e.g. a retail store and a restaurant? What does your analysis tell you about the processes by which customers evaluate quality and customer service?

Within your own organization list the main end-users of the output of your work and that of your staff. Then list the key responsibilities and tasks which you all have. Which of these key responsibilities and tasks relate most directly to meeting the needs of these end-users? How do you ensure that the end-users are satisfied with what you do? What ways are there in which you can adapt or improve the way you manage yourself and others in order to enhance end-user satisfaction?

Implement quality assurance systems

Using the systematic approach to quality management offered in this chapter evaluate your organization's performance at each stage of the model. What opportunities for improvement present themselves? How can you contribute, in the short, medium and long term, to these improvements?

Target an organization in the private sector which has a recognized quality assurance and management system in place (i.e. BS5750/ISO9000) and discover what you can about the way that the organization achieved the standard and maintains it. This may entail talking with people in the organization, reading reports of their approach in the press, books on quality management, getting hold of company reports and similar means. How does their approach to quality assurance differ from that which you have experienced in the public sector? What could the public sector teach them, and vice versa?

Review internal and external operating environments/Evaluate and improve organizational performance

Conduct some research into those organizations in your area of work, or associated areas, who have achieved a 'Charter Mark'. How did they achieve the award? How were customers/users and staff involved in the process? What have they done following the award to continue to improve standards of service delivery and value for money. What could your organization learn from this experience?

Establish strategies to guide the work of the organization

What are the major issues involved in managing the needs of overall corporate control of quality and customer care and the advantages for as much local autonomy as possible? How are these issues managed in organizations with which you are familiar?

Evaluate and improve organizational performance

How does your organization communicate with its customers? Which communication techniques are working particularly well, and why? How can communication with customers be improved? Who should be responsible for these improvements?

How do organizations attempt to influence customers' perceptions of quality and customer service? Are these management techniques always in the customer's best interests?

Determine the effective use of resources

How much (or what proportion) of your organization's budget is devoted to directly meeting the needs of its end-users or customers, i.e. how much of the total budget is spent on 'support services' and other activities? How much of the budget is spent on finding out (a) what customers want and (b) how satisfied they are with the services they receive? To what extent is this balance the correct one, in your opinion? How does it compare with other organizations?

How 'customer focused' are you in monitoring expenditure for which you are responsible? How do you measure the impact of your spending decisions on your customers? Decide one major step you could take personally to improve the cost effectiveness of your area of responsibility, and take it.

Develop teams and individuals to enhance performance

As a manager, to what extent do you encourage and reward your staff for taking a positive, proactive approach to quality and customer care? What opportunities for improvement in this area are you missing, and how can you take advantage of them in the future?

Further reading

Drucker, P.F. (1995). *Managing the Non-profit Organization*. Butterworth-Heinemann.
A general text for managers in not-for-profit organizations and charities, with chapters on marketing and performance management.

Gaster, L. (1995). *Quality in Public Services: Managers' Choices*. Open University Press.
A review of quality management across the public sector. A particularly useful text for managers pursuing management qualifications because it effectively bridges the gap which sometimes exists between academic research and review and the pragmatics of managerial practice. Thought provoking and offering no 'quick fixes'.

Local Government Management Board (1993). *Learning from Consumers and Citizens*. LGMB.
Offers some ideas on strategies and activities for involving customers.

Palmer, A. (1994). *Principles of Services Marketing*. McGraw-Hill.
Covers all aspects of marketing services, including market research, service quality and the human elements of service delivery. Good coverage of public sector services.

Part Four Broader Issues and the Public Sector

9 The strategic perspective

Aims and learning objectives

The aims of this chapter are to introduce you to the strategic perspective. Involvement in strategy distinguishes the middle level or more senior manager from her/his more junior colleague. Strategy is an area where there is no shortage of writers. It is easily possible to feel overwhelmed when confronted with such a selection of authors.

We have sought to focus this chapter very much upon the public and not-for-profit sector in the UK. That does not mean, however, that influences from across the Atlantic are irrelevant. Henry Mintzberg (whose work was discussed in Chapter 2) makes another appearance. You will also be introduced to John Bryson's key work on strategic planning in the non-profit sector.

A vital point to hold onto as you read this chapter is that strategy is only learned by practice. There are, we hope, sufficient demonstrations of the techniques in this chapter to encourage you to do this.

At the end of this chapter, and associated activities and reading, you will be able to:

- understand the context of strategic planning and management as it operates in the public sector setting
- understand what characterizes strategic decisions from operational ones
- be aware of different patterns of strategic development
- appreciate the variables which affect the strategic process
- be introduced to a series of steps in making and implementing strategy
- be able to carry out some straightforward analytical techniques
- be familiar with planning aspects in the change process.

The strategic perspective

The nature of strategic management

Strategic decisions are characterized by one of the leading texts on strategic management (Johnson and Scholes, 1993, pp. 5–10) as possessing the following characteristics:

1 They relate to the scope of an organization's activities.
2 They involve matching the activities of the organization to the environment in which it operates.

3 Similarly they involve matching activities to resources and in particular the resource capacity.
4 Therefore strategic decisions have major resource implications and affect the operational decisions which the organization takes.
5 The values and expectations of the stakeholders in the organization will have a significant effect.
6 A strategic decision is likely to have longer term implications.

Robert Smith (1994, p. 16) talks about the evolution from strategic planning to strategic management as a 'move away from centralized, mathematical and deterministic systems through coordinated systems employing soft rather than hard analytical techniques, to flexible delegated and supportive systems'.

In this chapter we will use the term strategic planning on occasion referring to the process by which strategy is formulated. We would stress that strategic management is implicit in this process.

In the public and not-for-profit sector the context of the organization is crucial. Some voluntary organizations are more able to make major decisions because they are freer from the legislative and political constraints which affect public sector organizations. An expert on the voluntary sector commented to one author that voluntary sector overseas aid organizations had been able to be more effective in famine countries than the governmental bodies. A key factor had been that they had been able to adopt a strategy of simply taking hard cash into the countries in suitcases. They then used that cash to directly purchase and distribute food stocks. Government overseas aid organizations were constrained in how they could use their resources by the need to account for spending and to direct spending through 'approved' usually official channels.

The political dimension is ever present in the public sector. The implication is that strategy is often guided by electoral or media considerations which are frequently short term. In the public sector there is often the absence of private sector (for-profit) success criteria such as return on equity or market share. This means that the effect of a strategic decision tends to be measured by the positive column inches it gets in the press and whether it receives a favourable sound bite on *News at Ten*. The rapid creation of the Cones Hotline was very much in this mould. In September 1995 the Cones Hotline was quietly consigned to the dustbin of history – a measure perhaps of making strategic decisions with an eye to short-term rather than long-term considerations.

Background of strategy

Box 9.1 provides a number of definitions of what strategy is about. They are listed in time sequence – that of Johnson and Scholes being an exception because their book has gone through three editions! You will observe that the definitions have changed over time.

Box 9.1   Definitions of strategy

The word comes from the Greek for *stratos* (army) and *ag* (to lead).

The art of war, especially the planning of movements of troops and ships etc ... into favourable positions; plan of action or policy in business or politics etc.

Oxford Dictionary

The determination of the long-run goals and objectives of an enterprise, and the adoption of courses of action and the allocation of resources necessary for carrying out these goals.

Alfred Chandler (1962)

Strategy in the pattern of objectives, purposes or goals and the major policies and plans for achieving these goals, stated in such a way as to define what business the company is in or is to be in and the kind of company it is or is to be.

Kenneth Andrews (1971)

A strategy is the pattern or plan that integrates an organization's major goals, policies, and action sequences into a cohesive role. A well-formulated strategy helps to marshal and allocate an organization's resources into a unique and viable posture based upon its relative internal competences and shortcomings, anticipated changes in the environment, and contingent move by intelligent opponents.

James Brian Quinn (1980)

What business strategy is all about is, in a word, competitive advantage...

Kenichi Ohmae (1982)

The direction and scope of an organization over the long term: ideally, which matches its resources to its changing environment, and in particular its markets, customers or clients so as to meet stakeholder expectations.

Johnson and Scholes (1993)

> Our framework departs from [the] linear model in a number of ways. It regards the linear rational model of strategy as at best providing a single probe. Yet in reality managers do not have the privilege of the comprehensive information such models assume. ... The processes by which strategic change are made seldom move through neat successive stages of analysis, choice and implementation.
>
> Pettigrew and Whipp (1991)

Indeed Robert Grant, an American writer, has neatly conceptualized the evolution of strategic management into time periods. Each period he regards as having a dominant theme, a main focus, principal concepts and techniques and organizational implications. Figure 9.1 shows Robert Grant's conception.

Robert Grant's conception of time periods is useful but it cannot be assumed that all organizations progress at the same speed irrespective of whether they are in the private, public or independent sector.

	Dominant theme	Main focus	Principal concepts and techniques	Organizational implications
1950s	Budgetary planning	Financial control	Budgeting and investment appraisal	Financial management as key
1960s	Corporate planning	Planning growth	Market forecasting	Planning department
1970s	Corporate strategy	Portfolio planning	Analyse strategic business units	Integrate strategic and financial control
Late 1970s and early 1980s	Industry and competitor analysis	Choice of industries and markets and positioning	Analysis of industry structure and competitor analysis	Divestment of unattractive business units
Late 1980s and early 1990s	Quest for competitive advantage	Sources of competitive advantage within firm	Resource analysis and organizational competence	Corporate restructuring and business process re-engineering

Figure 9.1 *The evolution of strategic management*
Source: Grant (1995).

Elsewhere in this book we make reference to the UK Government's 'Financial Management Initiative' (see Chapter 3). Arguably this would be seen as a Budgetary Planning and Control approach in Grant's typology. Grant writes about for-profit organizations. If such an organization was still trying, in strategic terms, to operate simply via budget planning then it would be regarded as still stuck in the 1950s.

The strategic focus in much of local government has been on financial control over the recent years. Should this be seen to imply that, strategically speaking, local authorities are forty years behind the current private sector strategic focus? Or is it more the case that the public and not-for-profit sector is strategically different. There are many stakeholders and strategy is often inextricably bound up with political issues. Success is not always measurable in the ways available in the private sector.

Later when we consider Bryson's approach we will look at how the definition of strategic planning in the public and not-for-profit sector may differ from definitions used by authors writing about the private sector.

Levels of strategic decisions

Strategy is applicable not only to organizations but also to parts of them or even to individuals within the organization. Robert Grant uses the interesting examples of Madonna and General Giap (the North Vietnamese military commander) to demonstrate the importance of individuals as much as organization in recognizing opportunity.

When people are asked to name individuals in the public sector who have been crucial to strategic decision making the tendency is to mention either military leaders (Eisenhower or Montgomery) or politicians (Margaret Thatcher or Mao-tse Tung). Within the voluntary sector there is wider scope – Mother Teresa, Leonard Cheshire, Chad Varah, Dr Bernardo. In part this is because the opportunity to create a whole new organization is available.

However strategic decision making takes place at a number of levels. At the highest level there is corporate strategy to determine the kind of business which the organization should be involved in or the global issues over allocation of resources and scope of activities. Issues concerning the overall structure of the organization would be corporate ones.

In the public sector in the UK the recent decision to merge the Department for Employment and the Department for Education would be at this level. There was surprisingly little discussion about the merits of the merger beforehand and comments made by the Permanent Secretary of one of the Departments concerned suggest that there had been relatively little consultation.

In the voluntary sector the decision which the Spastic Society made to change its name to SCOPE was clearly a corporate one. One of the authors was aware of discussions which had been going on for some years about a name change. The decision was a major one because it reflected a desire to change the 'scope' of the organization's remit to move it away from the parents as stakeholders and towards the disabled person as a stakeholder in the organization.

The second level is described in the literature as 'business level'. Strategy is seen as making decisions whether to compete in a particular market and over which products or services to offer and develop. Such decisions are obviously influenced by the 'global or corporate' objectives set at the higher level. In the public sector this often is demonstrated through decisions about whether to provide certain services. In the NHS there is a clear move away from the provision of hospital beds to meet chronic health problems – in particular those associated with old age. Rather the hospitals have been looking to private nursing homes as a more appropriate resource. In effect it is a decision to 'not compete' in that particular market. The reference point in terms of 'corporate strategy' is not necessarily any clear instruction to close down geriatric chronic provision. Rather it is implied in objectives which require maximum patient turnover and focus hospitals towards acute care.

The third level is the 'operational' one. Some writers (Johnson and Scholes) identify this as where the functional elements of the organization (finance, marketing etc.) make their own individual contribution. In the public sector there is a great deal of activity at the operational level. In local government and the health service the 'Care in the Community' focus gets translated into operational plans. In the Benefits Agency the intention to make the Job Centres more 'customer focused' took effect through the actions of local managers in removing the barriers and setting up carpeted foyers with staff sporting name badges.

Mintzberg on strategy

Henry Mintzberg has had a key influence upon the development of thinking about how strategy is formulated. He suggests that strategic formulation does not take place evenly; rather there are different patterns of strategic change. The patterns can in some ways be compared to the behaviour of the surface of an ocean. The water in an ocean offers the following kinds of behaviour:

- There is the incremental adjustments represented by the rise and fall of the tide.
- There are aspects which offer continuity such as the deep ocean currents which change little over time.
- There are periods of flux and uncertainty which could be typified by storms which agitate the surface of the sea.
- There are occasional major transformations such as perhaps a tidal wave caused by volcanic eruption.

Similarly there are different patterns of strategic change in the public sector. Examples in the UK might be as follows:

- Incremental: The regular review and adjustments to interest rates made through government policy.
- Continuity: The long period of post Second World War political consensus which accepted the welfare state.
- Flux: The ongoing strategic uncertainty in some areas of government policy such as health service funding.
- Transformational: The privatization of large areas of the UK public sector over the past fifteen years.

This model of patterns of strategy operates not simply at national government level but can be found throughout the governmental and voluntary sector.

Through his later work Mintzberg also looked at differences between intended strategies and actual outcomes. He suggests that there are pure forms of strategy which can help understand the way in which strategy is arrived at in organizations.

Deliberate strategy is defined by three conditions.

1 There must have been precise intentions in the organization to set out in some detail what was intended.
2 These intentions must have been held in common by the members of the organization.
3 Events must have worked out exactly as intended without any surprises.

Emergent strategy requires that there must have been no intention to have achieved the actual consequence from the actions taken.

Obviously it is unlikely that many strategic situations would fit in either of these categories – though it is possible. Few actions by public bodies come very close to the deliberate strategy model – such as the gradual reduction of the value of mortgage interest relief (MIRAS) by the UK Conservative Government over recent years. Emergent strategy seems more amenable to examples from the UK public sector. As Harold Wilson memorably observed a week is a long time in politics. Strategic decisions may be made as almost a knee-jerk reaction to current media issues. The sudden announcement by ministers of the merger of the Department of Employment and the Department of Education appeared to have even caught the top staff of these large government departments by surprise. Arguably the decision was made for largely political reasons to try to seize an initiative over unemployment as an issue.

Deliberate and emergent strategies are, as we said earlier, almost pure forms which mark the end points of a continuum of strategy. Mintzberg and Waters suggest that between these two extremes lie a

Type	Characteristics	Example
DELIBERATE	Totally intended and happens to plan	Reduction in Mortgage Interest Relief (MIRAS)
Planned	Detailed plans in a predictable environment	Relocation of government agencies outside London
Entrepreneurial	Plan directed by individual vision 'imposed' on organization (or part they control) – adaptable	Setting up of Live Aid by Bob Geldof
Ideological	Where the vision is shared by organization members	Conservative party policy on contracting out local authority services
Umbrella	Where control is relaxed perhaps because of a complex environment	Allocation of government research funds
Process	Leadership exercise control through influence	Appointments to quangos
Unconnected	Where part of an organization goes its own way	Personal agendas in universities
Consensus	Strategy emerges through consensus	Decisions of the synod of the Church of England
Imposed	Strategy is imposed upon the organization from outside the organization	Leaving the Exchange Rate Mechanism; capping the Council Tax
EMERGENT		

Figure 9.2 *A continuum of strategic types*

series of mid points. In a simple form Figure 9.2 demonstrates our interpretation of these mid points using examples from the UK public sector. The examples we offer may, we hope, lead you to try to match examples from your own experience.

Strategic planning for management in the not-for-profit sector

In 1988 in the USA John Bryson wrote an influential book aimed specifically at this sector and practically orientated towards managers and policy makers (Bryson, 1995). Subsequently authors in the UK have picked up on and developed Bryson's model (Willcocks and Harrow, 1992).

Strategy has been frequently defined and redefined by authors writing either about the private sector or with the movements of armies or nations in mind. (Box 9.1 gives a number of such definitions.) Though some definitions, such as that of Johnson and Scholes (1993), seek to be all embracing, much of the flavour of the definitions relies on concepts such as 'competitive advantage' and 'opponents'.

Bryson (1995, p. 5) took strategic planning to mean:

a disciplined effort to produce fundamental decisions and actions that shape and guide what an organization (or other entity) is, what it does, and why it does it. At its best, strategic planning requires broad scale information gathering, an exploration of alternatives, an emphasis on the present implications of future decision. It can facilitate communication and participation, accommodate divergent interests and values, and foster orderly decision making and successful implementation.

Writing more recently in a purely UK public sector context Robert Smith (1994) identified four main purposes of strategic planning as follows:

1 Clarity of purpose which involved establishing a sense of direction, setting priorities and sharing common values.
2 Obtaining a unity of purpose behind the mission statement, corporate objectives and core values through participation in the planning process. This means formulating strategy both from the top and from the bottom of the organization in order to win commitment. It also implies that strategy formulation should be a learning process.
3 Achievement of purpose which involves ensuring that the strategy is feasible, is adequately resourced and that responsibility for implementation is clearly apportioned and communicated.
4 Strategic planning provides a framework for day-to-day decisions using such concepts as delegation, monitoring and mechanisms to handle the unexpected.

Johnson and Scholes (1993) also consider the characteristics of strategic management in the public sector and not-for-profit organizations. They note that though there are some areas of the public sector which are similar to the private sector there are some fundamental differences. In particular they draw attention to the following factors (1993, pp. 28–29):

- the political dimension associated with funding
- the existence of monopoly or quasi-monopoly
- competition is often for resources rather than for markets
- ideology plays a greater role.

Where not-for-profit organizations are concerned Johnson and Scholes stress the impact of stakeholder groups and sources of funding. Figure 9.3 shows how they perceive the characteristics of strategic management in not-for-profit organizations.

In the next section we will take you through the key steps in strategic planning. This is based upon Bryson's model but utilizes some additional techniques which we feel are valuable.

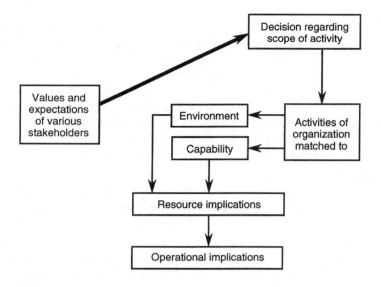

Figure 9.3   *Strategic decisions in the public and not-for-profit sector*

Source: Johnson and Scholes (1993).

Key steps in the strategy process

Bryson sets out an eight-step process to facilitate strategic thought and action. The stages are as follows:

1   Initiate and agree on a strategic planning process.
2   Identify what the organizational mandate is.
3   Clarify the organizational mission and values.
4   Assess the external environment (opportunities and threats).
5   Assess the internal environment (strengths and weaknesses).
6   Identify the strategic issues.
7   Formulate strategies to manage the issues.
8   Establish a vision for the future.

He compares successful strategic planning to telling a good story. A good story would possess the following ingredients:

● an appropriate setting
● relevant themes
● plots and subplots
● actors
● scenes
● a beginning, middle and conclusion
● interpretation.

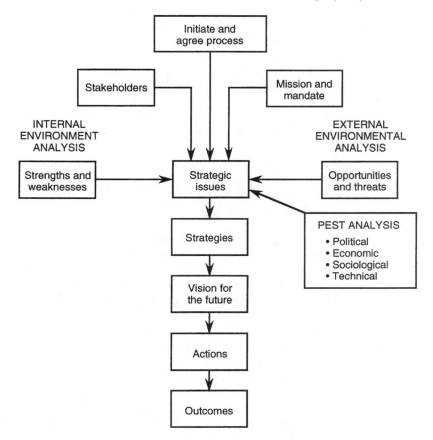

Figure 9.4 *A simplified model of strategic planning in the public and not-for-profit sector*

Source: Bryson (1995).

Bryson's framework is shown in diagrammatic form in Figure 9.4. We will now follow through this framework in more detail.

Initiate and agree

Bryson (1995, p. 73) notes that:

> the purpose of the first step in the process is to develop among key internal decision makers or opinion leaders (and, if their support is necessary for the success of the effort, key external leaders as well) an initial agreement about the overall strategic planning effort and main planning steps.

The agreement Bryson envisages would relate to four issues:

- the importance of the strategic planning itself
- those who should be involved
- the actual steps or stages in strategic planning
- the form which any reports would take
- when any reports would be required.

Robert Smith (1994) comments that strategic planning used to generate the following concerns:

- It had become an end in itself with the process owned by planners rather than managers.
- It had become an annual event which once completed was forgotten about until the next year.

In the late 1970s one of the authors attended a course where some of the other participants were planners in the National Health Service. The planners described the effort which they put into drafting strategic plans for their regions. When the author asked what happened to the plans afterwards there was an embarrassed pause and one of the planners finally remarked that they were 'stored in a cupboard' and, as far as he knew, hardly had any impact upon the strategic direction of his health authority. Further discussion revealed that the planners functioned as a separate part of their health authority and prepared the strategic plans with only limited participation from others outside their section. Their main communication with medical consultants and senior administrators lay in making requests for information from them. The planners had virtually no direct contact with members of the Health Authority who were supposed to make strategic decisions.

In contrast the Government set up the Resource Allocation Working Party (RAWP) which involved a range of key people and set a clear strategic direction for reallocation of health service resources between London and other health regions. The membership of the working party and the political commitment to the outcome made the planning process more effective.

The lesson is clear. Unless there is agreement over the process at the outset and key groups or individuals are involved then the outcome is likely to be another addition to a dusty shelf in a cupboard – even if the plan offers a desirable and appropriate strategy for the organization!

Mission and objectives

The term 'mission statement' has become widely used in the business vocabulary of management and management education. It is part of the organizational rhetoric of the 1990s. Many public sector and voluntary organizations have taken the notion of mission on board. But in reality the concept of 'mission' has a long and distinguished history in the voluntary sector.

Mike Hudson (1995, p. 93), writing about not-for-profit or 'third-sector organizations', points out:

> Missions are concerned more with an organization's **common beliefs** and the **reasons why it exists**. People who work in third-sector organizations are usually motivated by a deeply held desire to help change society. Consequently most third-sector organizations have a strong sense of mission.

Sometimes the mission lies with a strongly held view of the organization's founder. William Smith founded the Boy's Brigade with a distinctly Christian objective. He felt that by using military concepts he could reach out to boys who were otherwise reluctant attenders at Sunday School. Baden-Powell wrote a book for the Boys' Brigade entitled *Scouting for Boys*. Subsequently Baden-Powell founded the Boy Scouts. Why did Baden-Powell found a separate organization? It certainly wasn't to compete with Smith – by all accounts the two men were the best of friends. Rather it was because Baden-Powell saw a different mission – he was primarily concerned with the concepts of scouting and citizenship rather than with using scouting as a means of propagating the gospel.

The later history of the two organizations are shaped by the different mission of the founders. The Scouts have reached out well beyond the Christian faith and are to be found, for example, in Muslim countries, and they rapidly moved to offer scouting to girls. The Boy's Brigade has stayed close to both its male remit and Christian focus.

A mission statement for an organization helps answer these questions:

- *What* is the organization's purpose?
- *Why* should it be doing what it does?
- *What* should the organization look like?
- *How* should the organization behave?

Here values are often all important and the views of key stakeholders should be sought to ensure that these values are accurately recorded.

Stakeholders are people who wish to and are able to affect the future of the organization. Robert Smith (1994) identifies four categories of power or influence which stakeholders might possess:

- Resource power – often through seniority in the organization.
- Political power – which has an indirect (or sometimes direct) influence over resource allocation.

- Production power – often possessed by people whose actions are necessary for implementation of strategy.
- Environmental power – through influence on the regulatory framework or the marketplace of the organization.

Key steps in a stakeholder analysis would include identifying:

1 who they are
2 their significance to the organization
3 what they expect of the organization.

Therefore in Table 9.1 we set out a stakeholder analysis of a university. This is simplified and does not encompass all the stakeholders who could conceivably be considered. The governing board, publishers, local schools, careers service, etc. are amongst many stakeholders who could be added.

A stakeholder analysis will influence and inform what is described by Bryson (1995) as the 'mandates' of the organization. Mandates indicate what the organization is expected to do. Robert Smith (1994) suggests that it establishes the boundaries between:

1 What MUST be done.
2 What COULD be done.
3 What MUST NOT be done.

The university example is quite interesting to follow in this respect. Clearly there is a mandate to educate and award degrees to those who pass. There is also a mandate to promote research activity. What is the university not able to do? You would say that the university cannot sell degrees to students unless they meet the educational requirements. A suggestion that a university had in fact done this created much comment in the academic and popular press.

In the public domain managers must be constantly aware of the limit of their organizational mandate. Activity which in the private sector would be seen as entrepreneurial and rewarded if successful may, in the public domain, be penalized whether or not it is successful.

During one author's early days in social work he was aware of a practice for dealing with school truancy. Certain social workers used to take funds which were meant to cover outings and expenses for children in care and used the money to bribe persistent truants to go to school. It was highly effective. Yet if the use of the money had come to the notice of senior managers or politicians there is little doubt that it would have led to severe criticism. Advising and supporting children to help them back into school was part of the mandate – paying cold cash to the individual child was not.

Table 9.1 Stakeholder analysis of a university

Stakeholder	Strength	Importance	Main expectations
Current students	• Voice opinions and influence next intake • Limited ability to leave	• Limited power unless expressed collectively	• To be educated • To receive a degree • To have a social life • To have post university prospects
Prospective students	• Able to choose whether to come to university	• Seen as vital and courted assiduously	
Parents of students	• Able to influence student • Often power to influence others (polititians etc.)	• Seen as important in influencing student decision	• Quality of education • Career prospect • Reputation
Academic staff	• Knowledge of subject • Tenure (in some cases)	• Dependent on individual academic	• Research opportunity • Professional development • Job security • Academic freedom
Non-academic staff	• Knowledge of systems • Trade Union base	• Limited impact on organization	• Job security
University managers	• Authority of position • Control of budgets	• Key in setting strategic direction	• Career prospects • Control of resources
Employers	• Influence of managers • Provision of endowments • Careers for graduates • Work placements	• Depends on company (some very strong)	• Usable graduates • Useful research
Funding councils	• Ability to award funds • Require statistics • Conduct audits	• Vital to resourcing and academic standing	• Accountability • Efficiency • Reports and figures

Environmental analysis

Bryson (1995) builds his analysis around a simple technique with an easily remembered acronym – SWOT. It is an analytical technique which is taught to probably every management and business studies student in the UK and in the USA.

However we will start with another widely taught technique with an equally easily remembered acronym – PESTeL. The letters stand for:

Political
Economic
Social
Technical
Legal

It is used to identify the key trends in the environment *outside* the organization which would or could have an impact upon the strategy which the organization is following or might follow in the future. The key questions to be asked are:

1   What environmental factors are affecting the organization?
2   Which of these are the most important now?
3   Which will be most important in the future?

Figure 9.5 sets out a typical PESTeL analysis for a Local Authority Social Services Department.

Johnson and Scholes (1993) note that a PESTeL analysis which just leads to a list of influences is of limited strategic value. But it is useful in drawing out:

● the key environmental influences
● the long-term factors which are driving change
● the key trends identified by the influences.

So looking at Figure 9.5 it is apparent that political influences are going to be highly significant. The reorganization of the health service and changes in local government structure are going to be key factors.

Changing population demographics represent a continuing trend which will have implications for social services departments. An ageing population combined with poor educational attainment and a growing need for a more highly skilled work force to meet the challenge of more technology in social work.

Let us now look at a different approach to analysing the organizational environment. The Open University in its Strategic Management course describes a model of environmental analysis as a process

POLITICAL

- Possible change in government
- Change in structure of local authority
- Local government reorganization
- Health services reorganization

ECONOMIC

- Cuts in local authority finance
- Customer/value for £ focus – charters
- Negative equity amongst local homeowners
- Increased number of private sector care organizations

SOCIAL

- Ageing local population
- Poor education results
- Increase in family breakdown
- Concern about mentally ill in community

TECHNICAL

- Increased use of computers in social work
- Use of more sophisticated aids for handicapped
- Increased skills required of staff
- Calculating service charges

LEGAL

- Compulsory Competitive Tendering
- Community Care Legislation
- Child Care Legislation

Figure 9.5 *PEST analysis for Local Authority Social Services Department*

(Fahey and Narayanan, 1986). Environmental analysis is presented as four stages:

1 Scanning. There is an overall examination of all aspects of the environment to recognize signs of change at an early stage. The information available at this stage is often incomplete and ambiguous. For example the first signs of AIDS emerged in the 1970s. At that time little was known other than the growing belief amongst doctors and researchers that there was a new disease process at work. Because there is uncertainty over what is important the range of data collected is very wide.

2 Monitoring. During this stage data are collected with a view to establishing whether they indicate a definite trend. There is a focus upon particular kinds of information which are collected in

order to either confirm whether a particular pattern or trend exists. Using the example of AIDS some of the initial monitoring looked at whether it was a disease which was transmitted through gay sexual contacts linked to bath-houses.

3   Forecasting. The next stage is to look forward and try to predict what will happen in the future. Will the trend be short lived or will it prove to be long term? Is it linear or will it go in cycles? The early forecasts of AIDS mortality (death) and morbidity (illness) in the gay community have proven inaccurate in several ways. One explanation is that the gay community has very quickly adjusted to the disease and so limited the spread. On the other hand the spread of AIDS in the heterosexual community in some countries has been greater than anticipated.

4   Assessment. The final stage involves looking at what the implications of the trend or change might be for the organization. Using the AIDS example this would mean planning the number of hospital beds and community health facilities which will be needed now and in the future.

The SWOT analysis referred to previously is a convenient and simple technique which links both External and Internal Environmental Analysis. Figure 9.6 shows a SWOT analysis for a voluntary housing association. The strengths and weaknesses relate to internal aspects of the association's environment. The opportunities and threats are concerned with the association's external environment.

STRENGTHS

- Long-served staff
- Local knowledge
- Good links with local authority
- Good reputation with tenants

OPPORTUNITIES ——————————————— THREATS

- Bid for local authority work
- Merge with larger housing association
- Get government grant to expand

- Takeover by another housing association
- 'Right to buy' of current tenants
- Failure to secure government grant

WEAKNESSES

- Financial control
- High cost base
- Limited number of staff

Figure 9.6   *SWOT analysis for a voluntary housing association*

The external threats and weaknesses could very well be derived from a PESTeL kind of analysis as outlined previously. Bryson (1995), in his model, also suggests the following external forces which might be associated with threats or opportunities:

- Clients/customers/payers
- Competitors
- Collaborators.

We would also add the importance of stakeholders who are external to the organization. One of the London health districts became well known for its expertise in the AIDS field. As a result a number of people from outside its catchment area would travel in for both HIV testing and consultation. Clearly any proposal to limit geographically that district's resources would generate an angry response from this group of stakeholders.

The internal strengths and weaknesses analysis should, following Bryson (1995), examine the following:

- the inputs (resources)
- the present strategy (process of managing resources)
- the outputs (performance).

In the public sector organizations usually have a wealth of information about their inputs. Staffing, budgets, materials and supplies data are all available. This should not always be assumed though. One author has vivid memories of some business planning consultancy work for a London borough where a week was spent arguing over how many staff were employed.

The present strategy may be unclear, though. The top management of the organization may believe that resources are being managed in a particular fashion which in fact differs markedly from the way they are managed in reality. The succession of recent inquiries into residential homes certainly would suggest that this happens not infrequently.

Unlike the private sector where there is a clear and measurable outcome in terms of product or profit, the public sector has difficulty in establishing outputs. Norman Flynn has written cogently about this dilemma which confronts public services (Flynn, 1994).

The Audit Commission has sought to establish a wide range of performance indicators in local government and the health service. But the dilemma will of necessity continue. When do you measure the success of an outcome of a child coming into care? Most social work professionals find it hard to answer such a question. Some would say, and with just cause, that you can only really measure success of taking a child into care by looking at whether that child is able to become an adult and undertake the role of parent and citizen. Yet the operation of a Social Services child care strategy requires measures that we do not have to wait twenty years for.

Alan Lawrie in his 1995 guide to business and strategic planning for voluntary organizations offers the following hints in carrying out a SWOT analysis:

- People often find it easier to list weaknesses and threats. It helps if you insist that people list an equal number of strengths and opportunities.
- A weakness identified by one person might be perceived as a strength by another. It is important to probe the reasons behind such apparent contradictions.
- Sometimes it is unclear whether something is a threat or an opportunity.
- There is a tendency to spend too much time thinking how to redress identified weaknesses and not enough time analysing what is associated with a strength.

Issue identification

Bryson (1995) sees this step as having two outcomes:

1 A list of the strategic issues which the organization confronts.
2 Some prioritization of these issues.

In the example he offers (p. 140) of a local authority in the USA, what is involved is a brief outline of each issue, a discussion of the factors which make it a strategic issue for the organization and an indication of the implication of failing to deal with it.

Bryson then goes on to outline three approaches to identifying strategic issues:

- The direct approach. Here after carrying out the mandate, mission and SWOT you proceed to specify the strategic issues. This is demonstrated in Bryson 1995 (p. 140).
- The goals approach. Here the organization determines goals and objectives and then works out strategies to address them.
- 'Vision of success' approach. Here the organization seeks to imagine what it would look like as and when it succeeds in carrying out its mission. The strategic issues will relate to shifting the organization from where it is now to where the future vision is.

In Figure 9.7 we set out a 'best fit' guide based upon Bryson's (1995) model. This indicates the characteristics of organizations which fit best with the different issue identification approaches.

Bryson also stresses that you need to consider the priorities of dif-

	Direct approach	Goals approach	'Vision' approach
Nature of political environment	Dominant Coalition	Consensus over goals is possible	No current goals or objectives
Nature of organization	Pluralistic Partisan Fragmented	Hierarchical and top down	Loose and less hierarchy 'Community groups'
Number of stakeholders	Many but agreement possible	Limited	May be many sharing power
Example	Local authority with ruling party	Central Government Department/Next Steps Agency	Community-based voluntary group

Figure 9.7 *Identifying the best fit*

ferent issues. Some will not be urgent in the immediate future; they can be kept under review. Others can be dealt with under current procedures. Finally there are some issues which require special and immediate attention.

Strategy formulation

We must always remember that in the public sector strategy does not begin with an empty sheet of paper. There is a history of previous decisions or policy. This may, using Mintzberg's approach, have not been a deliberate formulation of strategy. Nevertheless it will have created a perception of how strategy is made and where the limits are.

Bryson (1995) suggests an approach which asks five questions about each issue which has been identified. The following questions are based upon Bryson but extended by us to be more practical for managers in the public sector.

1 What are the *alternatives* available to deal with the issue?
2 What are the *barriers*?
3 What *proposals* might either accomplish an alternative or overcome a barrier?
4 What *criteria* will be used to select from available proposals?
5 What must we do *within the next year*?
6 What must we do *within the next six months*?
7 What must we do *almost immediately*?

Alternatives

There is a wide range of techniques used to generate alternatives. Brainstorming is widely taught to managers (though often in an overly simplistic way). If done properly it should succeed in generating a wide range of ideas to address a particular issue. If you wish to look at an easily accessible discussion and description of a range of techniques then you might find it helpful to look at a more focused text, such as Murdock and Scutt (1994) – especially Chapter 4.

Barriers

In the for-profit sector the barriers are usually fairly straightforward. The required rate of return may be higher than the alternative offers; the organization may lack expertise or resources to carry it out.

However in the public and voluntary sector there are more diverse barriers. There is often a wide range of stakeholders whose concerns might represent a major barrier to a particular alternative. The proposal to change the name of the Spastics Society to SCOPE encountered considerable opposition from internal stakeholders. In contrast the decision to divide a huge UK company (ICI) into two parts and name the new part Zeneca was a market oriented decision.

The barriers are frequently less quantifiable in the public sector. Staff, especially in the voluntary sector, may be motivated by values and ethos. It is hard to think of any private sector organization whose staff would willingly and at considerable personal risk occupy abandoned oil rigs or sail boats into areas where nuclear tests are due to take place as Greenpeace staff have recently done. When staff are strongly value driven then this can create a barrier to change. Such people are not persuaded by personal gain (or threat) and may be resistant to factual evidence.

Proposals

Inviting proposals is the next key question. In the public sector there is a wide range of practices over how this takes place. Some organizations require that managers offer a choice of proposals to address an issue. When politicians are involved they feel that simply agreeing or referring back a proposal is not sufficient; rather they would wish to have several options offered. In our experience the frequent tactical response of managers to such a sentiment is to offer three proposals, two of which will almost certainly be rejected by the politicians. In short the politicians are given the illusion of choice.

But in the ideal situation the aim would be to generate proposals which genuinely seek to resolve the strategic issue in a range of ways.

Criteria to select from proposals

Robert Smith (1994) offers the following questions to decide between proposals drawing from the mission and SWOT analysis.

- How far does the proposal meet aims and objectives?
- Does it build on strengths and address weaknesses?
- Does it help seize opportunities and counter threats?

Johnson and Scholes (1993) suggest several criteria appropriate in selecting from proposals.

- Suitability. To what extent does the proposal address the SWOT? Does it fit with the organizations' values and objectives?
- Feasibility. Is there adequate sources of funding and/or resources to carry out the proposal? Does the organization have the skill to carry out the proposal? What is likely to be the reaction of other organizations? Is the proposal feasible in technical terms?
- Acceptability. Does the proposal meet any financial requirements (viz. return on assets or matched funding)? What are the implications for the key stakeholders in the organization? Is any risk involved acceptable to the organization?

The cost benefit analysis approach which we described in Chapter 5 is also a widely used method in the public sector and can be very useful here.

Actions within the next year

This will need to include such matters as plans for:

- resources (acquiring and disposing)
- staffing
- finance
- information
- operations.

Actions within the next six months

It is axiomatic that major strategic action in any substantial organization will need the active involvement and commitment of the people affected. A key factor in getting such involvement and commitment is to give such people a role in deciding *how* the strategy will be carried out.

A proposal which is too tightly specified at the outset denies people the opportunity to influence the process by which any change is carried out. Therefore a key action is to give affected people discretion to plan the steps involved in carrying out the strategy.

Actions almost immediately

The immediate actions involved will be associated with communication of the proposal to the various affected groups and individuals.

All too frequently senior managers in an organization overlook the impact of rumour and the grapevine. The need for quick and accurate information can hardly be overestimated. Politicians are often more aware of this than managers. Hence the way in which the major parties try to counter media rumours at an early stage.

Communication channels should be carefully chosen. The medium and the message should be matched. Information about terms of severance or redundancy should be provided in written form. Where staff may have questions which need to be answered then a manager (or accredited person) should be available.

Establishing a vision

Organizations need to have a vision of success. Perhaps one of the most enduring public sector visions in the UK has been that of the National Health Service. The concept of health care which is free to all and not dependent upon wealth is one which the Conservative Party had to acknowledge. 'The National Health Service is safe in our hands' is a statement which Margaret Thatcher would not have made about any other non-uniformed public service.

One of the major impacts of the 'private sector' upon public sector organizations has been the increasing stress upon mission statements and vision. Management gurus will frequently extol the virtue of inspirational messages.

Bryson (1995) states that a vision of success should probably include:

- Mission
- Basic philosophy and core values
- Goals
- Basic strategies
- Performance criteria
- Important decision rules
- Ethical standards expected of staff.

Further thoughts on strategic management and planning

Strategic management and planning in local government

One of the largest changes in local government has been the Local Government Reorganization. Shire and district councils in England, Scotland and Wales have been subject to review. In many cases this means that Unitary Authorities will be created where previously there were two levels of authority. In a number of cases authority boundaries will also be changed.

The Audit Commission published a paper (1994b) which offers advice to local authorities on how to deal with the change process which this reorganization will involve. The paper is very useful as a template to managing major strategic change in local government. It identifies the following elements as crucial in enabling the major reorganization to take place:

Co-operation/co-ordination

This takes place on both an internal and external level. The Audit Commission suggests that local authorities should use three tests to evaluate any actions which they propose:

- Is it legal?
- Is it financially sensible?
- Is it managerially sensible?

The checklist which they offer for local authorities includes many items which are useful for managing strategic change generally.

Records

The Audit Commission identifies five interlinked areas where records and information will be needed in order to manage reorganization effectively. These are: services, fixed assets, finance, staff and contracts/legal issues. We have covered these more explicitly in Chapter 7. Again there is a checklist which is useful as a general guide to strategic change.

Staffing

In local government staffing accounts for over 60 per cent of the budget and the Audit Commission suggest that the following three headings are particularly important:

- Regulations, particularly the implications of the 1981 Transfer of Undertakings (Protection of Employment) Regulations (TUPE) which will apply to staff who are affected by reorganization.
- Personnel records, which contain detailed information about staff and may show that some members of staff have conditions of service which are based on long standing and possibly outmoded practice.
- Key staff, whose knowledge and skills are vital to the success of reorganization, must be identified. This may require special conditions of remuneration to ensure that their services are retained.

Financial issues

The Audit Commission provides ample information on this in other publications. But where an authority is about to disappear they note that financial standards can 'quickly erode, leaving taxpayers vulnerable to addition costs, and service consumers to suffer a deteriorating service'.

We would comment that these comments may be applicable also when a local authority is undergoing major strategic change. There is the same uncertainty about whether departments, functions and staff will survive.

The financial areas on which the Audit Commission lay stress are:

- Prudential guidelines in particular where commitments, liabilities, balances and asset disposal are concerned.
- Systems and procedures where standing orders and debts are concerned.
- Checks and controls in respect of probity, fraud, misappropriations and theft.

Strategic management in the NHS

Pettigrew and his colleagues (1992) looked at making change in the NHS. He previously had looked at other large organizations in the private sector (such as ICI) as well as the NHS.

The work they engaged in was empirical – that means that they went out and interviewed people and gathered data from a wide range of documentary sources. The breadth of the research (eight Regions) and the duration (1987–90) together with the fact that it was supported at a very high level in the NHS makes it particularly significant.

The timing of the project was also significant coming as it did after the Griffiths report and the introduction of a management ethos into the NHS. The focus of the research strategy was case study based and particularly sought to examine whether the 'top down' management approach to change was effective.

The research found that the pattern and pace of change differed between authorities.

The importance of context

Pettigrew et al. argued that there were differences in the receptivity to change dependent upon context. They identified eight factors which were derived from the research they conducted:

- Quality and coherence of policy. Here they found that simply taking central policy and implementing it locally was not always enough. A vision was important even if that vision was imprecise. An absence of such a vision could promote inertia. Policy also had to be broken down into actionable 'chunks' and the tendency of short termism to push aside long-term issues was noted.

- Availability of key people to lead. This means the ability to gain continuity and a degree of stability. Their findings did not support the rotation of managers to maintain change. The loss of key people was associated with a draining of energy and could even put the change process further back than its original start point.
- Long-term environmental pressure. Environmental pressure can also drain energy and impede the change process. Financial crisis produced a range of reactions (such as delay and denial) and was often seen as a threat rather than an opportunity. However in some cases management were able to use the crisis to accelerate the rationalization process.
- Supportive organizational culture. They found a great deal of effort was required to change culture. This was attempted in a range of ways. One was to set up a 'management cadre' as opposed to simply general managers. The NHS was not seen as one culture but rather as a set of subcultures. Factors associated with a change culture at district level included:

  - flexible working across boundaries (skill rather than rank focus)
  - an open risk-taking approach
  - openness to research and evaluation
  - a strong value base
  - a strong positive self-image

- Effective managerial clinical relations. These were easier where negative stereotypes had broken down. It was important for managers to understand what clinicians valued. Also clinicians with managerial perspectives played an important role and considerable advantage could be gained from alliances. They found that relationships were slow to build up but quick to sour.
- Co-operative interorganizational networks. There were a number of agencies (DSS and voluntary bodies) where the NHS District Health Authorities (DHA) had only power to influence and not to control. The impact of individuals who 'spanned boundaries' was critical. Effective networks were those which informal and purposive. However they were also fragile and vulnerable to staff changes.
- Simplicity and clarity of goals and priorities. Managers varied greatly in their ability to narrow and focus the agenda down to a limited number of priorities and to protect these from short-term pressures. The risk was constant escalation of priorities until they became individually meaningless. Persistence and patience in pursuing a limited number of priorities over a long period bore fruit.
- The fit between DHA change agenda and its locale. The sort of factors which had a bearing on this were:

- degree of coterminosity with Social Services departments
- one large population centre
- teaching hospital
- strength and nature of local culture
- nature of local NHS staff.

Implications of the findings

- Turning problems and panics into sustainable action: The NHS tends to be 'panic driven' yet few of these panics are life threatening. The challenge is to separate the urgent from the important. If all things are crucial few get done. The origin of this 'panic culture' may be political or possibly from the importance attached to 'symbolic decision making' rather than action. A focus upon simplicity of goals and priorities is suggested as a way forward together with greater skill in environmental assessment.
- Managing incoherence: The NHS is enormous and segmented in many ways:

  - political–managerial
  - professional–managerial
  - professional–professional
  - regional, district and local
  - geography
  - care group.

- Segmentation such as this is linked to inertia and factors such as structural complexity and poor communication linkages create challenges to management of change.
- Incentives and politics: These are critical in mobilizing energy for change. Labelling change is often important – 'closure' becomes 'redevelopment ' and 'crisis' becomes 'opportunity'.
- Combining top-down pressure and bottom-up concerns: There is a debate as to how much of the Thatcherite era has survived her. Is public management in the NHS context more 'action oriented'? Has a new culture of public management emerged? Top-down pressures were apparent at DHA level. Often pressures were interlocking with 'Care in the Community' local issues adding to central pressures.
- Dualities and dilemmas in managing change: For example, the need to both create central policy whilst leaving room for local manoeuvre. Raising and sustaining energy was a constant challenge. Managers needed to know how to generate momentum. Change could be both seen as a threat or an opportunity. Managers needed to maintain continuity whilst also promoting change. Managers needed to build commitment from hierarchies and networks.

Strategic management in uniformed organizations

The Audit Commission (1994a) has produced a report on one of the largest public sector uniformed organizations in the UK: namely the police. It has major implications for the strategic management of this service.

The Audit Commission confirm the view expressed by Sir John Harvey Jones, 'The Troubleshooter'. Sir John Harvey Jones was concerned at the lack of delegation of practical resource management decisions in the South Yorkshire police force. The Audit Commission report is directly inspired by the Police and Magistrates Courts Act 1994 which they describe as 'the most far reaching reform of the management of the police service for thirty years'.

The 1994 Act changes the composition and functions of police authorities, delegates considerable authority to chief constables and encourages the maximum feasible delegation of responsibility. Thus day-to-day financial management should rest with the chief constable who is encouraged in turn to delegate further.

The strategic implications for the police manager is immense. Terence Grange in Willcocks and Harrow (1992) describes the strong cultures which operate in the police service. He notes (p. 299) that:

> Historically, police managers have imposed, through layer on layer of supervision, the policies of the chief officer . . . The overriding function has been that of supervision of the results of the actions of junior personnel.

In order for responsibility to be effectively held by managers the Audit Commission (1994a, p. 21) stresses that local financial management has to be accompanied by:

- clear roles and accountabilities
- specific objectives and quantified targets
- measurable performance indicators
- safeguards against excessive bureaucracy
- appropriate financial autonomy
- clear authorization levels
- rules about purchasing
- policy guidelines.

Research by the Audit Commission found that whilst overtime budgets were held at Basic Command Unit (about superintendent level) many aspects of training budgets were not so delegated. They noted early cultural resistance to local financial management but claimed that there is increasing acceptability.

Three phases of financial delegation were described in carrying through the strategic change (Figure 9.8). The Audit Commission

	Type of budget	Managerial characteristics
Phase 1	Overtime Lighting Minor repairs	Stress upon budgetary control
Phase 2	Civilian Pay Transport Training	Move to resource management
Phase 3	Maximum Feasible Devolution	HQ becomes strategic Basic Command Unit manager as key resource manager Business plans as basis for expenditure

Figure 9.8   *Identifying the best fit in the Police Force*

Source: Audit Commission (1994a).

sees the next stage as delegating staff budgets since police staffing consumes 55 per cent of a typical budget (73 per cent if overtime and civilian pay are included and no less than 82 per cent if pensions are also included!).

The development of business or service plans is also going to represent a major challenge for police forces. Interestingly the Audit Commission appears to recommend the use of consultants to help devise these.

Finally the Audit Commission (1994a) notes that 'forces need to prepare for Compulsory Competitive Tendering (CCT) by developing CCT strategies and should designate officers to fulfil client side responsibilities for defined activities'.

Strategic management in the Civil Service

Robert Smith (1994) describes the strategic planning process in the Lords Chancellor's Department. This is a central government department employing about 11 700 civil servants with a total expenditure in 1993/94 of £2066 million. Smith describes the 'hierarchy of plans' which exist in this department. They range from the strategic plan and departmental report which are published to management and divisional plans which are for internal consumption.

What is interesting is the description of how these various plans are produced. The Department has two separate parts which engage in planning. The Central Unit deals with the strategic planning and the Resources Division handles the management plan and department report.

An obvious question is why the Department separates responsibility for strategic from management planning. Robert Smith notes that it was done deliberately in order to distance financial considerations from strategic planning. The separation happens at the beginning of the planning cycle but then the management and strategic plans are brought together. The process is thus a simultaneous 'top-down bottom-up' one.

The written strategic plan which emerges is about forty pages long with about half devoted to challenges, objectives and targets. In brief the key challenges included such things as to:

- ensure access to justice whilst reducing the cost
- sustain improvements in the quality, efficiency and effectiveness of court services
- gain adequate control over the overall cost of legal aid whilst ensuring publicly funded legal services.

Each key challenge was linked to between two and six strategic objectives and each strategic objective is in turn linked to targets. Smith notes that the targets are generally not quantifiable though the plan often set out expected actions and dates by which such actions were to take place.

The plan is published in 'glossy document' format with a summary provided to junior staff.

The management plan in contrast is an internal document of which over 90 per cent is devoted to operational plans. The relatively short section which refers to the document to the strategic plan is set out mainly in the form of tables which link the strategic objectives, division of the Department and operational objectives.

The largest section on operational plans lays out the resources, operational objectives and operational targets over the next three years.

Strategic management in the voluntary sector

Butler and Wilson (1990) in an interesting and key work look at strategy and structure in voluntary and not-for-profit organizations. They see strategies as representing a choice on a continuum between competing and co-operating. Competitive strategies have been well described in the world of business but co-operating has had a more limited treatment.

Butler and Wilson suggest a typology of the environment of co-operating voluntary organizations as follows:

- 'Givers': These are the suppliers of funding, consumers/customers and raw materials.
- ' Commensals': These are organizations which seek to attract similar support and would in the 'profit sector' be described as competitors.

- 'Receivers': Those whom the organization exists to help or benefit.

They view the potential available strategies as being for competitor oriented voluntary organizations to either focus on efficiency or on innovation. For co-operating voluntary organizations they suggest mechanisms such as:

- co-opting (taking in members of the other organization)
- contracting (entering into legal or less formal obligations)
- coalescing (engaging in joint ventures etc.).

Butler and Wilson looked at thirty-one voluntary organizations to see if there was any pattern to the strategies which they followed. They concluded, using some fairly sophisticated statistical analysis, that certain strategic clusters could be identified together with the context in which they were likely to be found:

- Extenders. These are organizations which seek to find new givers and co-operate with commensal organizations for this purpose. However there is low co-operation over outputs and low concern with efficiency of input. Oxfam was given as an example at the time of the research. The strengths of this strategy lay in innovation and taking opportunities to grow. Its weakness was when the environment was more stable or expansion was less possible. They were likely to be in a dynamic context where there was a high voluntary sector share and expectations of efficiency.
- Competitive co-operators. These co-operate with commensal organizations over givers but compete over outputs. Christian Aid was seen as an example at the time of the research and it was also found in some organizations for the visually handicapped. The strengths of organizations in this cluster will be in developing close co-operative relationships. However weakness might arise over lack of resources. They were likely to be highly service oriented and have limited reserves.
- Output co-operators. These organizations co-operate over clients (receivers) and also seek efficiency on inputs (givers). The Royal National Institute for the Blind was an example. Such organizations can develop much goodwill from their clients but may neglect their inputs (givers). They are similar in their context to Extenders but tend to have more covenanted income and focus less upon efficiency and service norms.
- Acquisitors. Here there was a very high concern in improving methods to increase giving and obtain resources. There was very little focus upon competing for clients (receivers) or co-operating with receivers. The Royal National Lifeboat Institution was an obvious example and still is today. These are organizations which, in the words of Peters and Waterman (1982), stick to what they know best and aim to do it even better. They risk being

overtaken by changes in their external environment. They will tend to occupy a market 'niche' and will be content within it.

- Reactors. Here there was low concern with gaining new inputs either by reaching new givers or through efficiency. There was limited co-operation with receivers (clients). St Dunstans (an organization for the visually handicapped) was seen as an example at the time of the research. These are organizations which possess large reserves or assured sources of income. As long as these last the organization is safe though it may be vulnerable to criticism over failure to use its resources appropriately. As such they operate in a 'protected sub niche' type of context.

Summary

Strategic thinking is a factor which marks out first line from middle and senior level managers. It usually requires a certain detachment from the everyday action orientation of a busy manager. It is a well-used truism that when you are 'up to your waist in alligators you tend to forget that the aim is to empty the swamp'.

Much has been written upon the subject and in this chapter we have tried to equip you with some useful models and concepts. However armchair reading is a poor substitute for trying it out in the real world. In the delayered and demassed organizations of the current public sector one advantage is that it is often easier to gain access to strategic planning groups and teams. If you show interest and possess a useful knowledge or skill base, it is possible to become part of the strategic process in a way which would have been difficult in the procedurally driven hierarchies of yesteryear.

If we would leave you with just one thought then bear in mind the piles of dusty volumes produced by strategic planners in those old-style hierarchies. They now serve often only as a source of interest to researchers. The mere act of producing a detailed strategic plan is no guarantee that it will influence events. Planning which does not lead to meaningful and appropriate action is at best an intellectual exercise. At worst it represents a tragic misuse of valuable human resources.

Action points and discussion points

(Items in italics are intended to encourage the reader to develop a greater intellectual awareness, items in plain type are focused upon work-related activity.)

Review internal and external operating environments

Obtain and read an analysis of your industry or organizational sector. This may be a publication or government report. Alternatively it may be a survey or analysis undertaken by a quality magazine or broadsheet news-paper. Highlight the aspects of the analysis which you either strongly agree or disagree with and note down the reasons for your opinion.

For your own organization carry out the following analyses:

1 A stakeholder analysis where you assess the stakeholders onto a matrix of two variables (level of interest vs. amount of power, for example).
2 A SWOT analysis looking at the internal Strengths and Weak-nesses and the external Opportunities and Threats.
3 A PESTeL analysis setting out the Political, Economic, Social, Technical and Legal issues which impact or may impact upon your organization.

Establish strategies to guide the work of the organization

Obtain at least two strategic documents from public sector organizations. Compare what they say and try to identify which strategic model (if any) seems to best fit what they are doing.

Obtain past and current strategic documents or statements from your own organization. Use them to identify how strategy has evolved over time. Consider to what extent the mission and objectives as set out are still relevant. How might these be revised and how would you seek to go about this?

Further reading

Hudson, M. (1995). *Managing without Profit*. Penguin.
This is a recent book written by a practising management consultant who specializes in 'third sector' organizations.
Johnson, G., and Scholes, K. (1993). *Exploring Corporate Strategy* (3rd edn.). Prentice Hall.
A well-regarded textbook written from a UK perspective. It is used on a range of undergraduate and postgraduate management courses as the main strategic manage-ment book.
Lawrie, A. (1995). *The Complete Guide to Business and Strategic Planning for Voluntary Organisations*. Directory of Social Change.
This is a very practical and 'hands on' book written in an easy to follow style.
Pettigrew, A., Ferlie, E., and McKee, L. (1992). *Shaping Strategic Change: Making Change in Large Organisations*. Sage.
A well-researched and thorough account of strategic change in the NHS. This is written by experts on the NHS.
Smith, R. (1994). *Strategic Management and Planning in the Public Sector*. Longman.
This is part of a series commissioned by the Civil Service College. It offers some useful perspectives on central government departments and agencies.
Stewart, J. and Stoker, G. (1995). *Local Government in the 1990s*. Macmillan.
This is a recent collection of contributions covering the broad range of local govern-ment functions and services. It offers a valuable source to the strategically oriented manager looking for both an overview and for a focused approach.

10 Managing and measuring performance and the Citizen's Charters

Aims and learning objectives

As we have seen, one of the key issues facing managers in all parts of the public sector is to demonstrate that they are managing resources economically, efficiently and effectively. In order to demonstrate these achievements at the levels of the individual, team, department and whole organization the ability to measure, manage and report performance is required. This chapter aims to help you do this and builds on the work you have done in preceding chapters. Improving public sector performance is a key political objective at both national and local levels. This is reflected in the growing use of service 'Charters', so we will also be considering the impact of Charters on performance management.

At the end of this chapter, and associated activities and reading, you will be able to:

- identify issues peculiar to performance management in the public sector
- outline examples of good practice in performance management as the basis for evaluating and improving organizational performance
- review your own organization's approach to performance management and suggest ways to improve it
- outline the implications of the Citizen's Charter, and other Charters, for performance management in the public sector and managing activities to meet customer requirements
- develop teams and individuals to enhance performance
- relate these issues to your response to the poor performance of team members.

Managing performance – the public sector difference

The nature of the public sector, which we have already discussed, significantly affects the processes of assessing the value for money of the services provided. The public sector does not have the private sector's 'bottom line' measures of success, or failure in performance, such as profit or loss, market share, or increasing or decreasing product value. Traditionally in the public sector the emphasis was on *how* money was spent. Performing well involved spending the whole of an allocated budget, not overspending because that might lead to difficulties, nor underspending because that could lead to budget reductions in the next financial year. This approach has, largely, being overtaken by more concern with the effectiveness of expenditure rather than control merely over how it was spent.

This is as true for public services in countries such as America, for example, as for the United Kingdom. Reporting on the American experience of introducing performance measurement, Ammons (1995, p. 37) asserts:

> For many years, measurement proponents have urged local governments to report not only how much they spend, but also how much work they do, how well they do it, how efficiently, and, ideally, what their actions achieve.

Here Ammons is echoing the concern of the Audit Commission in England and Wales, and the Accounts Commission in Scotland, with the 'three Es' of Economy, Efficiency and Effectiveness. The Audit Commission was established in 1983 as part of the government's aim of making local authorities more accountable to their electorate. The Commission was partly created to take over the auditing functions of the District Audit service, but also to fulfil a wider role of providing advice and analysis generally to local government and, more recently, the Health Service as well.

The three Es are clearly interlinked. 'Economy' can be defined as the provision, and purchase, of services at lowest possible cost consistent with specified quantity and, which provides more of a challenge to managers, quality. 'Efficiency' seeks to ensure that the maximum output is obtained from resources devoted to an activity, or that only the minimum level of resources is devoted to a specified level of output. The concern of 'Effectiveness' is that the impact of the service or policy is actually meeting its stated aims.

It is possible to think of other 'Es' which might be added to this model such as 'equity', 'excellence', 'environmental impact' and 'enterprise'.

The concept of equity focuses attention on the impact of services, which may be achieved in an economic, efficient and effective way, on society. It encourages us to ask questions such as, is it a socially acceptable use of resources and are the differing consumer/client group needs being met by the service? Are decisions being made which are fair to all parties? Does the service involve any, unintentional, discrimination against any group? How do we know?

'Excellence' criteria would involve a review of current performance against standards of best practice, while environmental-impact requires us to assess, perhaps, the longer-term consequences of service delivery and the extent to which costs of provision are being 'externalized', i.e. met by somebody else, perhaps some time in the future. Hence a currently 'economic' solution to waste management may prove far less 'economic' to future generations who have to, for example, meet the cost of dealing with contaminated land. Criteria for performance on the 'enterprise' dimension could involve an evaluation of the impact of service delivery on the wider economic benefit of the community, focusing, for example, on the increase of human capital through a well-trained workforce.

Generally speaking it is the first three Es which are of most immediate concern to managers, so we will concentrate on them in this chapter.

Defining terms

Addressing these issues requires you as a manager to have your own working definition of some key terms. We will offer some definitions now, but these need to be carefully interpreted in the context of your own organization, which may have its own precise definitions within which you need to work.

We would define performance management as the process of communicating organizational mission and objectives to all stakeholders and setting and reviewing performance targets to measure the achievement of these objectives and ensuring that all this activity provides the basis for continual performance improvement.

Performance management requires performance measurement, because you cannot manage what you cannot measure. Selim and Woodward (1992) suggest the following classification of the main types of performance measures:

1 Workload/demand and performance measures
2 Economy measures
3 Efficiency measures
4 Effectiveness measures
5 Equity measures.

The first type, workload and demand, may be regarded as a fairly basic, some might even say crude, measure which links the volume of output with measures of input of resources. Take for example a voluntary agency offering advice to clients from a number of offices. At one location each member of staff (measure of input) may counsel fifty clients per week (volume of output), while at another office achieves sixty interviews/client/week. Obviously such measures need to be interpreted with a high degree of caution before final judgements can be made about the comparative 'performance' of the two offices; however they may provide a manager with some indication of where further investigation may be warranted.

Economy measures compare actual input costs with planned or expected input costs. As the manager of a 'meals-on-wheels' service, for example, you may have budgeted for each meal to cost £1 to prepare, before delivery. However your performance monitoring system is highlighting the fact that each meal is costing £1.25. Either you got your initial estimating wrong or perhaps there is some food being unnecessarily wasted, or the person responsible for purchasing is not getting the best deal possible from your suppliers.

Economy measures, then, are concerned with actual versus *planned* input while efficiency measures focus on the relationship between actual input and actual *output*. To continue with the meals-on-wheels example, if one kitchen produces 500 meals per day with five staff, while another takes ten staff to produce the same level of output then it appears, on these performance measures, that the first kitchen is twice as efficient as the second.

However, if upon further investigation you find that half of the food produced by the first kitchen is being returned as inedible by your clients, then you might have doubts about its effectiveness, despite its apparent efficiency. Effectiveness measures are concerned with the extent to which the overall objectives of a service or other production process are being achieved, that is actual output with planned output. It is unlikely that you planned for 25 per cent of the meals produced to be inedible!

Selim and Woodward (1992, p. 149) defined equity measures as drawing 'attention to present and potential unfairness by the enterprise in terms of its corporate policy and practice'. They give as examples of equity measures the proportion of policemen/women from minority groups and the proportion of teachers from minority ethnic groups working in areas with a large percentage of families from these same groups.

Box 10.1 gives an example of one police service which is attempting to explicitly link inputs, outputs and outcomes (i.e. the type of data needed to assess, at least, economy, efficiency and effectiveness), while Box 10.2 gives an international example as a comparator.

Box 10.1   Case example

Strathclyde Police

Strathclyde Police sees its primary aim as one of upholding the rule of law, protecting and assisting the citizen; and working for the prevention and detection of crime, so that public tranquillity is maintained, with the fear of crime and disorder being reduced or even eliminated.

Strathclyde have adopted an approach to performance management which it describes as 'continuously evolving and improved to address public satisfaction and the delivery of a professional service'. Strathclyde Police's process is based on the input/output/outcome model in Figure 10.1.

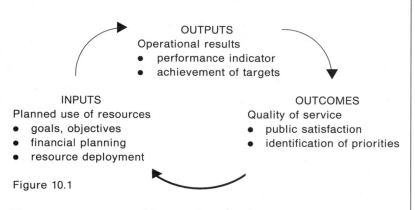

OUTPUTS
Operational results
- performance indicator
- achievement of targets

INPUTS
Planned use of resources
- goals, objectives
- financial planning
- resource deployment

OUTCOMES
Quality of service
- public satisfaction
- identification of priorities

Figure 10.1

The process starts with a variety of public consultation exercises, such as meetings with elected representatives and community groups and surveys, to identify public needs, concerns and expectations. These are addressed in a policy planning process, which results in the formulation of 'Force Goals'. For 1994 five Force Goals and associated targets were established, for example,

> Goal 1. To reduce crime with special attention being paid to those crimes which cause the greatest local concern. Target 1: To reduce the level of crime to that of 1984. Target 2: To sustain the long-term commitment to challenging the culture of violence involving knives and weapons.

> Goal 5. To wage a war on bureaucracy. Target 1: To reduce Force forms by 50 per cent. Target 2: To increase operational patrol time by continued improvements in technology.

Local, divisional, managers then consider how best to use their resources to achieve these goals and establish plans to deploy their resources accordingly. Regular checks, including activity sampling, are undertaken to check that the plans are being put into practice. Bids for extra resources are considered through the production of Divisional Management Plans which form the basis of a Force-wide forward-planning mechanism.

Results are assessed through the production of quarterly performance indicators focused on crime and detection; evaluation of the success of specific operations and initiatives and monitoring of qualitative aspects of service provision such as response times to urgent incidents. Overall effectiveness, or outcomes, are evaluated through an assessment of the extent to which local objectives have been met and public satisfaction via surveys of various categories of customers. For example in

1994 the Force reported a 10.8 per cent reduction in the overall level of reported crime, an increase in the overall detection rate to 30.6 per cent (from 28 per cent) and reductions in road accidents. These results were supported by, amongst other qualitative indicators, a 16.6 per cent reduction in complaints against police officers, a 91 per cent expression of satisfaction in the service they received by victims of crime and fifty-three submissions to the Force Suggestion Scheme.

These evaluations feed back into the goals and objectives in a continuing, circular, process.

Source: Strathclyde Police (1994).

Box 10.2   Case example

Policy and performance measurement in Tilburg, The Netherlands

Tilburg is a city with around 165 000 inhabitants. In 1995 its budget was in the order of 1.2 billion gilders. Local government budgets in the Netherlands, 90 per cent of which are made up of central government grants, have been subject to cutbacks since the 1980s. Both general and specific grants have been reduced, without a concomitant reduction in the requirement to provide services. These changes have forced local authorities to reassess their structures, methods of operation and attitude to performance measurement. Tilburg has been in the vanguard of these changes.

Until the end of the 1980s Tilburg operated a traditional 'input' budgetary process. It now operates a 'performance budget' and, although it still has some way to go, has established 'measurable policy goals' and presents performance data for almost every task it undertakes. Quantitative information is also provided on the underlying policy goals. Tilburg's administration is driven by a vision of being a 'Modern Industrial City'. This mission is translated into a 'General Policy Plan' with three main parts: 'Modern Industry'; 'Modern City'; 'Other'. For each part measurable policy goals have been established, which are expressed either in terms of outputs or effects. For example the plan to encourage a modern industrial base is presented in measurable policy goals such as to achieve an economic performance better than the country average; becoming a modern city includes the goal of delivering 1000 houses in 1995; while the 'Other' policies include targets for the reduction of crime and traffic accidents and increasing the participation of immigrant children in education to 30 per cent of the target group.

Each policy goal is illustrated with results from the previous year.

Each of Tilburg's seven major service divisions provides performance data in some combination of input, activity or output data. Overall it is estimated that some 95 per cent of Tilburg's budget expenditure is covered by performance data. The Environment and Public Works Divisions, for example, present data on real costs per unit activity or output such as costs per square metre for street cleaning or costs per kilometre for the installation of sewerage. Quality indicators such as average waiting times or the value of a service to customers are also presented.

Source: Haselbekke (1995).

Performance measures or performance indicators?

Without the potential advantage of a performance measure in terms of a 'bottom-line' profit or loss (or at least one which would be likely to be accepted by everyone with an interest in the service and in the context of some concept of the 'pubic good') it is probably the case that each of the performance 'measures' offered in the two case examples are better seen as 'performance indicators', i.e. as drawing managers' attention to areas where action may be required rather than purporting to truly measure the overall performance of their whole area of responsibility.

It is not possible, or perhaps desirable, to prescribe a generic set of performance indicators for public sector organizations. However drawing on the work of writers such as Jackson (1988), Palmer (1993) and Meekings (1995) we are able to produce a list of fifteen questions you should consider as a manager when formulating and reviewing performance indicators (PIs).

1   Consistency. Are the definitions of 'performance' inherent in the PIs consistent over time, and between units or divisions of the organization? Obviously if the definition of, say, customer satisfaction changes over time from the level of complaints received to the results of a more proactive customer satisfaction survey the validity of the indicator of performance between these two definitions will be very questionable.
2   Comparability. Are the PIs comparing like with like where necessary? To continue with the customer satisfaction example if one part of the organization uses complaints as a PI, and another uses survey responses, the two PIs cannot really be directly compared, i.e. you cannot conclude that one or other part of the organization is performing 'better'.

3 Clarity. Are the PIs as simple, well defined and easily understood as possible? This may be difficult to achieve in that the PIs may need to be understood by a range of people who do not necessarily share the same understanding of some of the terms used in a PI.

4 Controllability. Do the PIs relate to the specific responsibilities of a manager, or group of managers, who can control the achievement of the performance levels required? There are few, meaningful, areas in any organization where complete control can be guaranteed; however if a PI is patently beyond the control of a particular manager it is unlikely to be regarded as very credible by them.

5 Contingency. Are other factors likely to affect performance, such as organizational structure or environmental influences recognised by the PI? This criteria is related to that of controllability and recognizes that PIs can be a powerful tool in, and reflection of, a broader change in organizational culture.

6 Comprehensiveness. Do the PIs reflect all the areas of information required for effective decision making? It is tempting to establish PIs which are easy to identify and monitor, and while this may be a reasonable approach when first setting up a system, it must quickly develop into a truly representative set of PIs to be effective for performance management.

7 Boundedness. Have the key PIs, i.e. those which are most likely to give the biggest pay-off, been identified? Boundedness can be seen as an important limit to comprehensiveness. Too many PIs can lead to 'information overload'; too few to the danger of crucial areas being ignored.

8 Relevance. Do the PIs satisfy the need to take account of specific needs and conditions? This criteria can interrelate with the notion of contingency; PIs need to show responsiveness.

9 Feasibility. Do the PIs relate to areas which can be achieved by reasonable managerial action, based on realistic expectations of managers or the other people to whom they relate?

10 Scope. Do the PIs cover the areas of economy, efficiency and effectiveness? There is some suggestion that, driven as they are by pressures to reduce expenditure, PIs in the public sector organizations may concentrate on economy and efficiency, that is primarily cost-related areas, to the detriment of effectiveness, such as customer satisfaction and the achievement of policy goals.

11 Targets. Is each PI a reflection of an associated target? It is difficult to use PIs to evaluate performance if they are not related to a target to be achieved.

12 Timeliness. Do the PIs provide information in a sufficiently short timescale to allow management to take corrective action if necessary? The timescale will depend on the aspect of performance being measured; however for many activities it is unli-

kely that annual reporting is likely to be very helpful, while reporting on a monthly cycle may be a more appropriate guideline.

13 Construction. Are the people who will take decisions on the basis of the PIs involved in setting them? This criteria also relates to the other issues of controllability, clarity, relevance and feasibility. It may also be important to consider the roles of the work team, and teamwork in constructing appropriate PIs.

14 Communication. Is the information provided by the PIs communicated to the people with a need, or a right, to know it? It is likely that public sector managers may increasingly need to address the tensions between public accountability and commercial sensitivity.

15 Integration. Are PIs clearly derived from overall organizational strategy and are they integrated with the organization's planning and budgetary processes? A PI without a plan for achieving the performance required, or the resources to allow it to happen, is unlikely to be effective.

Box 10.3 gives an example of one local authority's approach to incorporating performance indicators in an overall performance management system.

Box 10.3   Case example

Redditch Borough Council

Redditch Borough Council introduced a system of performance monitoring in 1989. The system now covers all the council's activities and about 1000 performance indicators have been identified at corporate and service level. The council defines the objectives of its overall performance review system as 'To measure council services objectively through a set of numerical indicators and relate these to a set of policy objectives and core values laid down by members'. The corporate core values and objectives set the framework for the system and in this context each service has a set of policy objectives, annual key tasks and targeted performance indicators (which are also reflected in the performance appraisal process for individual employees).

Redditch places emphasis on quantifiable indicators and distinguishes between indicators of service activity or demand (e.g. the size of the housing waiting list) and performance indicators (e.g. the rate at which people are rehoused from the list). In selecting each indicator Redditch applies five tests:

1 Is it relevant as a useful guide to efficiency and effectiveness of the service?

2 Is it measurable and are any new information systems necessary to produce the required data?

3 Is the indicator 'pure', so that it really measures what it seems to indicate?

4 Is the target realistic, while aiming to stretch and improve the service?

5 Does it reflect the authority's core values and policy objectives?

Source: Audit Commission (1995c).

Measuring and indicating performance – whose performance?

Performance indicators are sometimes portrayed as if they were always objective and quantifiable, in practice this is seldom really the case, particularly in controversial areas such as the police service. Different people are likely to assess 'performance' from their own perspectives, using differing concepts of 'performance' and establishing their own, often implicit, assessment criteria. As a manager you are trying to respond to these differences, and, of course, at the same time you have your own concept of 'performance' and views on appropriate criteria from your particular perspective. In this part of your management task the concept of 'stakeholder analysis' may help make some sense of this complex area.

Stakeholder analysis involves identifying the individuals and groups who are affected by or can affect the future of the organization and trying to ascertain how they see the organization and the criteria by which they would measure its success. Taking as an example a voluntary organization involved in providing an advice service the stakeholders might include the organization's clients, paid employees, volunteers, the management committee, people representing the sources of funding. It would be possible, and in some cases important, to extend this analysis to, say, the families of clients, other agencies working in the same and associated fields and perhaps even to some broader concept of the 'community' which may ultimately benefit from the organization's work.

As well as the views and needs of the other stakeholders, as a manager it is important for you to gather and evaluate information that allows you to make some judgement about what is being achieved against what is planned and/or needed. Therein lies one of the managerial tasks – reconciling what is possible in the gathering and measurement of performance with the various needs and perceptions of the key stakeholders.

Performance – who sets the standards?

Perhaps one of the differences between management in the public and private sectors is the extent to which public sector managers are influenced and guided by performance targets, measurement and monitoring emanating from sources external to the organization. Clearly private sector managers are required to meet the demands of auditors, shareholders and other stakeholders; however the public sector is probably unique in the extent of central government interest in its detailed performance and being subject to the scrutiny, and advice and guidance of the Audit Commission. This interest is reflected in the growing use of 'Charters' covering service users. The process of establishing Charters and subsequently monitoring their implementation and reporting on the extent to which the performance standards included in the particular charter have been achieved represents a potentially interesting interaction between internal and external stakeholders. Therefore we shall consider the issue of Charters in some depth next.

The Citizen's Charter

Since the introduction of the concept of the 'Citizen's Charter' in a White Paper (HMSO, 1991) its intent and impact has been the subject of some debate. However, Goldsworthy (1994, p. 59), then the Deputy Director of the Citizen's Charter Unit in the Office of Public Service and Science, appears to be in no doubt about the link between the Citizen's Charter and performance:

> It [the Citizen's Charter] has been about delivery; the delivery of better public services. That may be too simple for some. But it is that simple – and that difficult.

It is, as Pollitt (1994, p. 9) suggests, necessary to see the 'Citizen's Charter' as a 'broad and developing *programme*' rather than one singular charter with a 'definitive list of rights, entitlements and commitments'. Certainly a large number of 'Charters' are in existence now, ranging from those covering a large number of people such as the Patient's Charter in the NHS and British Rail's Passenger's Charter, to Charters issued by individual local authorities, to those covering relatively small numbers of people, for example we have seen a Charter produced for an individual course in a university (Box 10.4 provides more details of the Patient's Charter as an example). It might be argued that the university example cannot be seen as part of the Citizen's Charter programme, but if that is so, what is? Perhaps the nearest we can get to an answer to that question is to consider the six principles included in the first report on the Citizen's Charter (HMSO, 1992) and reiterated in the guidelines for the

'Charter Mark' (HMSO, 1996). In order to apply for the Charter Mark, public sector organizations and the public utilities have to demonstrate that they have achieved the six Charter Mark principles, which are:

1 The publication of standards of service and performance against those standards.
2 Customer consultation.
3 Clear information about services.
4 Courteous and efficient customer service.
5 Complaints procedures.
6 Independent validation of performance and commitment to value for money.

Goldsworthy (1994) elaborated on these six principles, albeit with a slight change of emphasis, as follows:

> Standards: There must be explicit standards for the levels of service which individual users of services can expect to receive published in plain language in a form everyone can understand – and displayed at the point of delivery.
> Consultation: Decision makers must take account of the views of users in setting service standards. Final decisions remain in the hands of Ministers, local councillors etc., but the user must be heard.
> Information: Full, accurate information must be readily available in plain language about services, targets and results. Whenever possible this must be in comparable form so that there is pressure to emulate the best and do better next year.
> Openness: The public should know whether or not the service is meeting its standards and who is in charge. Public servants should normally wear name badges when they meet the public and should give their names on the telephone and in letters.
> Complaints: Pubic servants must respond quickly and appropriately if they fail to deliver the promised standards of service. There must be swift, user-friendly, effective remedies if things go wrong.
> Value for money: Public services must be run efficiently and give the taxpayer good value for money. Improving quality is not about what you spend but what you buy. There will always be a limit to the amount of money that any nation can afford to spend on public services, so it is vital to make sure that priorities are got right.

Goldsworthy (1994, p. 60) adds an important caveat to this statement of principles:

> They are intended not as a straightjacket but as an enabling framework to ensure that the exercise remains focused on *results* and does not get bogged down in process.

Box 10.4   The Patient's Charter

The Patient's Charter includes the following twenty-four rights, which all patients will receive at all times, together with a large number of statements of the standards of service that people can expect to receive from the National Health Service, unless prevented by exceptional circumstances. The rights are:

1 To receive health care on the basis of clinical need, not on the ability to pay, lifestyle or other factor.
2 To be registered with a General Practitioner (GP).
3 To be able to change GP quickly and easily.
4 To receive emergency medical care at any time through a GP or through the emergency ambulance service and hospital accident and emergency departments.
5 To be referred to a consultant, acceptable to a patient, when a GP thinks this is necessary and to be referred for a second opinion if a patient and GP agree this is desirable.
6 To choose whether or not to take part in medical research or medical student training.
7 To be given a clear explanation of any treatment proposed, including any risks and alternatives, before deciding whether to agree to it.
8 To have access to health records, and to know that those working for the NHS are under a legal duty to keep the content of records confidential.
9 To have any complaint about NHS services (whoever provides them) investigated and to receive a full and prompt written reply from the chief executive or general manager.
10 To receive detailed information on local health services, including standards of service, waiting times
11 To receive information about GP services and to see a copy of the GP's practice leaflet which sets out this information.
12 To be offered a health check when joining a GP practice for the first time.
13 To have a health check if you are aged between sixteen and seventy-five and have not seen your GP for the last three years.
14 To be offered a health check once a year if you are aged seventy-five or over.
15 To be prescribed appropriate drugs and medicines.
16 To obtain free medicines under certain circumstances.
17 To be guaranteed admission for treatment by a specific date no later than eighteen months from the day when the patient is placed on a waiting list.
18 To be told before entering hospital whether it is planned to offer care in a ward for men and women.

19 To receive advice in an emergency if you are registered with a dentist, and treatment if the dentist considers it necessary.
20 To receive a signed, written prescription from an optometrist immediately after an eye test.
21 To take an optometrist's prescription to any optometrist or dispensing optician.
22 To have a written statement from the optometrist if you do not need a prescription.
23 To decide which pharmacy to use for prescriptions.
24 To have prescriptions dealt with promptly.

Source: Department of Health (1995).

From a managerial perspective this pragmatic, enabling rather than prescriptive approach, may, perhaps, be welcomed. However it does open the Citizen's Charter programme to a number of criticisms and critiques, such as those offered by Pollitt (1994) and Beale and Pollitt (1994). These can be summarized as follows:

- At a philosophical level there is little attention to the rights and responsibilities of the 'citizen' as an entity; rather the Charter appears to be more concerned with the user, customer, client or consumer, of public services.
- Many of the Charters mix up pre-existing and new provisions, legal rights and administrative regulations and managerial promises.
- Despite presenting the Citizen's Charter as a move to decentralize management and empower the user of public services, central prescriptions, such as cutting the waiting lists for hospital treatment, have distorted local priorities, hence centralizing power in practice.
- An emphasis on the individual user and 'hearing the user' with a reluctance to extend the opportunities for users to present a collective voice.
- The need to distinguish between minimum standards, average standards and best practice standards and a clear indication of the consequences of the service provider for breaching any particular standard.

Using these issues, together with the espoused purpose of the Citizen's Charter, it is possible for a manager either to evaluate a Charter already in existence, or to consider what should be included in a proposed Charter. Even if this approach is adopted the manager is still confronted with the need to reconcile the particular requirements of a number of different stakeholders and stakeholder groups. Managers may be tempted to produce a Charter which is largely concerned with protecting their own vested interests, as Pollitt (1994, p. 11) comments:

like so many other recent developments forced through in the name of the consumer, the Charter is in many ways a charter for managers as much as for users. The standards which are crucial to the entire enterprise are to be set by managers, who are advised to *consult* consumers but are in no way obliged to comply with their wishes.

Under the Local Government Act 1992 the Audit Commission was given the power to produce a set of performance indicators to be used by local authorities in England and Wales. Local authorities, in turn, are required to publish annually details of their performance, against these indicators, in local newspapers. In Scotland the indicators are laid down by the Accounts Commission. The Audit Commission (1994c) produced a guide for the general public designed to help them interpret the indicators and assess their local authority's performance. This is a very credible attempt by the Audit Commission to present the complexity of performance review in plain language likely to be comprehensible to the 'average' citizen. However in doing so the guide also alerts the reader to some of the ambiguities and subjective judgements inherent in trying to measure performance and, in particular, to compare 'performance' across more than one local authority. So the introduction to the guide asserts (p. 7):

> To show if your money is being well spent, the Audit Commission has drawn up a set of 'indicators' to measure how well local authorities are doing their job. The indicators give all the information you need to see what standards your council is providing and how much they cost.

However the Audit Commission also appears to recognize the part played by subjectivity in performance review in the next sentence (p. 7, emphasis added):

> Together with *your own experience* of your council, they will help you decide whether you are getting a good service.

The guide also points out that when comparing the performance of two councils it is also necessary to bear in mind that any particular service may be harder or dearer to provide in one area compared with another and that also 'some of the circumstances which affect how councils do their job are beyond their control'.

Implementing performance management

There is obviously a wealth of experience now available to managers as a result of several years of attempts to introduce and improve performance management in the public sector. So what has been learnt and how can you benefit from these lessons?

The Audit Commission (1995b. p. 5.32) offers a set of ten Cs: Consultation, Clarification, Credibility, Commitment, Continuity, Communication, Conflict, Competence, Control and Consolidation. The Audit Commission sees the first three Cs as being concerned with 'making it real', the next four with 'making it happen' and the last three with 'making it work'. It is worth looking at each 'C' in more detail.

> *Consultation* is concerned with involving both staff and other, external, stakeholders from the very beginning of the performance management process. This not only helps ensure that the most appropriate objectives and priorities are set, but is also important in developing a sense of ownership of the process amongst all concerned. This consultative process was well illustrated in the Strathclyde Police case example (Box 10.1). Managed well this consultation stage can form the basis of a collective, team-building, approach which can be beneficial to the organization far beyond the creation and maintenance of the performance management system itself.
>
> *Clarification* is the stage were the broad objectives and priorities identified through consultation are translated into corporate, service level and individual aims and objectives. This reinforces the link between organizational and individual objectives which we outlined in Chapter 5.
>
> *Credibility* recognizes that these aims and objectives are unlikely to be accepted by the people charged with achieving them unless they are clearly financially realistic, measurable and operationally relevant. Indeed, as Meekings (1995) suggests, measures which are not credible can be counterproductive.

A well-communicated, clear and credible system should appear 'real' and important to all those involved in its operation and outcomes. The next stage is to put the system into practice, to make it happen, which requires:

> *Commitment*, starting at the top of the organization and developed by 'champions' at lower levels in the organization. Unless senior management commitment (including local councillors, governors, non-executive directors etc.) is communicated and demonstrated throughout other stakeholders are unlikely to make the efforts required to make the system happen.
>
> *Continuity*, which recognizes that introducing an effective performance management system is likely to be a long-term process. As with any major change effort initial gains can be quickly lost, especially once the novelty wears off unless there is follow-through, review and continuous improvement to the system. The

possible conflict here between 'continuity' and 'continuous improvement' is, of course, one example of the tension in managing change between the need to preserve what is useful while also confronting the anxiety in changing what needs to be changed. Meekings (1995, pp. 5–6) suggests that an effective performance management system can be a major pull-factor in change and improvement because:

> Managers are encouraged to *reach* for the tools of continuous improvement, instead of having them thrust at them, usually from above. People have the opportunity to *create* results, rather than simply react to circumstances. Those who have to live with changes become directly involved in shaping them.

Communication, which involves continuing the consultation process and perhaps extending it to, for example, training programmes, to ensure that staff continue to understand and be committed to the programme. To quote from Meekings (1995, p. 6) again:

> The actual *use* of performance measures is vital. Getting people to use measures properly not only delivers performance improvements but is the vehicle for a culture change that helps liberate the power of the organization.

Conflict, which as we suggested under 'Continuity', is likely to arise, perhaps between different stakeholder interests. This conflict, which can be a positive as well as potentially negative factor, needs to be recognized and resolved.

Once the system is real and happening it needs to be maintained through:

Competence by staff and management in the new approach and their responsibilities. This is likely to involve a significant training investment, drawing upon many of the formal and less formal approaches to training which we also discussed in Chapter 5, as well as continual communication.

Control recognizes the need for systems to ensure that the system continues to work and develop. There is another managerial tension here between the needs of a co-ordinated overview of the process which does not mitigate, through too much bureaucracy or the use of extended managerial hierarchies, against the need for ownership and commitment.

Consolidation uses the control process to monitor, review and improve the system in terms of both achieving objectives and the overall management and operation of the system.

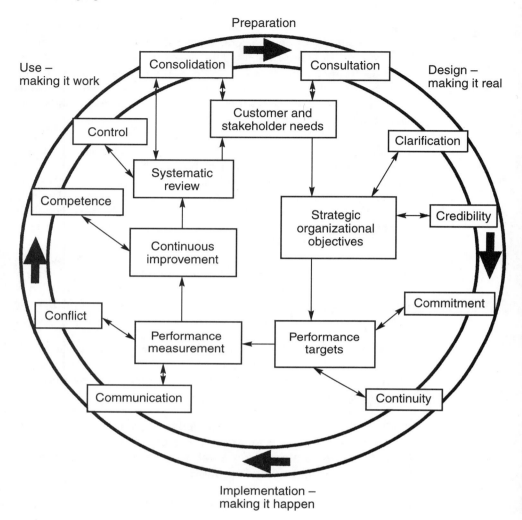

Figure 10.2 *Implementing a performance management system – a simplified model*

Source: Adapted from Audit Commission (1995) and Meekings (1995)

Figure 10.1 attempts to integrate a simplified version of Meekings' (1995) model of core management processes in performance management with the Audit Commission's (1995b) cycle of the ten Cs. Even in this simplified approach we think the complexities inherent in designing, implementing and maintaining an effective performance management system are illustrated.

The limitations to performance management

There are no simple and clear-cut methods of managing performance. Despite the views of some people who would try to present performance management as a 'rational' managerial activity, it is still essentially a political process which is not without its dangers. Hepworth (1995, p. 41) includes the following amongst a list of risks in his analysis of the 'new public management' reforms:

> The emphasis upon performance, coupled with performance pay, will tend to force management attention onto those aspects of service delivery which are measurable at a risk to the unquantifiable features of services.

and

> The capture by managers of the performance measures to suit their own interests rather than the interests of the service or the customer.

As with other aspects of managing in the public sector, definitions and measurements of performance are defined according to the dominant political parties at both national and local level, and the relative power of other stakeholders, particularly the senior management group.

Attempting to manage performance by trying to measure it is not a hopeless task, but you do need to take care in developing your performance management system. According to Flynn (1994, p. 113):

> The first imperative is to ensure that the purposes for measuring performance are clear and accepted by everyone. If measurements, especially of costs, are to be used punitively, then they will create a different atmosphere than if they are to be used creatively to help people improve their performance.

That is, perhaps, the target: to manage performance to empower rather than to control. Although even this prescription assumes that stakeholders such as employees and clients want to be empowered, this may not always be the case.

Summary

Despite its problems and limitations performance management is now a major issue for managers in all sections of the public sector. Managing and reporting performance is an important element of public accountability. An organization also needs to be able to define and assess its performance, and the performance of others, often as the basis of agreeing and monitoring a service-level agreement or contract.

Performance management needs to be integrated throughout an organization's management processes and procedures, involving all the relevant stakeholders as appropriate. At the very least it should have some performance indicators to assess its key activities. Once these have been established they need to be linked with performance targets, as an expression of the organization's commitment to continuous improvement.

If an organization is unable or unwilling to establish these systems then it will come under increased external pressure, from initiatives such as the Citizen's Charter and the work of the Audit Commission, to do so. As with most management activities a proactive and internally generated response is likely to be ultimately more beneficial than an externally imposed one.

Action points and discussion points

(Items in italics are intended to encourage the reader to develop a greater intellectual awareness, items in plain type are focused upon work-related activity.)

Manage activities to meet customer requirements

Collect two or three examples of 'Charters' and conduct a comparative critique of them. Consider, amongst other things, which stakeholder interests are addressed in the charters; what type of standards are included; what are the remedies available if standards are not achieved?

Conduct a similar evaluation of any Charters relating to your area of managerial responsibility. How could the Charter be improved? (If you are not yet currently covered by a Charter, draft one which you believe would meet the principles of the Citizen's Charter and be likely to be acceptable to your organization.)

Implement quality assurance systems/Evaluate and improve organizational performance/Determine the effective use of resources

Review the performance indicators available for your area of management responsibility. How were they established? How useful are they in providing you with the data you need to manage? How could they be improved? Is the range of indicators available adequate? Do you need to establish/agree new indicators? You may wish to incorporate Redditch's 'five tests' in your analysis (see Box 10.3).

Think of two services that you use, one in the private sector and one in the public sector. Decide what indicators you would set as a customer of those services to measure their performance. Then think about the process that you went through to establish those indicators. How did you define what you expected from the services? Did your expectations of the private and public sector organizations differ? If so, why, if not, why not? What are the implications of your analysis for the way in which your customers measure the performance of the service which you manage?

Review internal and external operating environments

Conduct a stakeholder analysis of your area of managerial responsibility. Who are the stakeholders? What are their requirements? What performance indicators would they be likely to establish to assess the effectiveness of the services you provide (remember that your staff are likely to be key stakeholders)?

Maintain effective working relationships

Reflect on the issues surrounding the 'voice' of the stakeholder. What means are generally available to stakeholders to make their needs and aspirations known? How are these means 'managed', e.g. through the political processes and the exercise of 'managerial prerogative'? How do stakeholder interests interact? What is your role, as a manager, in this web of interactions?

Further reading

Connor, A. (1993). *Monitoring and Evaluation Made Easy: A Handbook for Voluntary Organisations.* HMSO.
A useful guide derived from a research project conducted by the Scottish Office into the extent to which voluntary organizations could be responsible for monitoring and evaluating their own activities. The handbook is aimed at helping voluntary organizations describe, plan and review their work and performance.

Local Government Management Board (1993). *Performance Indicators: An Introductory Guide.* LGMB.
A short, 26-page book, which gives a explanation of the different types of performance indicators and how they can be used.

Martin, L.L., and Kettner, P.M. (1996). *Measuring the Performance of Human Service Programs.* Sage.
As you can tell from the title, an American book, but covers a number of important areas such as performance measurement, quality measures, and client satisfaction which it should be able to translate into the UK experience without too much difficulty.

Meekings, A. (1995). Unlocking the Potential of Performance Measurement: A Practical Implementation Guide. *Public Money and Management.* October–December, 5–12.
A clearly written and comprehensive guide to introducing performance measurement, usefully set in the context of broader change management. A practical guide, well illustrated with example of good practice drawn from British Rail's Network South East and Rolls-Royce.

Stewart, J., and Walsh, K. (1994). Performance Measurement: When Performance can Never be Finally Defined. *Public Money and Management.* April–June, 45–48.
Considers the limitations to performance management in the public sector. A good, short, critical article.

Part Five   Bringing it All Together

11 Conclusions

Aims and learning objectives

Now we are at the end of the book the aim of this chapter is to help you bring together the various themes and issues that we have been discussing and, importantly, to help you to plan for the future and manage your own continuous learning and development. To do this we will consider (a) what we can learn from the past, (b) how we can manage the present and, (c) how we can plan for the future.

At the end of this chapter, and associated activities and reading, you will be able to:

- encapsulate the major themes and developments across public sector management
- relate them to your own experience and development as a manager
- prepare a forecast of possible changes in public sector management generally, and your area of work in particular
- prepare an ongoing career and personal management development plan in the light of this forecast.

Learning from the past

If there was only one lesson that we were able to take from the history of the public sector over the last, say, twenty years it would be that it is dangerous to be lulled into a false sense of security based around a belief in the power of the professional acting from within a bureaucratic organization. We are sure that the public sector is never likely to revert to this closed-system way of operating and the impressive response of many public sector managers to the new, competitive, customer-centred environment in which they are now working supports our contention. In this book we have encapsulated the changes taking place across the whole public sector in the concept of the 'New Public Management'. We have reviewed how this new set of expectations on the public sector and its managers has been manifest in requirements for improved performance, quality, customer care, financial economy and efficiency, all to be reflected in reports of performance standards and indicators. These environmental factors impact individually and severally on the overall strategic management of any public sector organization and involve managers in developing new systems of operating, especially information systems.

Managing the present

This book has been based around the theme of competent management, partly in response to the developments outlined above, but also in anticipation of changes to come. Each successive chapter has identified areas where you need to develop and maintain competent practice. Put together they represent an extensive portfolio of knowledge, skills and behaviour. Learning from the past and managing the present requires change, and, as we said earlier, there can be no change without learning. Active learning, making and taking opportunities and carefully working through the experiential process of experience, reflection, theorizing and experimentation is, we believe, the best approach that we can recommend to deal with the challenges you face.

Planning for the future

So, at the time of writing there is an ongoing trend in the public sector involving factors such as downsizing (reducing staff) and delayering (cutting out management layers). We also observe further contracting out services, time-limited staff contracts and part-time working. These are trends which replicate well-established patterns in the private sector.

There is also much debate about the whole basis of the welfare state and this debate ranges far wider than the UK. The financing of pensions and health costs may move away from state provision and towards individual provision via insurance schemes and personal pensions. This is linked to a broader discussion about the change in the role of the state to that of 'enabler' rather than provider.

Much of this will be very familiar to you as a public manager. There is no lack of crystal ball gazers offering their views in the popular press and management journals. It has been said that a cautious futurologist will always forecast events far enough ahead that the futurologist will be comfortably in the grave by the time the forecast can be measured for accuracy. Alternatively, the forecast is ambiguous like that of many a fairground palm reader.

In forecasting the future we will offer some thoughts which are neither ambiguous nor located so far ahead that we will be long gone by the time they might come to pass. In doing so we provide the health warning that they are, like the long-term weather forecast, liable to be upset by unforeseen changes.

The renaissance of local government?

Local government is an area which is currently the subject of much upheaval following local government reorganization. One of the authors attended the 1995 Annual Seminar of Local Authority Chief Executives. The theme was around a perceived 'renaissance' of local government. After many years of successive reduction of powers it would seem that local government is well overdue for a rebirth. In the key publication for the conference Roger Harris (1995) offered the following reasons for a renaissance:

1 A perception that central government is out of step with the public mood.
2 The public have developed greater expectations of service quality and efficiency and in particular have become far more environmentally aware.
3 There is a growing unease over quangos and the lack of public (or local) accountability of such bodies.
4 Despite successive reports there is still a lack of clarity about what central government expects of local government.
5 The general approach of ministers and civil servants since 1979 has been to disparage and mistrust local government and seek to constrain it. This atmosphere of censure is rebounding upon central government itself.

Will Hutton addressing the same conference noted that the public sector in the UK had become very centralized with an obsession upon short termism – what he described as 'spot market capitalism'. He saw this as creating a problem whereby short-termism led to job insecurity which then impacted upon the housing market.

He felt that there were two possible ways to break this cycle:

● There might be constitutional change which would provide the sort of individual rights which citizens in other countries enjoyed. Such a 'bill of rights' could foster a new sense of positive citizenship.
● He saw a greater focus upon corporate governance and tighter financial regulation to offset the simple operation of the profit motive.

The growth of corporate governance

The concept of 'corporate governance' is one which is being bandied about in the public management literature. Hodges, Wright and Keasey (1996, p. 7) noted that:

There is no single authoritative definition of 'corporate govern-ance', although there appears to be some agreement that it is concerned with the procedures associated with decision-making, performance and control of organization, with providing structures to give overall direction to the organization and to satisfy reasonable expectations of accountability to those outside it.

The public accountancy body (Chartered Institute of Public Finance and Accountancy; CIPFA) is quoted in the same article as identifying the following principles underlying corporate governance:

- Openness to ensure that stakeholders can have confidence in the decision-making processes and actions of public bodies, in the management of their activities and in the individuals within them.
- Integrity which is based upon honesty, selflessness and high standards of propriety and probity in the stewardship of public funds and management of a body's affairs.
- Accountability such that public service bodies and the individuals within them are responsible for their decisions and actions, including their stewardship of public funds and all aspects of performance, and submit themselves to appropriate external scrutiny.

The Nolan Committee recommendations broadly concur with the CIPFA framework adding the requirements of 'leadership' and 'objectivity'.

We believe that the concept of corporate governance is likely to be very influential in the foreseeable future and will affect many if not all public managers. The implications of this is that the end will no longer justify the means. The concepts of corporate governance do not sit easily with a purely outcome-driven approach to management.

The importance of alliances and relationships

In 1989 an American professor, Rosabeth Moss Kanter, wrote a book entitled *When Giants Learn to Dance* in which she advised large companies to develop alliances and partnerships. The book made virtually no reference to the public sector though it was generally well received by the business community.

In the UK the public sector has wrestled with the introduction of Compulsory Competitive Tendering, purchaser–provider splits and the internal market in the National Health Service.

However we may now be seeing a move towards the sorts of alliances and partnerships Rosabeth Moss Kanter described. For example GP Fundholders are forming purchasing groups to negotiate with Hospital Providers. Instead of simply shopping around for the lowest price they are getting into consultation with the hospitals in order to discuss and influence the nature of the service which is offered. Writing recently in the *British Medical Journal*, Jonathan Shapiro (1996, p. 652) comments:

> In all the experiments with general practitioner (GP) commissioning, a consistent finding is that GPs' attitudes are changing. Fundholder or not, GPs are moving from short term 'gung ho' purchasing towards more thoughtful longer term relationships with their provider and health authorities.

Ferlie and Pettigrew (1996), two very experienced observers of the NHS, have also recently noted a move towards 'network-based management' which they see as associated with the emergence of 'relational contracting'. Relational contracting involves social exchange and trust-building activities which implicitly leads to a restriction upon competitive behaviour. The purchaser and provider see a common interest and work towards a long-term association rather than a limited duration contract which is awarded to the lowest bidder.

Relational contracting and corporate governance fit together well in value terms. Both involve developing trust and a recognition of a broader accountability as opposed to the narrower 'value for money' concept. If relational contracting is a trend which develops and extends more widely across the public sector it could transform the whole nature of Compulsory Competitive Tendering.

Voluntary sector – a shake out and merger movement?

Whilst the voluntary or charitable sector in the UK is certainly active, the impact of the recession and the growth of the 'contract culture' has had a marked impact. We believe that the key to success will be organizational learning. It is quite likely that there will be further mergers (or takeovers) as it becomes harder for certain charities to survive.

The Charities Aid Foundation (1994) conducted a survey which identified the middle income range charities (income between £7500 and £50 000) as most affected by a drop in income. Housing-based charities were doing well whereas advocacy-based charities were worst off.

What factors may incline a charity to seek a merger? A recent study (Cowin and Moore, 1996) suggests that most voluntary sector mergers were inspired by a range of reasons. However local mergers tended to be about resource provision whilst national mergers were more focused upon improving image and impact. However, strong leadership was a critical factor in whether the merger was successful. Perhaps significantly the study found that mergers of voluntary sector organizations tended to be more successful than mergers in the private sector.

Action points and discussion points

To continue the theme of this chapter we have organized these final action suggestions around learning from the past, managing the present, and planning for the future. Please note that we have not allocated Units of Competence to these particular action points because we see them as integrative and essentially future oriented. This means that we have offered a wide range of action points with the intention that you choose those most relevant to yourself – we do not expect you to do them all!

Learning from the past

Identify the sort of job that, in time, would attract you. It may be an advert or perhaps you could obtain some job specification for it. Then ask two friends or discreet colleagues who know you well to give you a frank opinion as to what sort of reference they would give you for such a job based upon their knowledge of your background and current abilities. Using this information consider what are your areas of strength and areas for improvement.

Identify your most positive work achievement and your biggest foul-up in the past three years. Write down the factors which were associated respectively with success and disaster. Identify the lessons in terms of improvement for you as an individual.

Without making any reference to your files write down all the courses or conferences which you can recall attending in the past three years. Beside each note down what significant lessons, information or skills you acquired from each event.

Chart the progress of your career from the time you left school until the present day. Identify key points or crises in your career. What do they tell you about you and what lessons can you draw from them?

Think back to a time when you felt especially fulfilled and positive. What were the factors associated with this? How might these be recreated (if they don't already exist)?

Find the longest serving member of staff in the organization. It will probably not be a senior manager! Spend some time with this person and try to learn from them their perception of the history of the organization.

Locate where the oldest records of the organization are stored. Take samples from the records over a period of years from then until the current day. Ask yourself how they represent changes in the sort of issues and strategic decisions which the organization has made. Identify where the organization has apparently learned or failed to learn from its experiences.

Contact people who have left the organization. Find out why they left and what their opinion of the organization is. What lessons should the organization draw and in particular what implications do they have for you as a manager?

Compare the success of your organization with its closest competitors (or with similar organizations). What are the similarities and differences? To what extent do these account for differences in the success of the organizations?

Identify and describe the historic role of the following forces on your organization:

- Competitors
- Customers/clients
- Suppliers
- Development of alternatives to what your organization offers.

Examine the impact of innovation upon your organization. What technological and skill developments have taken place in your environment?

Look back at the main issues in the environment which impacted upon your organization over the past month, year, five years and ten years. What issues have remained constant and which ones have changed?

To what extent could the changes in the environment be said to be 'chaotic'? Has your organization contributed to this sense of chaos? How effectively has it managed the chaos?

Conduct a review of your organization's relationship with other organizations over time. How have these changed? Have some relationships become more or less important? Why? How has the relative impact of other organizations on your own changed? Why?

Compare the history of your organization with another similar one. To what extent are the two histories similar, and how do they differ? What factors seem to contribute to these differences and similarities?

What mistakes did your organization make when responding to the environmental changes you have identified (e.g. decisions it took which subsequently had to be overturned or proved ineffective; changes in services which had to be reversed; posts deleted from the establishment and then reinstated)? Why, with the benefit of hindsight, did these mistakes occur? What can be learnt from them?

What are the major lessons that your organization has learnt over the last ten years? How have these lessons been disseminated and incorporated into the organization's culture? To what extent has your organization's system of values and underlying assumptions changed over this period?

Draft a short autobiography, concentrating on your work history and relating it to other important aspects of your life such as family and social life. What trends can you discern from this autobiography? What were the major turning points in your career to date? What decisions did you take which, with hindsight, proved to be particularly correct, and which do you regret?

Review the career history of someone whose work and progress you particularly admire. How have they achieved what they have? What can you learn from this comparison?

Update (or prepare) your curriculum vitae. Make sure that it contains all your major achievements and successes. Concentrate on your work experience, but do not omit important aspects of your life outside work if they are likely to be of interest to an employer.

Prepare a précis of what your organization and yourself have learnt from the past? What are the major lessons which you both need to take into a review of the present, and planning for the future?

Managing the present

Review how you spend your time. This may involve keeping a log of your activities over an period of a typical week. Compare how you use your time to a list of your key accountabilities or tasks. What lessons can you draw from this comparison?

Get frank opinions from your manager, your subordinates and your colleagues over which areas are your strengths and where you could improve. Compare the data and see where there are similar messages coming through. (This technique is sometimes called 360 Degree Appraisal.)

Make a practice of having lunch occasionally with someone who works in a different part of the organization. Try to learn something about their work and perception of the organizations' situation.

Develop a network both within and outside the organization. Collecting and filing business cards (with brief comments about the card donor written on the back) is a good way to do this. When a piece of information crosses your desk which might be of interest to someone in your network then send it to them. You'd be surprised how such actions can build up a reservoir of goodwill which can pay dividends in the future.

Conduct a review of current press coverage of your area of the public sector both nationally and locally. Which issues are being given prominence and why?

Compare press coverage with issues in the trade and professional journals? How do they differ, in both content and emphasis?

How customer-focused is your organization currently? What methods does it use to ensure that it is managing and meeting customer expectations?

How effective are your organization's current procedures for scanning the environment? How does it collect, interpret and report trends and changes in the environment? How could these processes be improved?

Who are currently the key decision makers in your organization? How do they influence the decision-making process? What information are they working from? How do they gather their information? How effective are they as decision makers?

Review all the activities that you have completed while working through this book and prepare a 'competency audit' of your own managerial performance. What are you currently doing well? What are the main managerial problems which you are currently confronting? How competently are you dealing with them? How well do your current competencies fit with the managerial audit you conducted in the last exercise?

How powerful are you in the organization? What are the bases of your power? How effectively are you currently making good use of your power position?

How actively do you network (i.e. use other people, professional associations, electronic communications and similar means to update your knowledge and influence your work)? How effective is your networking? What results have you achieved from your network of contacts over the last six months?

What are your current strategies for continuous personal and professional development? How effective are these strategies in ensuring your competence as a manager? What resources do you use? What procedures do you have in place for monitoring your own development? How much time do you currently devote to your own development?

How effective are you at learning from experience? Do you always take time to reflect on things that happen (especially those which went particularly well or particularly badly), drawing conclusions from these reflections and planning new ways of dealing with similar situations should they arise again?

How effective are you at managing time? What are the major activities at work on which you waste time (e.g. ineffective meetings, 'social loafing', interruptions from staff and colleagues)?

Prepare a précis of the results of your work in this section as the basis for preparing plans for the future in response to environmental changes. What are the major learning points for your organization in your opinion? What are the major learning points for yourself?

Planning for the future

To what extent is the emerging 'Green Agenda' likely to be of concern to your organization?

What changes do you expect in the technological resources available to your organization, and you, over the next three years?

What new European and wider international trends do you expect to encounter over the next five years? Is an increasingly mobile workforce likely to be of any importance? Will international sources of income and funding become more or less important? Is there any potential for a wider international customer base for your organization's (and your own) products and services?

How is the power of the various stakeholders in your organization likely to vary over the next three years (e.g. will professional groups become more or less important, do you expect more or less direct intervention from central government, how will consumer demands change and how will these be articulated)?

What changes do you expect in your own career over the next one, three and five years? What do you want to be doing in five years' time? What part will work play in your overall lifestyle? Do you need to revise (or prepare) your career plan in the light of these anticipated/desired changes?

To what extent is your current skills/competences mix likely to fit you for the changes you anticipate in your organization and its environment? Are there particular gaps in your competence that you need to address over the next year or so? Do you need to pursue new qualifications, both formally to recognize the skills, knowledge and competences you already have, as well as preparing you for new tasks, jobs or careers?

Are there areas in which you could become multiskilled (e.g. if you are currently employed as a finance specialist could you expand your portfolio into strategic forecasting)?

If the trend towards the 'portfolio worker' continues, what would be in your current portfolio, and what opportunities are there for you to enrich your portfolio, thereby increasing your value in the job market? Can you see any opportunities for you to diversify into new areas of work, or reskill in areas which may be more in demand?

Are your current levels of commercial skills and competence at business planning and management likely to be adequate for the changes you envisage?

How adequate are your professional and personal development systems? Do you have a mentor? If so how well is the relationship working, if not, can you identify a potential mentor to help you in planning and achieving your career goals?

Do you need to increase your level of networking activity in your organization, your area of professional/managerial interest and further afield? What opportunities are available to you to network further?

In other words – if it all goes horribly wrong have you got a good parachute?!! What is your personal survival plan?

Further reading

Hopson, B., and Scally, M. (1991). *Build Your Own Rainbow: A Workbook for Career and Life Management.* Mercury.
Not designed specifically for managers, but especially useful if you want to undertake a more general review of your career and life plans.
Johnson, M. (1996). *The Managers' Survival Guide: How to Achieve Success and Career Fulfilment in a Changing Workplace.* Butterworth-Heinemann.
Addresses some of the current realities of organizations, including delayering and being required to take on extra responsibilities, and helps you review your situation and plans in this context.

Pedler, M. (1994). *A Manager's Guide to Self-Development* (3rd edn.). McGraw-Hill.

A well-established and well regarded resource book which helps you plan your own development and suggests a wide range of activities to put the plan into practice.

Reeves, T. (1994). *Managing Effectively: Self Development Through Experience.* Butterworth-Heinemann.

Based around the experiential approach to development which we have featured in this book and covering important areas such as coping with organizational politics and managing change.

APPENDIX A Matrix mapping competence units onto chapters

Competence Units	Chapters of this book										
	1	2	3	4	5	6	7	8	9	10	11
Manage activities											
Manage activities to meet customer requirements			✓		✓		✓	**✓**	✓	**✓**	✓
Implement quality assurance systems				✓	✓		✓	**✓**		**✓**	✓
Implement change and improvements in organizational activities			✓	✓	✓	✓	**✓**	✓	✓	✓	✓
Review internal and external operating environments		**✓**	✓	✓		✓	✓	**✓**	✓	✓	✓
Establish strategies to guide the work of the organization				✓	✓	✓	✓	✓	✓	**✓**	✓
Evaluate and improve organizational performance		✓					✓	✓	✓	✓	
Manage resources											
Determine the effective use of resources					✓	**✓**	✓	**✓**	✓	✓	✓
Secure resources for organizational plans			✓		✓	**✓**	✓		✓	✓	✓
Manage people											
Manage self to optimize performance	**✓✓**			**✓✓**							**✓✓**
Maintain effective working relationships					✓	✓	✓	✓	✓	✓	
Respond effectively to poor performance of team members		✓	✓	✓	**✓✓**	✓	✓	✓	✓	✓	
Provide required personnel for activities		✓	✓	**✓**		✓	✓			✓	
Develop teams and individuals to enhance performance	✓				**✓✓**		✓			✓	
Determine the work of teams and individuals to achieve objectives	**✓**	✓	✓	**✓**						**✓**	
Develop management teams											
Delegate authority for programmes of work		✓			✓		✓	✓	✓	**✓**	✓
Establish organizational values and culture					✓	✓	✓	✓		✓	✓
Manage information											
Facilitate meetings and group discussion	✓	**✓**			✓	**✓**	**✓**	✓	✓	✓	✓
Provide information to support decision making					✓	**✓**	**✓**	✓	✓	✓	✓
Establish information and communication systems						**✓**	✓				

Ticks in bold show a major focus within the chapter

Bibliography

Adirondack, S. (1992). *Just About Managing: Effective Management for Voluntary Organisations and Community Groups*. London Voluntary Service Council.

Ammons, D.N. (1995). Overcoming the Inadequacies of Performance Measurement in Local Government: The Case of Libraries and Leisure Services. *Public Administration Review*, January/February, **55**(1), 37–47.

Andrews, K. (1971). *The Concept of Corporate Strategy*. Irwin.

Asher, K. (1987). *The Politics of Privatisation: Contracting out Public Services*. Macmillan Education.

Audit Commission (1994a). *Cheques and Balances*. Audit Commission.

Audit Commission (1994b). *Paving the Way: Helping Councils Prepare for the Future*. HMSO.

Audit Commission (1994c). *Watching Their Figures: A Guide to the Citizen's Charter Indicators*. HMSO.

Audit Commission (1995a). Making Markets: A Review of the Audits of the Client Role for Contracted Services. *Audit Commission Bulletin*, March.

Audit Commission (1995b). *Paying the Piper . . . Calling the Tune: People, Pay and Performance in Local Government*. Management Handbook. HMSO.

Bate, J. (1993). *Managing Value for Money in the Public Sector*. Chapman & Hall

Beale, V., and Pollitt, C. (1994). Charters at the Grass-Roots: A First Report. *Local Government Studies*, **20**(2), 202–225.

Best, D. (1994). *Purchasing and Contracting Skills*. Central Council for Education and Training in Social Work.

Bramham, J. (1989). *Human Resource Planning*. Institute of Personnel Management.

Brand, H., and Gill, S. (1995). Road to Recovery. *Health Services Journal*, 22 June, 34–35.

Brittan, S. (1988). *A Restatement of Economic Liberalism*. Macmillan.

Bryson, J.M. (1995). *Strategic Planning for Public and Non Profit Organisations: A Guide to Strengthening and Sustaining Organisational Development* (2nd edn.). Jossey Bass.

Buchanan, D., and Boddy D. (1992). *The Expertise of the Change Agent*. Prentice-Hall.

Butler, R., and Wilson, D. (1990). *Managing Voluntary and Non-Profit Organisations: Strategy and Structure*. Routledge.

Butt, H., and Palmer, B. (1985). *Value for Money in the Public Sector: The Decision-maker's Guide*. Blackwell.

Cabinet Office (1996). *The Charter Mark Awards 1996: Guide for Applicants*. HMSO.

Cameron, S., and Pearce, S. (1995). *The Management Studies Handbook*. Pitman.

Chandler, A. (1962). *Strategy and Structure*. MIT Press.

Charities Aid Foundation (1994). *Resourcing the Voluntary Sector*. CAF.

Chartered Institute of Public Finance and Accountancy (1994). *Councillors' Guide to Local Government Finance*. CIPFA.

Colling, T. (1995). Competing for Quality: Competitive Contracting and the Management of Quality in Local Government. *Local Government Policy Making*, **21**(4).

Common, R., Flynn, N., and Mellon, E. (1993). *Managing Public Services: Competition and Decentralisation*. Butterworth-Heinemann.

Constable, J., and McCormack, R. (1987). *The Making of British Managers*. British Institute of Management/Confederation of British Industry.

Coombs, H.M., and Jenkins, D.E. (1994). *Public Sector Financial Management* (2nd edn.). Chapman & Hall.

Cowin, K., and Moore, G. (1996). Critical Success Factors for Mergers in the UK Voluntary Sector. *Voluntas*, **7**(1).

Crozier, M. (1964). *The Bureaucratic Phenomena*. University of Chicago Press.

Curry, A., and Monaghan, C. (1995). Service Quality in Local Authorities. *Local Government Policy Making*, **21**(4).

Deakin, N., and Gaster, L. (1995). Local Impact of Contracts for Service Delivery on Social Cohesion. *Local Government Policy Making*, **21**(4).

Deal, T.E., and Kennedy, A.A. (1982). *Corporate Cultures: The Rites and Rituals of Corporate Life*. Addison-Wesley.

Deming, W.E. (1982). *Quality, Productivity and Competitive Position*. MIT Press.

Department of Health (1995). *The Patient's Charter and You*. Department of Health.

Dixon, R. (1994). *Investment Appraisal: A Guide for Managers*. Kogan Page.

Dopson, S., and Stewart, R. (1990). Public and Private Sector Management: The Case for a Wider Debate. *Public Money and Management*, Spring, 37–40.

Downs, A. (1967). *Inside Bureaucracy*. Little, Brown.

Drucker, P. (1990). *Managing the Non Profit Organisation*. Butterworth-Heinemann.

Edmonstone, J., and Havergal, M. (1991). Business Planning: New Wine in Old Bottles? *Health Services Management*, February, 33–35.

Edmunds, L., and Bowler, I. (1995). Partners in Action. *Health Service Journal*, 9 February.

Efficiency Unit (1988). *Improving Management in Government: The Next Steps*. Report to the Prime Minister. HMSO.

Elcock, H. (1995). *Public Administration: Change or Decay?* Longman.

Fahey, L., and Narayanan, V.K. (1986). *Macroeconomical Analysis for Strategic Management*. West Publishing Co.

Farnham, D., and Horton, S. (1993). *Managing the New Public Services*. Macmillan.

Ferlie, E. (1994). *Characterising the "New Public Management"*. Paper presented at the Annual Conference of the British Academy of Management, University of Lancaster, September.

Ferlie, E., and Pettigrew, A. (1996). Managing Through Networks: Some Issues and Implications for the NHS. *British Journal of Management*, **7**, March.

Flynn, N. (1994). *Public Sector Management* (2nd edn.). Harvester Wheatsheaf.

Friedman, M., and Friedman, R. (1980). *Free to Choose: A Personal Statement*. Penguin.

Gaster, L. (1995). *Quality in Public Services: Manager's Choices*. Open University Press.

Goldsworthy, D. (1994). The Citizen's Charter. *Public Policy and Administration*, **9**(1), 59–64.

Grant, R. (1995). *Contemporary Strategic Analysis* (2nd edn.). Blackwell.

Griffiths, E.R. (1983). *NHS Management Inquiry*. Department of Health and Social Security.

Gunn, L. (1988). Public Management: A Third Approach. *Public Money and Management*, Spring/Summer, 21–25.

Ham, C., and Shapiro, J. (1995). The Alliance of Scions. *Health Service Journal*, 18 May.

Hambleton, R. (1992). Decentralization and Democracy in UK Local Government. *Public Money and Management*, July–September, 9–20.

Handy, C. (1987). *The Making of Managers: A Report on Management Education Training and Development in the United States, West Germany, France, Japan and the UK*. Manpower Services Commission.

Handy, C. (1993). *Understanding Organisations*. Penguin.

Harrow, J., and Shaw, M. (1992). The Manager Faces the Consumer. In *Rediscovering Public Services Management* (L. Willcocks and J. Harrow, Eds.), McGraw-Hill.

Harvey Jones, J. (1992). *Troubleshooter 2*. BBC Books.

Haselbekke, A.G.J. (1995). Public Policy and Performance Measurement in The Netherlands. *Public Money and Management*, October–December, 31–38.

Henley, D., Likerman, A., Perrin, J., Evans, M., Lapsey, I., and Whiteoak, J. (1992). *Public Sector Accounting and Financial Control* (4th edn.). Chapman & Hall.

Hepworth, N.P. (1995). The Role of Performance Audit. *Public Money and Management*, October–Devember, 39–43.

HfM/CIPFA (1993). *Introductory Guide to NHS Finance in the UK*. Healthcare Financial Management Association/CIPFA.

Hind, A. (1995). *The Governance and Management of Charities*. Voluntary Sector Press.

HM Treasury (1991). *Economic Appraisal in Central Government: A Technical Guide for Government Departments*. HMSO.

HMSO (1991). *The Citizen's Charter: Raising the Standard* (Cmd. 1599). HMSO.

HMSO (1992). *The Citizen's Charter: First Report, 1992* (Cmd. 2101). HMSO.

HMSO (1994). *Public Expenditure Projections* (cmnd. 2519). HMSO.

HMSO (1995). *Economic Trends* (cmnd. 495), January. HMSO.

HMSO (1996). *Guidelines to the Charter Mark*. HMSO.

Hodges, R., Wright, M., and Keasey, K. (1996). Corporate Governance in the Public Services: Concepts and Issues. *Public Money and Management*, April–June.

Hodgson, P., and Hodgson, J. (1992). *Effective Meetings*. Century Business.

Holtham, C. (1992). Key Challenges for Public Services Delivery. In *Rediscovering Public Services Management* (L. Willcocks and J. Harrow, Eds.), McGraw-Hill.

Hood, C. (1991). A Public Management for All Seasons? *Public Management*, **69**, Spring, 3–19.

Hudson, M. (1995). *Managing without Profit*. Penguin Books.

Hunter, D., and O'Toole, S. (1995). Rosy Outlook. *Health Service Journal*, 11 May.

IDS (1994). *Quality in Practice* (Study 563, October). Income Data Services Ltd.

IDS (1995a). *Customer Care* (Study 582, July). Income Data Services Ltd.

IDS (1995b). Performance and Objectives. *IDS Focus*, **75**, July.

IRS (1995a). Annualised Hours at Northallerton NHS Trust. IRS *Employment Trends*, **575**, 12–15.

IRS (1995b). Performance-based pay at James Paget Hospital. IRS *Pay and Benefits Bulletin*, **380**, 2–4.

Isaac-Henry, K., Painter, C., and Barnes, C. (1993). *Management in the Public Sector: Challenge and Change*. Chapman & Hall.

Jackson, P.M. (1988). The Management of Performance in the Public Sector, *Public Money and Management*, **8**(4), 11–16.

Johnson, G., and Scholes, K. (1993). *Exploring Corporate Strategy* (3rd edn.). Prentice-Hall.

Joss, R. (1994). What Makes for Successful TQM in the NHS? *International Journal of Health Care Quality Assurance*, **7**(7).

Kanter, R.M. (1983). *The Change Masters: Corporate Entrepreneurs at Work*. Allen & Unwin.

Kanter, R.M. (1989). *When Giants Learn to Dance*. Unwin Paperbacks.

Kent Ambulance NHS Trust (1994). *Business Plan 1994/95*. Kent Ambulance NHS Trust.

Kouzes, J.M., and Mico, P.R. (1979). Domain Theory – An Introduction to Organisation Behaviour in Human Service Organisations. *Journal of Applied Behavioural Science*, **15**(4), 449–469.

Lawrie, A. (1995). *The Complete Guide to Business and Strategic Planning for Voluntary Organisations*. Directory of Social Change.

Lawton, A., and Rose, A. (1991). *Organisation and Management in the Public Sector*. Pitman.

Leach, S., Stewart, J., and Walsh, K. (1994). *The Changing Organisation and Management of Local Government*. Macmillan.

Local Government Training Board (1987). *Getting Closer to the Public*. LGIB.

McKevitt, D., and Lawton, A. (1994). *Public Sector Management: Theory, Critique and Practice*. Sage/Open University Press.

Manley, K. (1994). *Financial Management for Charities and Voluntary Organisations*. ICSA Publishing.

Mead, G. and Goss, S. (1995). Learning Verve. *Local Government Chronicle*, 10 February, 18–19.

Meekings, A. (1995). Unlocking the Potential of Performance Measurement: A Practical Implementation Guide. *Public Money and Management*, October–December, 5–12.

Mellett, H., Marriott, N., and Harries, S. (1993). *Financial Management in the NHS: A Managers' Handbook*. Chapman & Hall.

Metcalfe, L., and Richards, S. (1990). *Improving Public Sector Management* (2nd edn.). Sage.

Mintzberg, H. (1979). *The Structuring of Organizations*. Prentice Hall.

Mintzberg, H. (1983). *Structuring in Fives*. Prentice Hall.

Mintzberg, H. (1994). *The Rise and Fall of Strategic Planning*. Prentice-Hall International.

Morgan and Murgatroyd (1994). *Total Quality Management in the Public Sector*. Open University Press.

Murdock, A., and Scutt, C. (1994). *Personal Effectiveness*. Butterworth-Heinemann.

New Ways to Work (1995). *Flexible Working in Local Government*. New Ways to Work.

Oakley, P., and Greaves, E. (1995). A Catalyst for Change: Fundholding. *Health Service Journal*, 16 February.

Ohmae, K. (1982). *The Mind of the Strategist*. Penguin.

Osborne, D., and Gaebler, T. (1992). *Reinventing Government*. Addison-Wesley.

Pedlar, M., Burgoyne, J., and Boydell, T. (1991). *The Learning Company: A Strategy for Sustainable Development*. McGraw-Hill.

Palmer, A.J. (1993). Performance Management in Local Government. *Public Money and Management*, October–December, 31–35.

The Personnel Manager's Factbook, Vols. 1 and 2 (1996). Gee Publishing Ltd.

Peters, T.J., and Waterman, R.H. (1982). *In Search of Excellence: Lessons from America's Best-run Companies.* Harper & Row.

Pettigrew, A., Ferlie, E.B., and McKee, L. (1992). *Shaping Strategic Change: Making Change in Large Organisations.* Sage.

Pfeffer, J. (1992). Competitive Advantage Through People. *California Management Review,* Winter, 9–28.

Pollitt, C. (1993). *Managerialism and the Public Services* (2nd edn.). Blackwell Business.

Pollitt, C. (1994). The Citizen's Charter: A Preliminary Analysis. *Public Money and Management,* April–June, 9–14.

Pollitt, C., and Harrison, S. (Eds.) (1992). *Handbook of Public Services Management.* Blackwell Business.

Pugh, D.S. (Ed.) (1990). *Organisation Theory: Selected Readings.* Penguin.

Quinn, J.B. (1980). *Strategies for Change: Logical Incrementalism.* Irwin.

Ranson, S., and Stewart, J. (1994). *Management for the Public Domain.* St Martin's Press.

Selim, G., and Woodward, S. (1992). The Manager Monitored. In *Rediscovering Public Services Management* (L. Willcocks and J. Harrow, Eds.), McGraw-Hill.

Shapiro, J. (1996). Global Commissioning by General Practitioners. *British Medical Journal,* **312**, 16 March.

Sheaff, R., and Peel, V. (1995). *Managing Health Service Information Systems: An Introduction.* Open University Press.

Smith, R.J. (1994). *Strategic Management and Planning in the Public Sector.* Longman/ Civil Service College.

SOLACE (1995). *The Renaissance of Local Government: A Series of Papers Presented at the 1995 Society of Local Authority Chief Executives Conference.* SOLACE.

Stewart, J., and Stoker, G. (Eds.) (1995). *Local Government in the 1990s.* Macmillan.

Stewart, J. and Walsh, K. (1992). Change in the Management of Public Services. *Public Administration,* **70**, Winter, 499–518.

Strathclyde Police (1994). *Report of the Chief Constable of Strathclyde 1993.* Strathclyde Police.

Thomson, R., and Mabey, C. (1994). *Developing Human Resources.* Butterworth-Heinemann.

Tomkins, C. (1987). *Achieving Economy, Efficiency and Effectiveness in the Public Sector.* Kegan Paul.

Torrington, D. (1989). Human Resource Management and the Personnel Function .In *New Perspectives on Human Resource Management* (J. Storey, Ed.).

Torrington, D., and Hall, L. (1991). *Personnel Management: A New Approach.* Prentice-Hall.

Vinten, G. (1992). Reviewing the Current Management Ethos. In *Rediscovering Public Services Management* (L. Willcocks and J. Harrow, Eds.), McGraw-Hill.

Voss, C., Armistead, C., Johnston, B., and Morris, B. (1985). *Operations Management in Service Industries and the Public Sector.* John Wiley.

Walsh, K. (1995). *Public Services and Market Mechanisms: Competition, Contracting and the New Public Management.* Macmillan.

Weightman, J. (1995). *Competencies in Action.* Institute of Personnel and Development.

Willcocks, L., and Harrow, J. (1992). *Rediscovering Public Services Management.* McGraw-Hill.

Wilson, J., and Hinton, P. (Eds.) (1993). *Public Services in the 1990s: Issues in Public Service Finance and Management.* Tudor Business Publishing.

Winstanley, D., Sorabji, D. and Dawson, S. (1995). When the Pieces Don't Fit: A Stakeholder Power Matrix to Analyse Public Sector Restructuring. *Public Money and Management,* April–June, 19–26.

Wright, P.C., and Rudolph, J.J. (1994). HRM Trends in the 1990s: Should Local Government Buy In? *International Journal of Public Sector Management,* 7(3), 27–43.

Index